EUROPE UN-IMAGINED

Nation and Culture at a French-German Television Channel

Europe Un-Imagined examines one of the world's first transnationally produced television channels: Association relative à la télévision européenne (ARTE). ARTE, which calls itself the "European culture channel," was launched in 1991 with a French-German intergovernmental mandate to produce television and other media to promote pan-European community and culture.

Damien Stankiewicz's ground-breaking ethnographic study of the various contexts of media production work at ARTE (newsroom, editing studio, screening room) reveals how ideas about French, German, and European culture coalesce and circulate at the channel. He argues that the reproduction of nationalism often goes unacknowledged and unquestioned, and asks whether the creation of a "European imagination" is indeed achievable. Stankiewicz describes the challenges that ARTE staff face, including changing media technologies and audiences, national stereotyping, and unwieldy bureaucratic infrastructure, which ultimately limit the channel's ability to cultivate a transnational, "European" public. *Europe Un-Imagined* encourages its readers to find new ways of thinking about how people belong in the world beyond the problematic logics of national categorization.

(Anthropological Horizons)

DAMIEN STANKIEWICZ is an assistant professor in the Department of Anthropology at Temple University.

D1089179

ANTHROPOLOGICAL HORIZONS

Editor: Michael Lambek, University of Toronto

This series, begun in 1991, focuses on theoretically informed ethnographic works addressing issues of mind and body, knowledge and power, equality and inequality, the individual and the collective. Interdisciplinary in its perspective, the series makes a unique contribution in several other academic disciplines: women's studies, history, philosophy, psychology, political science, and sociology.

For a list of the books published in this series, see page 283.

EUROPE UN-IMAGINED

Nation and Culture at a French-German Television Channel

DAMIEN STANKIEWICZ

UNIVERSITY OF TORONTO PRESS
Toronto Buffalo London

© University of Toronto Press 2017
Toronto Buffalo London
www.utppublishing.com
Printed in the U.S.A.

ISBN 978-1-4426-3716-0 (cloth)   ISBN 978-1-4426-2879-3 (paper)

Printed on acid-free, 100% post-consumer recycled paper with
vegetable-based inks.

(Anthropological Horizons)

Library and Archives Canada Cataloguing in Publication

Stankiewicz, Damien, 1980–, author
Europe un-imagined : nation and culture at a French-German
television channel / Damien Stankiewicz.

(Anthropological horizons)
Includes bibliographical references and index.
ISBN 978-1-4426-3716-0 (cloth).   ISBN 978-1-4426-2879-3 (paper)

1. Association relative à la télévision européenne.   2. Mass media
policy–Europe.   3. Mass media and culture–Europe.   4. Television
programs–Social aspects–Europe.   5. Nationalism–Europe.
6. France–Relations–Germany.   7. Germany–Relations–France.
I. Title.   II. Series: Anthropological horizons

P95.82.E85S73 2017   302.23094   C2017-903068-X

University of Toronto Press acknowledges the financial assistance to its
publishing program of the Canada Council for the Arts and the Ontario
Arts Council, an agency of the Government of Ontario.

 Canada Council   Conseil des Arts
for the Arts   du Canada

ONTARIO ARTS COUNCIL
CONSEIL DES ARTS DE L'ONTARIO
an Ontario government agency
un organisme du gouvernement de l'Ontario

Funded by the   Financé par le
Government   gouvernement
of Canada   du Canada

contents

figures and tables

figures

tables

acknowledgments

This book has benefited from so much support, of so many kinds, from so many sources. I have to thank, first, those at ARTE who welcomed me and taught me and helped me to understand the channel's unique project and circumstances. At ARTE France, Adrienne Fréjacques and André de Margerie were instrumental in finding me a way to participate in the daily life of the channel and in helping me to develop contacts that would open doors throughout my fieldwork. Cédric Hazard was a colleague and a friend who met me for many a beer to chat; his friendship and laughter helped me to adjust to life in the field and at ARTE. Most of all, I have Claire Poinsignon to thank for my landing at ARTE France. Claire answered one of the first emails I sent off to ARTE inquiring about the possibilities of conducting fieldwork there, and I cannot thank her enough for the meals, coffees, and conversation that were always deeply generous. Her bright spirit and sincere openness and keen intellect I hope to have somehow imparted to these pages. I have also to thank, in and around Paris, the staff of *ZOOMEuropa*; Claire Doutriaux and the staff of *Karambolage*; and Frédéric Martel, who included me in his course on the sociology of media at *Sciences Po* and who was otherwise a good friend who thought to introduce me to Jérôme Clément and a number of other interlocutors in the world of French media. Finally, Thierry Garrel went out of his way to open a door to ARTE's headquarters in Strasbourg by way of its documentary unit.

In Strasbourg, I must thank the staff of the documentary unit for their hospitality and their adaptability in accommodating an awkwardly American anthropologist. Various staff went out of their way to find interesting projects for me to work on, and ones that I suspect they understood would allow me engage with some of the thornier aspects of production work at ARTE. I thank them for their willingness to answer so many of my questions; for their explanations solicited and unsolicited; and the many shared lunches and espressos. At ARTE INFOS I must thank Gabrielle Siegrist and Pascal Guimier for allowing me an internship, editors in chief Uwe Müller and Hugues Jardel, and all of the journalists at ARTE for their patience and willingness to have me hover about. Peter Geiger deserves special thanks for his help both in the newsroom and on our ARTE canoe trip. In Audience Studies, Brigitte Hofstetter was incredibly generous with her time, and Christophe Jung was both a source of deep understanding of ARTE and of cherished conversation after the workday would draw to a close. Finally, several ARTE administrators – including Jérôme Clément, Emmanuel Suard, Hans-Walter Schlie, and Christophe Hauser merit my deep gratitude for their willingness to allow me to participate in meetings and in the daily life of the channel. There are too many others at ARTE to thank by name, who granted me interviews or their time, but they should know that I am sincerely grateful for the attention they paid me. To my fellow interns: Thank you for improving my German and my French, for the Strasbourg strolls and *flammekueche*, and the sometime commiseration.

The conception and execution of this research project, as well, owes many scholarly debts. Ayşe Öncü and the participants of the Social Science Research Council's Predissertation Fellowship for International Collaboration greatly helped to refine this project, and the Fellowship provided funding to establish many of the contacts that I would need to pursue it. A fellowship from New York University further allowed me to lay the groundwork of this research. Grants from the Wenner-Gren Foundation for Anthropological Research and the National Science Foundation enabled sixteen months of fieldwork. A Provost's Summer Research Award from Temple University allowed me to return to Strasbourg for follow-up research in 2014.

While in Paris I was lucky to have a working relationship with the LAIOS research group of the CNRS, and I owe deep gratitude to Marc Abélès for his support of this project, and also to his colleagues Irène Bellier and Catherine Neveu.

During my time at NYU, the Program in Culture and Media was instrumental – literally – in affording me familiarity with the tools and technical knowledge needed to conduct research at a television station. Thank you especially to the wonderful, funny, award-winning Cheryl Furjanic for teaching me how to make a documentary film – and how to think about (documentary) film.

I follow in the footsteps of a great many Culture and Media Program graduates (and "honorary" graduates) before me who have largely pioneered the study of media in the discipline of anthropology – too many to name here, but Ulla Berg, Amahl Bishara, Lucas Bessire, Lydia Boyd, Omri Elisha, Danny Fisher, Tejaswini Ganti, Aaron Glass, Brian Larkin, Deb Matzner, Pilar Rau, Stephanie Sadre-Orafai, Naomi Schiller, Ayako Takamori, and Pegi Vail have provided inspiration and support – sometimes with their presence, sometimes with their words.

I owe an ocean of gratitude to Faye Ginsburg, who has not only taught me how to be an anthropologist who studies media but also a scholar who understands the stakes of representation for people's everyday lives, and, ultimately, a human who practices humility and kindness and looks for the same in others. In other words, well beyond the long hours in classrooms and office hours and dozens (and dozens) of letters of recommendation, Faye has shown me that a brilliant, critical, world-renowned scholar can also be funny, humble, warm. She is as much a friend as a mentor and the kind of broadminded, engaged scholar that I hope to be.

My Culture and Media colleagues continue to inspire me and to provide valuable intellectual interlocutors. My graduate cohort has been a source of inspiration; thank you to Anya Bernstein, Robert Chang, Emily Cohen, Adam Nilsen, Jason Price, and April Strickland for all you have taught me and continue to teach me. Becca Howes-Mischel deserves special mention for the generous support and feedback she has always been willing to provide, and for her friendship in both good times (wine!) and bad (wine). I must single out Christopher Fraga for joining me in new collaborations in these post-doctoral years and especially for co-organizing a generative Wenner-Gren Workshop on Media Theory in Anthropology at Swarthmore College in the spring of 2017.

Various scholars with whom I have had the pleasure of conversing and working have nourished pieces of this project in ways for which I cannot fully or individually account, but Thomas Abercrombie, Lila Abu-Lughod, Arjun Appadurai, Craig Calhoun, Herrick Chapman, Nina Glick-Schiller, Michael Herzfeld, Jeff Himpele, Ruth Mandel,

Emily Martin, Fred Myers, Catherine Raissiguier, Rayna Rapp, Martin Schain, Bambi Schieffelin, Annabelle Sreberny, Lok Siu, Katherine Verdery, and Frédéric Viguier have each in their own way provided this project momentum and direction. As an undergraduate at the University of Chicago I had the privilege of first conceiving this project alongside courses and conversation with Begoña Aretxaga, Dominic Boyer, Bert Cohler, Andreas Glaeser, Claudio Lomnitz, Flagg Miller, Saskia Sassen, and Lisa Wedeen – to them also, thank you. I am especially indebted to Bruce Grant and Anna McCarthy for their gracious participation as committee members, and for their deep insight, candid advice, and ongoing support.

Without the generosity and vision of my advisers – Susan Carol Rogers, Faye Ginsburg, and Sally Merry – I could hardly have completed this project. To them I owe a great deal of learning and understanding, and can only tell them that they will always be for me models of intellect, but also of thoughtfulness.

To Susan Carol Rogers, who not only taught me about the anthropology of Europe and France, but also the value of cross-Atlantic collaboration and collegiality, I owe especial gratitude. She has suffused my education, and this research project, with consistency of purpose and steady(ing) encouragement, not to mention untold hours of extraordinarily painstaking reading, editing, and feedback. To Susan I owe, as one might put it in French, "piles and piles" of gratitude. *Tout est bien qui finit bien*, but Susan has been a constant and kindly companion on the road to this book.

When I joined the Department of Anthropology at Temple University, I was welcomed by a new set of colleagues who have helped me to find balance (and even harmony) between the challenges of teaching and writing. To my former chair Mindie Lazarus-Black, current chair Paul Farnsworth, fellow visual anthropologist Jayasinhji Jhala, and fellow junior colleagues Inmaculada Garcia-Sanchez and Kimberly Williams (as well as Naomi Schiller, whom I dearly miss): Thank you.

At the University of Toronto Press, I am beholden to Anne Brackenbury and Douglas Hildebrand, who offered interest in, and support of, this project at our very first meeting together. My editor, Doug, has (almost) kept me on schedule and on target – so important for a first-time author – and made this not only a feasible project but helped me to think about it as an exciting and timely one.

Finally, to my family (siblings Jamie, Mara, Justin), and especially my mother, Joanne, and my father, James, who have supported me emotionally, intellectually, financially, and otherwise, I dedicate this book. It is but a small token of the deep gratitude of a brother and son well-loved, who loves you deeply.

EUROPE UN-IMAGINED

Nation and Culture at a French-German Television Channel

introduction

To change mentalities, frame of mind, and to create the conditions of a verita-
ble united Europe, it isn't enough to have a currency, an army corps, and legal
directives, though they may be well made. What's necessary is a *common imagination*. To think Europe together. So that the Germans, French, Italians, Spanish,
and all the others, even the English, learn to look at the world and to think the
world together ...

– Jérôme Clément, First President of ARTE

It was a question I had asked dozens of times before: "So I'd like to
talk a bit about ARTE's 'transnational' mission – its 'European'ness' and
whether, or how, it's trying to 'build Europe.'"

"Okay," said Serguei, who spoke to me in French, but whose parents
had moved to France from Eastern Europe when he was young.

"Do you think your department has been successful in helping to
build Europe ... or a European identity?"

Serguei's department was responsible for political documentaries,
which also included European "current events" programming.

"People won't watch programs about Europe," he responded, without reflection.

"I know ... I've heard this before from people, but ..."

"We've tried to interest audiences in all kinds of ways, but they don't watch."

"Is it because – other people have told me – Europe isn't interesting – that it has to be more local, or 'hidden' in programming about food, for example?"

"It is a little bit of that … but … let me put it to you this way: Do you consider yourself a global citizen?"

"Um. Maybe. I think I do."

"Would you be interested in watching a weekly program about the United Nations, or the International Court of Human Rights?"

"Well … if it were on at the right time maybe …?"

He turned up the corner of his mouth with scepticism.

"Yeah, probably not."

"See, so [the problem] isn't obvious … Even if people think they're interested in something, or even *identify* with something … they don't necessarily engage with this interest or identity, not like that … And we cannot *make* them. You see, that's the *challenge* [*le challenge*] of this channel."

"I see. ARTE's 'challenge.'"

"Yes, well, it's us against 500 or 1,000 years."

"[*laugh*] … I see."

My conversation with Serguei encapsulated so much of my time learning about ARTE, a remarkable trans-border television channel founded twenty-five years ago to help cultivate a European identity and "imagination." In the form of cliché, it was a little channel with big dreams: a collection of buildings in downtown Strasbourg, on the French-German border, where staff from France, Germany, Alsace, Spain, the UK, and elsewhere came to work every day to walls postered with slogans like "ARTE: Everyday Europe" and "Welcome to the culture channel of Europe!"

ARTE's headquarters (usually referred to as "la Centrale") are located in Strasbourg, a city of about 300,000 people nestled in the border between France and Germany, in the region of Alsace, which has changed national hands four times since 1870. ARTE's rooftop satellite dishes, shared by France and Germany, stand as potent symbols of what the countries have achieved in six decades. Indeed, Strasbourg was completely evacuated and partly destroyed during the Second World War, and the city's landscape is everywhere marked by its tumultuous past and annexation to Germany in 1870. Though the French army did much to erase the Kaiser's forty-odd years of "improvements" to the city, entire neighbourhoods of this border town – many of the buildings comprising the University of

Figure 0.1 Map of Strasbourg at the border of France and Germany.

Strasbourg, for example – remain testament to German imperial architecture. Near a shopping mall, a small plaque marks where the city's main synagogue stood before it was burned and then razed by Nazis in 1940. Bullet holes still pock many of the city's buildings.

At first glance, ARTE would seem to be a kind of vestige of twentieth-century propaganda machines that worked to disseminate political ideologies and to impart a sense of collective belonging. In some ways, ARTE's project runs parallel to Soviet media industries, for example, which once laboured to encourage loyalty to communist state ideals, or to Second World War American cinema newsreels and media exhorting citizen sacrifices for the war effort ("I want you!"). And its revisionist narrations of French-German and European history aren't dissimilar from nineteenth-century history books seeking to inculcate the "timelessness" of Swedish, or Mexican, or Bantu character and valour (cf. Schissler and Soysal 2005) (see chapter 4). Here it would seem an integrating Europe was arriving late to a rather old game, differentiated, perhaps, only by its transnational, post-national, or supra-national impetus. Otherwise, ARTE's publicity materials, one of which depicts Europe as a giant puzzle-map being assembled by young children, seem little different, in basic intent, from Mao-era Chinese posters depicting children piled together onto a smiling, soaring dragon.

But in this book I will argue that what makes ARTE unique has to do with the emergence of late twentieth-century ways of understanding and "seeing" the world – as these have circulated in popular thinking, but have also been reflected in academic social theory – which have produced an enduring linking-together, correlation, even conflation, of *identification* and *mediation*. In particular – and to avoid entanglement in all kinds of scholarly debates that this might otherwise unleash (note that I am *not* making an argument about "media effects," not least because this is, in the main, a study of media *production*) – I want to suggest that a late twentieth-century co-emergence of particular theories of nationalism, imagination, mediation, and globalization have aligned and converged in such a way as to *produce* ARTE. That is, particular ways of thinking about the "World" – both academic and mundane – have made this media organization (and other institutions like it) feasible, even inevitable, constructivist projects.

We might understand this blending and co-assembling of theories as a kind of "trans-cultural mediationism," which this ethnography of ARTE will, I hope, help us to untangle and explore. "Trans-cultural mediationism" is not at all graceful, but points to two key aspects of this book's argument:

First, "trans-cultural mediationism" encompasses a set of assumptions that the world (a singular World) is increasingly interconnected in all kinds of ever more complicated, if multivalent ways, which are sailing us towards ever greater (if more "complicated") trans-planet communication and mutual intelligibility (as a result of the spread of the internet, for example).

Second, it takes for granted that there is a positive correlation between this greater breadth and/or density of communication, and the emergence of trans-human understanding, trans-border solidarities, and large-scale collective identities (e.g., cosmopolitan identities, transnational identities, global identities, post-national identities). This "trans-cultural mediationism" is perhaps most clearly (and enduringly) articulated in Arjun Appadurai's (1990) article "Disjuncture and Difference in the Global Cultural Economy." Over almost three decades, certain assumptions and suggestions of that essay have been exhaustively extrapolated. Appudu-rai discusses "mediascapes" in the following way:

> Many audiences throughout the world experience the media themselves as a complicated and interconnected repertoire of print, celluloid, elec-tronic screens, and billboards. The lines between the realistic and the fictional landscapes they see are blurred, so that, the further away these audiences are from the direct experiences of metropolitan life, the more likely they are to construct imagined worlds which are chimerical, aes-thetic, even fantastic objects ... Mediascapes ... tend to be image-centered, narrative-based accounts of strips of reality ... out of which scripts can be formed of imagined lives, their own as well as those of others living in other places. These scripts can and do get dis-aggregated into complex sets of metaphors by which people live ... as they help to constitute narra-tives of the Other and proto-narratives of possible lives ... (9)

Whether we wish to emphasize Appadurai's theoretical innovation and influence, or would prefer to argue that Appadurai merely gave voice and form to some broader zeitgeist, we cannot ignore how compelling his formulation has been. In the twenty-odd years since Appadurai penned these words, I would argue that his evocation propelled a widespread theoretical (if not also practical) orientation that variously juxtaposes and superimposes such phenomena as cell phones, cinema, advertising industries, inexpensive travel, supra-national governmental institutions, the internet, multinational corporations, trans-border migration, and global finance. In this premise and formulation, the World is more *techno-logically* interconnected (digitally, etc.), and, therefore, more socially and culturally interconnected (albeit alongside processes of disjuncture and differentiation).[1] Of course, Appadurai was not the only theorist arguing for a convergence of new forms of mediation with new forms of identifi-cation. Many (if not most) anthropologists and social scientists were sud-denly turning their attention to globalization and beginning to argue for new permeabilities and "flows" (of people, image/sound/text, capital, ideas, etc.) across various kinds of borders (e.g., Basch, Schiller, and Blanc 1993; Kearney 1995; Nelson, Roberts, and Veit 1992).

If there seems much mixed together in this transnational-global soup – technologies, post-nations, migration, capitalism, human rights, movies, diaspora, social movements, cosmopolitan identity – much of the power of this description and explanation of global processes, I propose, boils down to an underlying (and quite compelling) thesis that *lived experi-ences* were (are?) converging with *mediated representations thereof*. Indeed, anthropologists (and others) have been fairly enthusiastic to argue that this distinction cannot always be deciphered, or else does not much matter. The argument goes like this: Broadcast news images of boats capsized off the coast of Italy, and the actual events (or first-hand experience or witnessing of such events), cannot fully be disentangled (even sometimes for the witnesses themselves), so that the (unhindered) circulation of media across the globe – which constitute the only means of access that we have to other places and peoples – amounts more or less (the argument concludes) to the *constructed reality* of today's World. Globalization is therefore a kind of mediatization, and vice versa.[2]

Alongside this trans-cultural logic, I would like to suggest that what has emerged – and what has warranted ARTE's project – is what Martin Heidegger might today refer to as a twenty-first-century "Age of the World Picture." We live in a World imagined as it is imaged, and imaged as it is imagined. But I will circle back to Heidegger in a moment.

One of my earliest experiences studying ARTE was in the fall of 2007 when, having only just arrived to the field, I attended one of ARTE's sponsored *actions culturelles* – "cultural actions [events]" – held at La Ferme du Buisson, outside of Paris, called Temps d'Images (which I would variously translate as The Time of Images, The Image Époque, or Image Times). Here is some of the language from the festival's description in brochures and on its website (my translation):

Initiated in 2002 by ARTE and La Ferme du Buisson, TEMPS D'IMAGES was originally created out of the observation of one issue in particular: the worlds of moving image and performing arts are not separate, but interact constantly wherever technology is used as a bridge rather than a boundary.

TEMPS D'IMAGES has developed into a European network. Through its commitment to the policy of production, TEMPS D'IMAGES has played an active role in developing the potential for creative exchange and collaboration ...

TEMPS D'IMAGES has opened territories little or poorly mapped, and has explored them in letting itself be guided by adventurers of all origins who, often, navigate in pairs, the one at watch at the helm, the other steering the rudder.

TEMPS D'IMAGES ties together music and cinema, dance and video, comic books and television series ... The festival gives the spectator time to see otherwise [*voir autrement*] and invites immersion into a world where the image multiplies dimensions, shatters the borders between genres, and creates new narrative modes.

Two of the most obvious tropes that run through these and other descriptions of the multi-day Time of Images festival, and which work in tandem, are those of trans-mediation (or multi-mediation) and trans-border/trans-World collaboration. The opening up or cross-fertilization of *images* is tied, especially in the second and third excerpt, to the opening-up and broadening of bordered *territory* (both geographical and metaphorical). Images and social space are, in this Image Times festival, not only superimposed, but the one is always defined in terms of the other – border crossings among the visual arts inspires (or at least engenders) social, trans-border collaboration; reciprocally, collaboration among a network of multinational artists gives rise to innovative artistic realms and modes.

This argument or belief – not only that media and sociality are mutually contingent, but also that the one can (and even should) instrumentalize and engender the other – leads us back to Heidegger ([1954] 1977). Although his essay, "The Age of the World Picture," is often glossed as an argument about the modern proliferation of images, he is in fact more interested in particular *beliefs about* images that this proliferation has entailed. One of the most interesting sections of the essay is Heidegger's exegesis of the phrase "to get the picture":

> "To get the picture" throbs with being acquainted with something, with being equipped and prepared for it. Where the world becomes picture ... in its entirety, is juxtaposed as that for which man is prepared and which, correspondingly, he therefore intends to bring before himself and have before himself, and consequently intends in a decisive sense to set in place before himself. Hence world picture, when understood essentially, does not mean a picture of the world but the world conceived and grasped as picture. (128)

Heidegger argues that there is an interesting kind of logical relationship between *images* (and their creation and dissemination) and a sense of control: Man [sic] brings these images "before himself" and so is able to act decisively through them. Through images, he is "equipped" and "prepared" to act not only *in* the World, in other words, but *on* the World (cf. Mitchell 1991, 1–62).

What I have learned from sixteen months of working with television and media producers at ARTE, in part, is that we must reconsider our assumptions about media (image/sound/text) and their relationship to the reconfiguration of culture(s) and collective identities. This assumption (about the *power* of media) – about the natural symbiosis of media and identity – has been so taken for granted that the efficacy of image/sound/ text as a tool for the building of nations and collective identities is rarely challenged.

Which brings us to the title of this book: What if television, film, cinema, radio, and the internet are not as puissant as we might believe (or as they once were)? What if they do not quite (or no longer) have the power to connect us – across nations or across the World – as Appadurai (1990) and others have suggested? What if, despite our best efforts to cultivate togetherness and commonality, image/sound/text remain just that – a collection of sensorial experiences that may amount to diversion or information, but which do not amount to coherent narratives or "imagined worlds" (cf. Stankiewicz 2016)?

If ARTE has earnestly invoked and deployed transnational mediationism in the hope of fostering European collectivity, this book argues that there is little evidence for Clément's (1992) "common imagination." It argues that Europe remains largely "unimagined" not only because at ARTE there is no cohesive sense of European-ness, but also, and more fundamentally, because mediation and identification simply do not align in ways that would make the self-conscious production of a common European "imagination" possible. In this book, I explore the un-imaginability of Europe through close attention to, and sustained critique of, Benedict Anderson's (1991) argument – at least as influential as Appadurai's (1990) and not altogether distinct – that large-scale communities like the nation coalesce (i.e., they are collectively "imagined") because of the widespread circulation of texts (newspapers, novels, but to which we are likely to add television and digital media), which are shared and engaged among people in common, in a common vernacular language.

In building a case that Europe remains un-imagined at ARTE, I propose that we need to reconsider, and add caveat and nuance to, the taken-for-granted relationship between media and large-scale collective identities that we presume media not only represent but which also, to a great degree, *construct* and *make "real."* If this is (as I will argue) precisely the logic of, and warrant for, ARTE's creation and existence – a media organization charged with the task of helping to forge transnational and post-national imaginaries and loyalties – ARTE staff (like Serguei) tend to feel it is a mission that has largely stagnated or failed. This book explores why constructivist projects like ARTE do not succeed – at least not as intended – and how their failures (or mitigated successes) suggest needed revisions to our sense that media can and do reorganize the world.

anthropologies of media

The ideology that image/sound/text can, and do, transform society[3] is not new, and is not particular to Europe or the West. As a number of scholars have described (see Critcher 2006), there have been waves of moral panic as communication technologies have appeared over the course of the twentieth century (and before), as each technology (radio, television, the internet) was understood to loosen and warp social cohesion. As William Mazzarella (2013) has recently noted about cinema in his excellent (and apposite) book *Censorium*:

> On April 13, 1937, the Indian film writer and actor Dewan Sharar ... noted that "the immense power of the cinema, either for good or for evil, is so well known that reference to it is a platitude" ... Dewan Sharar did not ... feel moved to inquire into the basis of this "immense power" ... Again and again, from the cinema's first appearance in the 1890s through to the time of my fieldwork more than a century later, the unique and inherent power of the cinema, for good or for ill, has been asserted. It is the basic premise on which the cinema has been mobilized as a means of education, entertainment, nation building, and propaganda. (1–2)

Mazzarella's (2013) attention to the *belief* in the power of cinema (and mass mediation), and his subsequent inquiry into the basis and substance of this belief, is something of an exception to the rule, however (cf. Peterson 2003, 86–121). Many media studies scholars and anthropologists tend to take this mediational power for granted – often as the fundamental justification for the study of media institutions and mediators (journalists, filmmakers, artists, advertising professionals) more broadly. While few media studies scholars or media anthropologists believe that media are the only thing we should be studying to understand social life – and while few would argue that media messages rain down upon social worlds in entirely coherent and persuasive ways – it is nonetheless the case that many argue (or presume) that mass media (of many kinds) are ever more present in social worlds across the planet, and are ever increasingly powerful in establishing social norms and values, whether in Pakistan or Peru. There are more anthropologists and ethnographies of media/tion than ever before[4] and it has become commonplace for an ethnography to feature (at least) a chapter on media, even when its focus is predominantly elsewhere (see, e.g., Richardson 2008; Verstraete 2010; Edmonds 2010; Kim 2010).

In part this has to do with the history of anthropology's engagements with media. For much of anthropology's history, despite the pervasive presence of media technologies like cinema, radio, and television in the places anthropologists were working, these were either ignored (often to avoid descriptions that would spoil otherwise "traditional" or pure-seeming societies) or else given only cursory attention.[5] Germane here is the famous scene in Robert Flaherty's classic docu-fictional *Nanook of the North* in which Nanook (played by a man named Allakariallak) "bites" a phonograph record, seemingly amazed by the white trader's technology – when in fact such technology was already well known among the Inuit (as a result of trade with merchants and others, as was and has been true for many "traditional" and indigenous societies across the world). In *Tristes Tropiques* (1955), Claude Lévi-Strauss notes the importance of the Rondon telegraph line as a conduit for interaction between Brazilian government agents and indigenous groups, but does not otherwise discuss the role of communication technologies in his lengthy ruminations on modernization and modernity. Even an ethnography written in 1991, Alan Sandstrom's *Corn Is Our Blood*, about a village in Veracruz, Mexico, mentions only twice, briefly and without elaboration, that radio in the village is a common "personal item" that villagers often buy with money they have set aside for recreation (202). Whether and how radio matters to the village and their identifications (especially as this might propel or inhibit social change and shifting identifications, which is central to the book's argument) is not addressed.

The scholarship of Lila Abu-Lughod is illustrative in this regard. Although Abu-Lughod's ethnography *Veiled Sentiments* (1986) makes no extensive reference to the presence or role of mass media, in her watershed 1997 article, "The Interpretation of Cultures after Television," she argues,

> We are only beginning to find the right point-of-entry for the ethnographic work – in the field and in our studies – that it would take to draw out the significance of television's existence as a ubiquitous presence in the lives and imaginaries of people in the contemporary world ... What can anthropologists offer when we begin to take television seriously? (110–11)

Abu-Lughod eventually and eloquently answers her own question with the 2004 publication of *Dramas of Nationhood: The Politics of Television in Egypt*, in which she writes, more emphatically,

> My argument in this book is that, for various reasons, television is a key institution for the production of national culture in Egypt; it is certainly an

institution whose careful exploration allows us to write an ethnography of the Egyptian nation. At the simplest level, it is salient in national processes because of the special place it seems to have in defining Egypt as a unique cultural center, dominant in the Arab region. (7)

By the time *Dramas of Nationhood* was published, Abu-Lughod was building on an already and suddenly broad amount of anthropological work focused on mediation.[6] Consolidated by Debra Spitulnik-Vidali's 1993 *Annual Review of Anthropology* article, "Anthropology and Mass Media," propelled by Kelly Askew and Richard Wilk's reader, The Anthropology of Media (2002), and galvanized by Faye Ginsburg, Lila Abu-Lughod, and Brian Larkin's widely read volume, *Media Worlds: Anthropology on New Terrain* (2002), anthropologists lost no time in turning their scholarly attention to ethnographies of media. Between 1998 and 2010, at least a dozen ethnographic monographs (written by anthropologists) appeared focusing on television and film alone.[7]

To some extent, of course, this mushrooming of interest in media can be attributed to the proliferation of communication technologies around the world, understood to be one of the key elements of a near-ubiquitous globalization. But it bears asking: If there are "more" media technologies and texts that operate and circulate in "today's world," to when and where are we making comparisons? For example, people in some parts of the world read fewer newspapers or novels than they used to, while broadcast and digital technologies have changed, but not necessarily enhanced, the ways people access news and information. Some places in the world have seen an explosion of interest in internet gaming; others, in Bollywood, Nollywood, or Kollywood film; in still others, cell phones matter most, both for communication and media consumption. These various, uneven permutations and distributions of technology and genre matter. More access to media does not necessarily entail more "mediation," and more mediation does not mean media somehow "matter more" to people, or that their narratives (presumed to be stable) are holding more sway in the constitution and playing out of social life. In any case, whether the "empirical" global growth of the role of media technologies in everyday people's lives fully merits, or is consonant with, a swell in scholarship on media is more or less beside the point (or in any case not the question I want to pursue here).

Rather, what I would like to think about further is where we as anthropologists, social scientists, and media scholars "draw the line," as it were, between the premise that mass media can craft and shape identities, and the ways in which people's engagements with mass media substantially *mitigate* and *limit* how media operate to build, define, or remake and redefine large-scale communities and cultures.

We know that both assertions can be true, of course, to some degree, and it may be the case that anthropologists should let 100 flowers bloom. Anthropologists of media may need considerable latitude in assessing the ways media operate in any given context (and indeed what constitute "media" in a given context), and whether and how they are vectors of widespread social change (or are ignored/ineffectual). That is, *The Simpsons* may in one place cultivate desires for the trappings of middle-class suburban life, but in another it may be that people either do not watch *The Simpsons* or watch it nightly but aren't very much affected by its stories. Perhaps they only find it funny. Perhaps they don't fully understand its references. Or perhaps their middle-class sensibilities are far more piqued by their real-life neighbour's recent home renovations.

Such an approach, which views mediation as one piece (larger or smaller) of a complex social puzzle, is very much in keeping with the spirit of Abu-Lughod's 1997 article:

> How do we trace this enmeshment of television in other social fields? The key, I would argue, is to experiment with ways of placing television more seamlessly within the sort of rich social and cultural context that the sustained anthropological fieldwork that has been our ideal since Bronislaw Malinowski is uniquely able to provide. The special challenge we face in doing so is that the cultural forms transmitted by television have no obvious and simple community and are always only a part – sometimes larger, sometimes smaller – of people's complex lives. (112)

Similarly, Ginsburg, Abu-Lughod, and Larkin (2002) noted in their introduction to *Media Worlds: Anthropology on New Terrain*:

> The anthropological studies of media presented in this book challenge stereotypes of media ethnography as narrowly empiricist versions of market research – querying television watchers in their living rooms about what they *really* think of certain programs, without placing them in wider structures or recognizing their complexity. The contributors, drawing on a range of scholarly traditions, take for granted the necessity of linking media production, circulation, and reception in broad and intersecting social and cultural fields: local, regional, national, transnational. (6)

Yet while Abu-Lughod's article and the editors of *Media Worlds* are careful to position mediation within "broad and intersecting social and cultural fields" in which a television set may or *may not* be relevant to understanding, say, religion in Uzbekistan (in an overall context involving agriculture, local moral economies, state education, ritual practices, etc.), I would argue that the more or less unmitigated success of anthropological and sociological interest in media has encouraged scholars to assemble less careful arguments – to naturalize the power of image/sound/text to shape large-scale collective identities. Great liberties have been taken with the premise that mediation is *sometimes* (or in *particular* sociocultural contexts) important to understanding sociality. The provocation of media anthropology (and media/cultural studies) that we need to *also* pay attention to media and assess their place in social life has sometimes been reduced to the assumption that media are always worth studying because they help us understand the constitution of social worlds. Sherry Ortner's *Not Hollywood* (2013), for example, features the subtitle, *Independent Film at the Twilight of the American Dream*; although the book argues that independent film sheds light on American neoliberalism and the emergence of a "dark side" of American capitalistic society, the extent to which these films and these narratives index *actual* social realities and on-the-ground debates simply cannot be ascertained from the book's evidence (much of which draws upon the narratives of films). Rather than framed as a *question* about whether and how social orders and mediation intersect – how independent film producers draw upon certain experiences of sociality, and attempt to influence social life in (certain parts of) the U.S. – mediation is presumed wholesale to "explain" how particular collective identities and social orders have come to be, or are coming to be. Social worlds and media are often assumed, in this way, not only to be dialogical, but often coterminous or synonymous, even conceptualized as metaphors for one another.

Indeed, consider how anthropologists have taken up the question of new and digital media. On the one hand, they have, perhaps in parallel with popular discourse, attempted to decipher the ways in which technology is changing the way people understand themselves and others, and the nature of interpersonal communication. These kinds of arguments are more sophisticated than brute technological determinism, but they take as their warrant that ever-denser experiences of mediation are making us more or less social, more or less capable of things like intimacy and love, and, indeed, more or less "human" (Turkle 1997; Boellstorff 2008, esp. 118–201; Nardi 2010). On the other hand, speaking back to the momentum of these arguments, anthropologists like Tom Boellstorff have argued that, to a large degree, humans have *always* been mediated, not least of all, by *culture* itself (Boellstorff

2008, 1–30). I sketch out these two positions because neither really challenges the tight entwinement of sociality and mediation; instead, the "new media" debate is largely cast in terms of the role of *technology*: either, these scholars argue, media technologies are increasingly pressing upon and changing collective social life, or else mediation is inherent to the human condition and technology is merely extensive of this mediation (à la Marshall McLuhan). Whichever side you take, media and sociality are compound and mutually contingent (or synonymous).

In the time since Abu-Lughod and the *Media Worlds* editors penned their arguments for why an anthropology of media was necessary, anthropologists (and others) have, I think increasingly, yoked together mediation and sociality without fully considering the theoretical or analytical consequences. There is a pervasive sense, and assumption, that though media does not *always* reshape or even affect people's identities or sense of place in the world, it "often does" or does "to some degree." Why else study the popularity of westerns in Japan, reality TV in Brazil, or the rise of independent film in the U.S.?

The "to some degree" is my concern in this volume, for although mediation may in certain times and places be "all around us," it is not everywhere, hardly to the same degree or in the same ways, and hangs in tension with non-mediated social and material realities. While popular thinking tends to presume that, *grosso modo*, "the media" both constitute social worlds and interconnect them, I want to propose in this book that we (re)consider processes and practices of mediation in more nuanced ways – not only to challenge the sometimes facile superimposition of mediation onto all things social (and vice versa), but also to think about *when* and *how* media texts and narratives come to matter (or are understood to *not matter*) through close attention to ethnographic contexts in which these are being negotiated, assembled, and disseminated.

In this study of mediation and mediators at ARTE, I ask: How does a concatenation of production activities lend itself to composite, incoherent, or even contradictory kinds of logics and orientations? Why do people seem to care about, or become emotionally attached to, some media texts, but less so others? How and when do media producers' intentions and personal commitments matter – and why do these sometimes not make it into the final cut? How do assumptions about who is watching (or not) sometimes contradict the very engagements that a program is supposed to encourage? How might we pay closer attention to structural, infrastructural, institutional, and linguistic constrictions that stymie the construction and dissemination of coherent national, transnational, or post-national "imaginations"?

In paying attention to the mitigated successes and failures of mediation at ARTE, we might be able to better specify *how* and *when* particular processes of mediation are able to remake commitments, loyalties, identities, and collectivities – and when they cannot or do not. It is not my argument that media are not effective or that they do not always "affect" people – I think that mostly they are, and that mostly they do – but rather to ask after the socialities and solidarities that they are presumed to build, maintain, or revise.

In this book I explore a context in which – despite a mission statement promising to foster transnational community – media do not necessarily suture social cleavages, but instead may leave a bifurcated social community *more* fragmented and oppositional; in which media do not seem to move across borders, or at least only with great difficulty; in which they are therefore unable to "produce" transnational or trans-cultural sensibilities; and, in which, indeed, *immediation* – a lack of mediational influence – may better name much of what is happening.

Europe

Though scholarship on European integration today fills whole libraries, books on those shelves have predominantly been written by political scientists, legal scholars, and political sociologists. Anthropologists and ethnographers have played a much smaller part in studying what Jacques Delors, prominent European statesman, once called an "Unidentified Political Object," which includes not only the central institutions of the European Union (the Council, Commission, and Parliament), but also parallel institutions such as the Council of Europe and the European Court for Human Rights. Radiating from this UPO are widespread programs and policies, including the ERASMUS university exchange program, the EURIMAGES cinema fund, and so on; and connected to this UPO, too, are a number of auxiliary organizations and institutions – including schools and universities (the European University Institute, ESCP Europe), think tanks (the Jacques Delors Institute, Notre Europe, the Centre for European Reform), and transnational media outlets (Euronews, Eurovision, Eurozine, ARTE).

When anthropologists did begin to study European integration (Borneman and Fowler 1997; cf. Boyer 2005), they, too, tended to set their sights on formal political institutions and politics (e.g., Abélès 1992,

1996, 2000; Bellier 2000; Wilson 2000; Neveu 2002), where they have for the most part argued that Europe constitutes a novel and still-inchoate project (cf. Shore 2000). As Marc Abélès (2000) has expressed it, "It does not seem possible to be European without projecting oneself into a world which does not yet exist" (31). In the flurry of interest in the transformation of the European Community into the European Union (whose new charter notably added "social Europe" and "European identity" to its mandate), expansions to fifteen (1995) and then twenty-five members (2004), and the adoption of a common currency (1999), a number of anthropologists and political sociologists argued that we were witnessing not only the emergence of a supranational polity but also the coalescing of a European identity – at least among European technocrats and those closest to the EU's administrative and bureaucratic structures (e.g., Herrman et al. 2004; Hedetoft 1998; Landau and Whitman 1997; Zabusky 1995). An integrating Europe seemed to offer the exciting possibility that the wars and massacres of the twentieth century – largely attributed to nationalism – were not only in abeyance but were also being superseded by a greater post-national human collectivity committed to a shared peace, prosperity, and the "ever closer union" proclaimed in the 1992 Maastricht Treaty. In this mode, Jeremy Rifkin (2004) writes in *The European Dream*:

> European foreign policy [is] so utterly different from anything that came before it in human history that it requires a leap of human imagination to even entertain it. European foreign policy is built on spreading peace rather than amassing power ... Europeans reject the kind of power politics that has dominated foreign policy for centuries and has led to so much death and destruction in the world. European leaders ask rhetorically: Who knows better than us the terrible consequences that can result from nations attempting to assert their will over others by means of coercion and force? And to those who say that human behaviour will never change, Europeans retort, Look at what we've accomplished in Europe. (297–8)

The scholarship on European integration and the "new Europe" has, then, to a great degree been crafted around tropes of singularity, novelty, and possibility. "Integration" suggests both inevitability and a dynamic quality, echoing Abélès's (2000) evocation of Europe as an "unfinished project" ever set against an unfolding horizon. We cannot quite make out what Europe means, or where it will lead, but there is a sense of constant movement and mutation as nation-states meld, converge, or are otherwise (re)assembled – with all the attendant consequences for interhuman politics, identities, and even (as Rifkin asserts) human nature itself.

This "dream and vision," at least as I write, has substantially receded. For one, the EU's efforts to strengthen its institutions through the introduction of a European constitution fizzled when, in 2005, French and Dutch voters shelved the document with "no" votes in national referenda. Observers and scholars have argued that the hulking bureaucratic machineries of European integration have tended to squelch or ignore everyday Europeans and their concerns. According to recent Eurobarometer surveys, less than half of polled Europeans report understanding the European Union, and only rarely has the number of Europeans saying that they feel "their voice counts in the EU" risen above 35 per cent of those polled.[8] The recent fallout from the Greek financial crisis has, for many, evidenced the contradictions and weaknesses of the Eurozone. The recent refugee crisis has revealed deep fault lines in EU countries' willingness to accommodate migrants – which must be understood against the backdrop of the newfound (and continued) momentum of far right and extremist political groups across the continent (Amselle 2003; Miller-Idriss 2009; Partridge 2008; Hellström 2016). And finally, Britain's decision to leave the European Union in June 2016 has led many to ask if we are witnessing the advent of European *dis*-integration. Detractors have argued, and do so today with new zeal, that Europe has never quite shed its nationalist and even xenophobic inclinations (Mandel 2008; Schiller 2005; cf. Bunzl 2004; cf. Habermas 2009).

There is, I want to argue, a certain homology between European integration and what I am calling "trans-cultural mediationism." Both are predicated on the constructibility and malleability of large-scale human communities. Mediationism assumes that, because social collectivities and audiovisual texts are so enmeshed, one can shape and pivot image-and-sound in order to influence people's identities and loyalties; European integration assumes that nation-states, and people living across Europe, can be politically reshaped through supra-national institutions, law, and policy. Fundamentally, both are invested in particular assumptions about how sociality and social change operate; in the view of each, people and their commitments can be influenced and modified through self-consciously forged, then widely disseminated, ideologies and principles. Douglas Holmes (2000), following Paul

Rabinow (1989), has argued for the origins of this logic in French social modernism:

> The project of French social modernism was centrally concerned with the conceptualization of society as a field of human interdependence suscepti-ble to planning and administration through the application of "scientific" principles ... Various reformers sought to orient the project of the French state around issues of social interdependence and integration. They sought to make the notion of collectivity ... the dominant preoccupation of the state. (40)

The notion that national and transnational social collectivities are malleable – amenable to reconfiguration by institutions, organizations, a common coin – is not, of course, unreasonable, but like the assump-tion that global media mean a globalized world, it is a broad, vague premise that is only sometimes and partially correct. European political and social integration – inasmuch as it grows out of a particular belief in the possibility of engineering or cultivating a new kind of large-scale political and social collectivity – only "works," when it does, with greatly uneven results.

At least at ARTE, the "European culture channel," the devil was most certainly in the details.

The self-conscious integratability of Europe was an assumption that was doubly in play at ARTE; first, as ARTE staff attempted, through its programming, to draw together French and German viewers, and, second, in the everyday interactions at a channel whose very existence was premised on the social emergence of transnational and European solidarities. As I hope to demonstrate, ARTE's European project, both on- and off-screen, took many forms and drew upon a number of strat-egies but – which will be crucial to the argument of this book – never quite coalesced as a singular "imagination," "vision," or consistent set of sociopolitical ideas and commitments. Some modes and mechanisms of integration seemed, in my view (or as measured by audience viewer-ship), successful; others were, by most everyone's admission, laughable failures or, worse, un-laughable failures.

In chapters that follow, I examine some of the integrative successes and failures of ARTE (both in my view and in the view of others) to argue for the limits (and even obsolescence) of the long-standing belief that a transnational Europe can be promulgated and engineered. I hope to build my argument about Europe alongside the contours of my argument about trans-cultural mediationism. I hold them in tension, first, because they are brought together in the project of ARTE. But their resemblance also calls back to my argument about the ways in which social theory, in the late twentieth and early twenty-first centuries, reflects and/or enables particular kinds of institutional projects; that is, theories of European integration and the fluidities of political subjectivity are not altogether dissimilar from those of supposedly fluid *mediated* subjectivities.

I argue that neither is as viscous as concomitant social theory (and its application) would have us believe, and I hope through close ethnographic description to demonstrate why not. In my conclusion I will suggest that we are coming away from assumptions of fluidity as a result, perhaps, of a concomitant rise in critiques of modernist humanism. But we cannot fully understand the relationship of mediation and integration unless we also, finally, pay attention to nationalism.

nation and culture

Despite claims to the contrary – that the world is becoming unbordered, transnational, rescaled, globalized – at ARTE, explicitly charged with the task of remaking borders (co-founded by two countries especially well poised to join together in collaboration and integration given their history of shared European leadership), objectification of national cultures and identities was ever-present. Despite the self-consciousness of ARTE's mission to cultivate French-German cooperation and/or a sense of European belonging, national cultural stereotype and national ways of explaining people's behaviour most surprised me about work and life at ARTE. I found at the media organization that there was a deeply rooted (we might say "hegemonic") sense that national ways of organizing and understanding the world were fundamental and natural. These ideas informed most every activity at ARTE, in which people's appearance, behaviour, aesthetic choices, and work ethics were cast and organized in terms of national predilections and cultural difference.

It is easy to get lost in the woods of *nationalism*, without even mentioning, for the moment, *culture*. The nation-state, nationalism, national identity – these are concepts that are slippery to engage. For one, they are among the most written about phenomena in the social sciences, if not among all writing (over the past few centuries) *tout court*. There is little one can write about the nation-state without echoing, or contradicting, arguments that have already been made if not in anthropology then in political science, sociology, history, or a dozen other disciplines that regularly think and write about the nation. Nationalism – which I will here define simply as the belief that nations, or countries, are natural, contained units through which to organize human community and politics – remains a fundamental aspect of daily life for a large percentage of human beings across this planet. And yet this still-dominant ideology seems no longer to be as interesting to scholars as it once was. Nationalism did have its time in the scholarly limelight – especially in the wake of new nationalist movements in the 1950s and 1960s (e.g., Kahin 1952; Coleman 1958) – and though a good number of important refinements to theories of nationalism were produced in the 1970s and 1980s (Smith 1971; Fallers 1974; Gellner 1983), by the 1990s scholarly interest had begun to migrate towards transnationalism, globalization, and cosmopolitanism.

Scholarly interest in nationalism has never fully receded, however, especially because over the past few decades it has regularly been a kind of retort to those claiming that borders were coming undone. In an exchange in a 2005 issue of the *American Ethnologist*, for example, Matti Bunzl argued that Islamophobia in Austria was evidence that exclusionary ideologies had moved from the national context (in the form of anti-Semitism) to the European context, in which Christianity was being pitted against Islam. In other words, racialized exclusion was no longer the privilege of the nation-state, but of the supra-nation. In her response to the article, Nina Glick Schiller (2005) wrote,

> Although the current moment is marked by the restructuring of global capitalism, the world continues to be divided up into nation-states ... The anti-immigrant sentiment that is so widespread in every state in Europe is one way that national identities are being maintained within a broader European identity context. Bunzl's portrayal of Austrian nationalism as only European identity writ small, without reference to the growth of nationalist rhetoric in all states of the expanded European Union, is puzzling. His insistence that nationalism has seen its day keeps him from noting that it is by delineating themselves from foreigners that people in each European state display their nationalism. (529)

As a number of scholars produced work arguing for the weakening of national sovereignty (Sassen 1996; Appadurai 1993; Tsing 2000; Stoller 1997; Castells 2000), others wrote against them (Billig 1995; Calhoun 2003, 2007; Nairn 2003).

I implicitly take a side in this debate by arguing, alongside Schiller (2005), that the nation-state not only remains worthy of scholarly scrutiny but that the nation-state – now renewed, retooled, reconsolidated – obligates us to augment and sharpen our ethnography and theory. Although I certainly have my own opinions about national identity and the work it does in the world, I have tried, in the context of ARTE, to evaluate national sentiment first, in terms of the channel's own project(s), and, second, in terms of the political implications of its representations of (national) difference against the backdrop of a fast-changing, diversifying continent. In other words, I am not interested in arguing that commitments to ideas of national character are, *ipso facto*, chauvinist or problematic; rather, I found during my fieldwork that objectifications of national character and commitments to national identity tended to cause conflict among staff; thwarted collaboration that might have aided the channel in its project to build trans-European understanding, and gave rise to simplistic and problematic representations of societal diversity and pluralism. While I might have found that national identities at ARTE actually contributed to collaboration (the argument has often been made that Europe works *because of* and not *in spite of* strongly differentiated national identities), and that nationism (to set aside nationalism) provided a means of exchanging ideas and brokering compromise, I simply did not find this to be the case. Instead, ideas about the nation, national audiences, national identities, and national character tended, from my perspective, to muck things up and limit (political-pluralistic-accommodative) possibilities. In these pages I try to decipher, ethnographically, how and why.

To avoid falling down a theories-of-nationalism rabbit hole, I will merely remind the reader of anthropology's particular contributions to theories of the nation-state. For many years, the nation-state was more or less the bailiwick of political science and history, where it was approached mostly through studies of conflict and war, governments, and institutions. In the latter decades of the twentieth century, anthropologists, not least ones who were working in Europe, tended to find that the nation-state – rather than omnipresent and monolithic – was in fact quite an uneven presence in people's lives, variable in its legitimacy, and contingent on more locally produced ideas about belonging (e.g., Fallers 1974; Borneman 1992a, 1992b). Anthropologists argued that the nation-state needed to be approached not as a top-down institutional arrangement or leadership structure, but rather as socially constructed and negotiated (Barth 1969; Verdery 1991, 1993). In other words, people made the nation, not the other way around.

In the late 1980s, Benedict Anderson introduced one of the most eloquent and coherent anthropological treatises in this regard, arguing in

Imagined Communties (1991) that nationalism, as an ideology (rather than an institutional arrangement or economic system), largely supplanted religiosity. With the introduction of the printing press and the emergence of vernacular languages, which replaced "sacred languages" like Latin, readers of newspapers and novels could finally begin to read together and therefore come to understand the world together. These readers developed, to use the language of *both* Anderson and the first president of ARTE, a "common imagination" comprised of common referents, nationally circulating tropes and protagonists, and a sense of forward movement (alongside and simultaneous to other national communities) through what Anderson calls "empty" time. The theory has been revolutionary to anthropology's engagements with national communities as well as many other kinds of large-scale communities: much has been written about various shared "national" imaginations as well as local imaginations, regional imaginaries, and global imaginations. The theory became a warrant for anthropologists to look at how people's lives were being collectively mediated – through newspapers, soap operas, movies, and so on – to understand how collective identifications were being produced, circulated, and consumed (see Stankiewicz 2016 for more on theories of imagination/imaginaries).

While Anderson's (1991) theory continues to be influential, I call this book *Europe Un-Imagined* because, in certain ways, I think the time has come to rethink some of the theory's suppositions and implications. I am hardly the first do this (e.g., Lomnitz 2001; Wogan 2001; Sneath, Holbraad, and Pederson 2009), but I propose in this book to reconsider the "imagined community" of the nation with a set of objectives that differ somewhat from those of other scholars who have sought to challenge or innovate Anderson's theory. First, if there have been plenty of arguments about the obsolescence of the nation-state, and assertions that other kinds of identities and loyalties now compete with that of nationalism ("transnationalism," "globalism," "post-nationalism," "cosmopolitanism"), there hasn't been much effort to think carefully about how the rise of these other *-isms* fits into or alongside Anderson's theory. The operative assumption seems to be that transnationalism or supra-nationalism would operate very much like nationalism – through mediation, shared narratives, temporalities, common imagination – but through a net that is cast more broadly, gathering together people across, rather than within, national boundaries. (This is to some degree Appadurai's [1990] argument about global "mediascapes.")

Based on what I found at ARTE, I will challenge this kind of proposition, arguing that there was little concrete evidence for a "transnational

imagined community" at ARTE (or among its audiences, for that matter, at least in the opinion of most ARTE staff).[9] Staff at ARTE certainly
had quite disparate understandings of how best to represent Europe
on the screen, and there was often little agreement about whether a
particular ARTE-produced series was "good" or not. But I also want to
argue that transnational and post-national identifications may operate through different kinds of modalities and experiences altogether –
some of which do not correlate to forms or processes of mediation,
or which are much less self-conscious or narratively coherent than
Anderson's (1991) theory might imply.[10] Part of my goal, then, is to
hold in tension *national* imagined community with the supposition of
transnational or *post-national* imagined communities in order to prod
at the implications of imagined community and to think about how
the theory remains (or does not remain) relevant at a media organization in the twenty-first century. How can we specify transnationalism
and/or transnational sociality (and perhaps belonging) if it does not
look like, or function like, national (or indeed transnational) "imagined community"?

But second, as I have already made clear, what I mostly found at
ARTE, rather than the construction of a transnational imagined community, was a prevalence of national talk, national assumptions, and
national stereotype. Because ARTE is an organization explicitly charged
to be *not* nationalist (or at least to work against cultivating national sensibilities in its audiences) there is much to chew on here. Instead of
arguing that nationalism and national stereotype constitute a "strategy" for ARTE staff to navigate life and work at the channel (which
I will disagree with as a theoretical orientation to stereotype), ARTE
asks us to rethink how we understand people's awareness of nationalist orientations or ways of making sense of the world. I would guess
that many at ARTE would deny some of my characterizations of certain
actions or comments as being nationalist, but I would respond that a
person or idea can be nationalist even if he/she denies being so, and
even if he/she never explicitly invokes nationalist logics (cf. Schiller
and Wimmer 2002).

This is not such a radical idea. In studies of race and whiteness,
scholars talk about "colour-blind racism" through which people develop
a number of defences and excuses for claiming that they are *not* racist
("One of my best friends is black/white/Muslim"), while it is clear that
they are uncomfortable with or distrustful of people who they deem to
be of a different race (Bonilla-Silva 2006). Likewise, nationalism at ARTE
did not often appear as outright flag-waving or jingoism (cf. Billig 1995).

Not unlike colour-blind racism, people at ARTE tended to understand blatant nationalism to be socially unacceptable, and so it became otherwise expressed – often through irony or humour (see Hill 2007 for an interesting comparison) or through being "leaked" into situations in ways that were often tacit, as I mean to illustrate in chapters 2 and 3. In a world that is increasingly understood as transnational and global, in other words, I would argue that there is a considerable amount of what we might call "flag-blind nationalism." Although it may be that no one wants to admit to having national pride or being committed to national identity (don't we all want to be cosmopolitan, global citizens?), our socialization into national ways of thinking and being (in schools, through media, in our families) remains potent. Ways of categorizing other people, of forming ideas and opinions about them, predicting what they will say or how they will act, remain saturated in ideas about an "us" and a "them" that may draw upon a variety of subtle boundary-making strategies and ideologies, but in which national borders continue to play a leading role.

So what?

Well, if nationalism – a belief in the reality and ubiquity of "countries" that not only organizes people but also determines what they are like – has effects in the world (good or bad), it may behoove us to pay closer attention to how nationalism seeps into everyday situations, even (or perhaps especially) when we are in places and contexts in which it is supposedly eschewed in favour of other kinds of transnational, "world-open," and cosmopolitan orientations (cf. Mandel 2008, 47–50). In thinking about national ways of thinking as sometimes implicit rather than explicit, non-intentioned or non-intentional, or as "collateral" to non-nationalist identifications, we might better understand how people organize and make sense of other people (sometimes despite what they may say about how they do so).

Finally, a note about "culture."

Early during my fieldwork at ARTE, a story was related to me. An outside consulting firm had been hired to conduct team-building workshops and exercises at the channel. One of the exercises asked separate teams of self-identifying French and German ARTE staff members[11] to each build a miniature model house with materials that they were given. The punchline of the story is that the Germans took inventory of the materials they had, thinking first about what to do with them, while the French went immediately to work building the house, pausing periodically to discuss and debate how to proceed. "This is ARTE in a nutshell!" an animated woman with whom I was sharing an office at ARTE told me during one of my first weeks at the channel: "The Germans plan, everything in lists [*mon dieu, les listes!*], and you have to follow *each* step or else they panic [*sinon, c'est la panique!*]." She continued, "With the French, it's 'say one thing, turn around and do another' – they agree, and then you're on the phone with them two days later arguing with them about why they did something else completely different."

As this example suggests, "culture" at ARTE was most often deployed to describe and organize French-German national difference. At its most rudimentary, this schema could be characterized as a Lévi-Straussian continuum of "hot" to "cold" (Lévi-Strauss 1955): the French were "hot," emotional, argumentative, subjectivist, quixotic, and so on, but the Germans were methodical, phlegmatic, objective, rational (cf. Boyer 2000, 464–8). Nearly every behaviour could, and was, explained with and through this schema – for example, the Germans didn't like the French documentary proposal about histories of colours? Typically German! For Germans, "colour" is too touchy-feely and "artsy." The French director of programs refused to hire a German to head the new music programming department? To be expected! The French are too attached to their nationalist pride in the arts to pick the objectively best person for the job. One assistant told me, without blinking, that the French were "Latin" and were much more kindred to the Italians and Spanish than to the "cold" Germans. France is a culture of the "south," I was once told by a programmer, while Germany is a culture of the "north." (And into this thermodynamic spectrum could be fit almost any nation in Europe – Poland and the Netherlands were closer to chilly Germany; Croatia and Portugal were warmer, more Mediterranean, more French.) With these categories and cultural geographies discursively in play, and mobilized/mobilizable in everyday conversation, everything from taste in music to economic policy could be explained in warmer/French versus colder/German "cultural" terms, and often was.

This book is not interested in parsing or defining French culture or German culture – indeed, this is close to the *opposite* of my intention – but in talk and ideas that people hold *about* "culture" (as a concept through which people understand and make sense of the world). It asks after the pervasiveness of culturalism, culture talk, and national cultural dichotomy at a multinational organization ostensibly charged with producing a "common imagination" and post-national or counter-national ways of understanding the world – founded, in part, to undo what Gayatri Spivak (2010) has called the "possessive spell" of chauvinist nationalism (86–7).

Why, among a self-consciously transnational, trans-cultural, and mul-tilingual staff, does talk about romantic French and bellicose Germans (continue to) pervade and prevail? Why are "French culture," "German culture," and *culture(s)*, more broadly, consistently set in opposition and contradistinction when one might predict that staff at ARTE would emphasize similarity, intersection, and complexity, or at least not incom-mensurable difference? Why do invocations of (bounded) *culture(s)* – at ARTE, and in a great many other institutions and settings – remain more compelling ways of explaining appearance and behaviour than others that might pay attention to historical contingency, geography, socialization, education, politics, language, and life experience (or other features of interlinking human communities that escape our attention or wherewithal)?

With these questions in mind, I attempt in this book to better under-stand how and why "culture" – both as an implicit category and an explicit one, both as an emic-folk category and (also, still) an etic-analytical one – remains so convincing a concept for understanding social difference, even in the face of social and linguistic variegation, complexity, and unevenness.

On the one hand, I mean to shed light on what I argue is a broaden-ing (or deepening) pattern across much of Western Europe, especially in the wake of recent political-economic pressures and fissures, in which *culture* is deployed to imply and (re)construct social unifor-mity and consensus. Culture not only remains a key idiom through which European sociality and society are understood, but indeed today seems one of the only means through which similarity and dif-ference can be fathomed. On the other hand, well beyond Europe, this book seeks to probe at the awkward and unresolved homologies between culture at ARTE and anthropology's ongoing invocations (whether explicit or implicit) of this key concept: In what ways does culture at ARTE mirror social theory's predilections for conceiving of circumscribed, "rounded" sociality, and shared-patterned behav-iour? If we tend to think the concept is outmoded or problematic – that anthropologists and others have in fact "moved on" – how do we contend with contexts in which it remains compelling and explana-tory, perhaps especially among educated people and experts (Holmes and Marcus 2005; cf. Handler 1988)? Finally, in even embarking on a study of Europe, to what extent are we always already mired in culture as insides/outsides? To this question I turn in the book's conclusion.

about this ethnographic study

This ethnographic study of the television channel ARTE took place, in the main, over approximately sixteen months, from October 2007 to January 2009 (funded by the National Science Foundation and the Wenner-Gren Foundation), with an additional two months of pre-dissertation fieldwork in the summer of 2006 (funded by the Social Science Research Council and New York University's Graduate School of Arts and Science).

Having initially made contacts at ARTE France, just outside of Paris, I spent the first four months of my fieldwork with the ARTE Development office there, before moving on to ARTE's headquarters in Strasbourg in February 2008. At ARTE's headquarters, I completed a string of internships, over approximately a year, including stints with ARTE's news department (one month), its documentary unit (four months), the programming department (two months), the audience studies office (one month), and viewer relations department (le service téléspectateurs/ Zuschauerdienst) (one month). I also spent intermittent weeks with the various production teams of *ZOOM Europa*, *Karambolage*, and *Philosophie*. Immediately after completing fieldwork in Strasbourg, I spent two weeks at the offices of ARTE Germany, located in Baden-Baden (in January 2009). With support from a Provost's Summer Research Award from Temple University, I returned to ARTE for a month of follow-up research and interviews in May 2014.

Participant observation at ARTE took many forms. Throughout the fieldwork period, I carried out the regular duties of interns – organizing, fetching, emailing, and mailing. But I was also given a variety of other tasks, drawing on my prior knowledge of film production work, English-language skills, or familiarity with American audiences. Most often I was employed as a researcher: at ARTE France I was asked to think about which of ARTE's films might appeal to an American academic audience; in ARTE's documentary department I did fact-checking and read through script proposals, providing summaries for department programmers and editors (but always alongside the regular duties of an intern – organizing, fetching, and so forth). When English was involved, I often provided translation or proofreading services. And sometimes, as in the case of ARTE *Info* (news) and the audience studies department, I was allowed to mostly watch and ask questions (though there is an ARTE news report on the financial crisis of 2008 that includes my name in its production credits).

In the chapters that follow, I have, whenever possible, included direct quotes from interviews or from my notes in which I attempted to reproduce as accurately as possible something that I heard. But I did not employ a recording device except in formal interviews (of which I recorded about twenty-five), and I often did not have a notebook in tow during some of the most interesting moments of my time at ARTE. Yet because television and media work often requires that one have a notebook open and a pen at the ready – especially during meetings – I was often able to take careful notes on what was happening and being said. Each night I then reviewed my handwritten notes and kept an ongoing electronic diary of what transpired on a given day.

Most people I encountered at ARTE knew exactly who I was and what I was doing there; I was most often "the American" and sometimes "the anthropologist" (or, to some German-speakers, the doctoral student in "Medienwissenschaften"). Not unlike a village, ARTE was a place where news and gossip travelled quickly. I often encountered individuals whom I had never before met who knew surprisingly a lot about me – that I was from New York, that I knew Thierry Garrel (ARTE France's former, well-known director of documentary), that I had spent time at Sciences Po, an elite French university, that I was a little bit nosy (or so someone told me in my final month at the channel). Various aspects of "who I was" mattered more to people than others, and I always found it revealing to note which of these roles I was called into in various interactions at the channel.

I have tried, in the chapters that follow, to provide a sense of movement through ARTE's buildings and offices that reflects my own motion through the channel's offices and studios, from chapter 1, which begins in Paris at ARTE France, through ARTE's documentary and news departments in Strasbourg (chapters 2, 3, 4), to ARTE's audience studies department, where I completed some of my last weeks of fieldwork, in chapter 6.

"no one watches ARTE": why ARTE matters

A number of readers who are already familiar with ARTE may, throughout their engagement with this book, think to themselves, "But nobody watches ARTE!" It is, after all, a relatively marginal channel and, especially in Germany, something of a narrow sliver in a wide range of available television channels (not to mention on-demand channels, etc.). But

I want to make two things clear: first, as I reiterate elsewhere, I am not interested in the question of reception. Ascertaining whether or not ARTE somehow influences people in one way or another – to feel more "European," to know more about the Middle East – is not my project. I simply did not study audiences, except through the lens of the audience studies department at ARTE itself. Partly this is because I am more interested in how producers think about meaning as they make concrete, observable decisions about scripts, scheduling, editing, and other material aspects of production work. Partly this is because producers and audience members (as I argue again in chapter 6), especially at a channel like ARTE, are not entirely distinct groups (as Barry Dornfeld [1988] argued in his study of the PBS) – and we can learn much about ARTE's audiences (and whether or not they cohere) through ethnography at the channel itself.

But second, ARTE's size and audience numbers belie its influence. ARTE is a state-funded, governmental project whose Strasbourg building abuts that of the European Parliament. Unlike what one would find at HBO or NBC, many of its highest-level administrators have held government posts or go on to hold government posts, both national and supra-national. ARTE is regularly held up – in French, German, and other European contexts – as a successful example of European cultural cooperation. It is cited in government reports and referred to in speeches on parliament floors. ARTE France is widely recognized by cultural elites in France, Germany, and elsewhere in Europe as a highly legitimate and respected media outlet, producing some of Europe's most lauded and award-winning films, television, and even books. Perhaps this is why ARTE staff enjoyed telling me that when they told someone they worked at ARTE, the response was inevitably, "Oh, I watch ARTE all the time!" Near-universal viewership despite ARTE's more or less steady 4–5 per cent audience share …

All this is to say that ARTE is far more than its audiences, which are a fraction of those of TF1, Das Erste, or HBO. What it produces and programs – what it *does* – is watched closely – if not on television – by large numbers of media professionals across Europe, and by many influential cultural and political elites. As I mention later in this text, this is precisely what Faye Ginsburg (2003) meant by the importance of the "off-screen" aspects of media's influence (cf. McCarthy 2010, esp. 1–30). What is of equal importance to how many viewers watch a documentary about headscarves in French schools is how the film may get mentioned in a European parliamentary debate; or at a dinner party of cultural elites in Munich; or if a government official, even the president himself/herself, gets the notion that ARTE is pushing against conventional understandings of Muslims in Europe, or even of "European culture" itself. The political visibility and legitimacy of ARTE, in other words, must be considered alongside its "normal" audiences, which, while hardly those of HBO, still number in the millions.

organization of chapters

Chapter 1 provides a general discussion of ARTE's transnational organization and history, and introduces readers to the complexity and compromises of the channel's administrative structures. Chapter 2 provides ethnographic vignettes of four television production contexts at ARTE, introducing the daily texture of work at ARTE and how particular kinds of decision-making, often at the level of micro-practices, come to shape ARTE's programming and representational politics. Ethnographic anecdote and analysis of production practices demonstrates a range of sensibilities and imagined audiences on the part of producers, from the program *Karambolage*, which aims to construct Europe through French and German mutual understanding; to *ARTE Info*, which works at the intersections of French and German knowledge and the selective treatment of certain current events as distinctly European; to *ZOOM Europa*, which attempted to present explicitly European topics in a way that was broadly accessible and which aimed to be relatively free of nationally specific perspectives or knowledge.

Through a discussion of how French and Germans at ARTE tend to "read" one another (e.g., what sorts of shoes are typically "German"), how they construct categories of French-ness/German-ness, and how they read French-ness and German-ness into aesthetic styles and production practices, chapter 3 argues that French-ness and German-ness were everywhere reified into a set of overly coherent stereotype and cultural schemata. But the chapter moves to contrast these objectifications with interview material demonstrating the complexities and modes of belonging and solidarity at ARTE.

One of the clearest strategies ARTE programmers deploy in efforts to fulfil the channel's European mandate, and to bridge national audiences' interests, can be seen in the channel's engagement with programming about twentieth-century history and, especially, war. Chapter 4 explores ARTE's engagements with history (and the problem of nationalist historiographies) not only through the channel's heavily historical programming but also in the ways in which staff talk about the fraught historical context of France-Germany. Chapter 4 examines the complex semiotic work underlying the production and programming of documentaries about the Second World War in particular.

In chapter 5, I explore the problem and meaning of "culture" at ARTE, demonstrating that "culture" is a highly ambiguous category at ARTE and yet is vital to its self-understandings as the "European culture channel." In particular, I examine the strategic semantic slippage, pervasive at ARTE, between European "culture" and European "Culture," while foregrounding the "cultural" analysis that I myself am performing throughout.

Ethnographic evidence in chapter 6 focuses on ARTE's audience studies department, highlighting the ways in which one staff member talks about why programs do or do not "work" for French or German audiences based on what she understands to be "national" preferences for particular genres, kinds of narratives, or political themes. It then moves to consider how conceptions and approaches to audiences at ARTE are changing in light of a neoliberalizing and digitalizing media landscape; it closes by asking whether trans/national public media like ARTE have a future, and argues that they should.

The book's final section attempts to gain distance from ARTE's cameras and spreadsheets, offering, by way of conclusion, three theoretical "riffs" and provocations towards which I think ARTE gestures.

I hope to lead the reader through various studios and offices and meeting rooms of ARTE in a way that overlays theoretical issues with the lived realities of everyday life and work at this trans-border channel. I must re-emphasize here my gratitude for those *ARTEsans* who helped me understand what they do and why they do it.

1

bienvenue à ARTE / wilkommen bei ARTE

I began my work with ARTE at its French headquarters, ARTE France, at the very last stop of *métro* line number twelve, whose dark green line across Paris's subway map wends towards a little satellite village, Issy-les-Moulineaux, just beyond the city's southwestern limits. I had already taken the *métro* to this last stop many times before my official arrival at ARTE, having conducted pre-dissertation fieldwork in an attempt to line up some sort of internship or other form of welcome from someone, *anyone,* who would be willing to allow an anthropologist to lurk about. I had been able to make a number of acquaintances who assured me that they would "find something" for me to do when I would return for my year or more of fieldwork, but people who work with the near-sighted deadlines of television are not, unfortunately, prone to planning things much beyond a few months into the future. So, when I stepped off of the plane into Paris in the fall of 2007, I found that much remained to be negotiated: What could I do, an *American* whose French was good but whose German was shaky, in the offices and studios of a French-German and European television channel? How would I make myself *useful*? I argued that I had received advanced training in documentary film production as part of my doctoral program; that I could help evaluate films, or just organize them; that I would do whatever sort of clerical work would allow me to get a foot in the door, to hang out a bit. "But you're a doctoral student," replied a woman who would eventually be my supervisor at ARTE France. "We can't just have you making copies. We have to find something that's *appropriate* for you to do."

From the beginning, who I was, and what I was doing at ARTE France, was thus marked – I was *l'américain* who had something of a quaint research project about ARTE. Yet, as an American, and as a researcher from an American university, senior staff at ARTE France eventually decided that I was in a unique position to assess how ARTE might become a more recognized audiovisual "brand" in the United States, especially among academics who might see in ARTE's programming useful tools for teaching or for their own research. So after weeks and weeks of waiting and exchanges of emails, a project finally emerged suitable for an American graduate student at a self-consciously European television channel: "We would like you to promote ARTE's image in the United States, to think about what ARTE might have to offer certain educated audiences and academics," explained Patrice Antoine-Duprès, in ARTE's development department. "You'll need to think about what's *different* about ARTE's programming, its unique editorial lines, the different areas of programming that are ARTE's strong points," added Guillaume Rondeaux, the head of ARTE's international relations office. "We have a certain focus on the arts, European history, and so forth," Patrice explained. "We're too 'in it.' We don't know why ARTE might be interesting to American academics ... we need an *outsider* to think about how we might put together a catalogue for the United States market, someone who can assess ARTE's programming with a fresh eye." The project was in many ways ideal; it allowed me to sift through catalogue after catalogue, familiarizing myself with several years of ARTE's programming, and to think about what made it compellingly different, in what I will call its "trans/national" model, from national public television in France, Germany, and most anywhere else in the world for that matter.

My first days and weeks at ARTE were also spent explaining away my presence and summarizing why a cultural anthropologist might be interested in a channel like ARTE. "You think ARTE's interesting?" was a half-rhetorical question posed to me a dozen times in the first weeks. "Well, yes," I would reply, tentatively. "French and Germans working together, all the history of it, the idea of building something European together ..." My answer was usually met with some combination of smiles and smirks, or else a facial expression that resembled something like a slow remembering: "Yes ..." people would respond, turning up their eyes and scrunching their foreheads into reflection. "I suppose it *is* interesting ..." But almost just as often I would hear, "Well, it *was* interesting ..."

"You see, what you have to understand about ARTE," explained a journalist at ARTE France who had been at the channel since its inception, "is that many people at ARTE feel like its original mission and mandate have gotten a bit obscured over time. At the beginning there was a lot of excitement for the project, for what it meant for Europe. But over time, things sometimes seem, they've gotten to be quite ... *difficult.*"

The word the journalist used, in fact, was *lourd;* later, at ARTE's Strasbourg headquarters, Germans would use the German near-synonym *schwer.* A more appropriate translation, in either language, would perhaps be "heavy." Things at ARTE were always very heavy, it seemed. While business at ARTE France was complicated enough, at ARTE's Strasbourg headquarters the work of coordination was even more byzantine.

"It's just so [*lourd*], ARTE," a French secretary in Strasbourg would tell me on an almost weekly basis, complaining to me about some bureaucratic snafu or other that would mean an afternoon spent on the phone trying to coordinate people at ARTE's French and German national headquarters in Paris and Baden-Baden, respectively. A week earlier, a German member of the documentary department had explained to me, "What's really [*schwer*] is how production is organized at ARTE, all the people you have to deal with, between ARTE's headquarters, the German stations, ARTE *Deutschland* – if you're trying to get proposals from the German stations, you have to know whom to contact at ten different offices. You really just have to *know* who people are, whom to contact."

French and Germans, I was told even in those first weeks at ARTE France, could agree on very little at ARTE. And yet it was almost immediately clear that they also agreed on a lot: ARTE's bureaucratic organization and infrastructure, the way in which the channel straddles France, Germany, and a wider intra-European network of producers, was understood almost by everyone to be at least unwieldy, and, at worst, so cumbersome as to be crippling to the station's daily work.

"The channel has only recently begun to address the 'structural question,'" said Thierry Garrel, the longtime head of ARTE's famed documentary department. "We began with a clear mission and idea of our editorial line ... but that's becoming blurry [*flou*] now. The channel's structure is ... the organization ... well ... maybe it would be easier ..." He drew me a picture on a corner of his *Libération* newspaper, which I reproduced in my notebook.

Thierry's sketch would be the first of many, as ARTE producers and programmers tried to concretely illustrate for me, with boxes, arrows, columns,

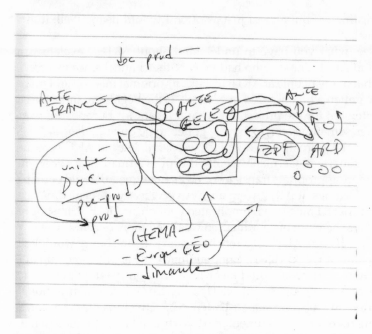

Figure 1.1 Thierry Garrel, then-head of ARTE France's documentary unit, sketches how production is organized at ARTE; the arrows and loops indicate the circulation of a documentary through ARTE's organization. (From author's notebook)

and sometimes loops, how production activities and decision-making were organized at ARTE, through an elaborate distribution of responsibilities and competencies between ARTE's headquarters, its national "poles" in France and Germany, and various production studios. During a week I spent at the production studio of one of ARTE's current events programs, *ZOOM Europa*, I often heard the production team complaining about their very complex interactions with ARTE's organizational structures.

"This channel is killing me!" one director of production half-shouted as she walked briskly through the studios of *ZOOM*, no doubt on her way to make a phone call to someone at the channel's headquarters, either in Paris or Strasbourg (or both). One afternoon I asked her to explain why, in fact, the organization of ARTE was "killing her" – why it was so *lourd*. She, too, began to sketch.

She explained that each week the various reports and features comprising each *ZOOM* program would arrive from France and Germany;

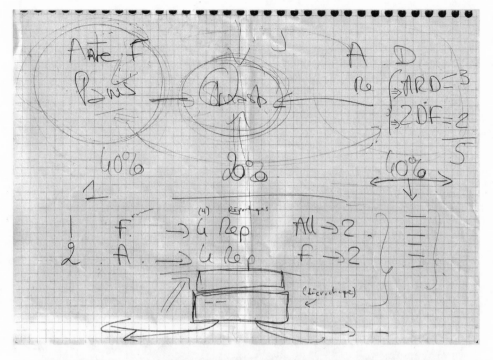

Figure 1.2 A director of production at ARTE's *ZOOM Europa* program sketches how production activities are divvied up among the three administrative structures of ARTE. (From author's notebook)

one week, four reports would come from France, two from Germany; the following week, four would be sent from Germany, two from France. For those coming from Germany, things got even more complicated, since these would have to be further divided between production by Germany's ZDF public channel and the ARD regional public German channels. Whereas the ZDF is centralized (in Mainz), the ARD stations are distributed into Germany's federal states, Länder, so that "German" reports were in fact produced in collaboration and rotation by a handful of regional production offices – by Bayerischer Rundfunk in Munich; Westdeutscher Rundfunk in Cologne; the Sender Freies in Berlin; and six or seven other stations. So if *ZOOM*'s reports were roughly divided in half between France and Germany,[1] the German reports were further subdivided between the ZDF and the ARD; and the ARD reports had to be assigned to the various regional channels, in

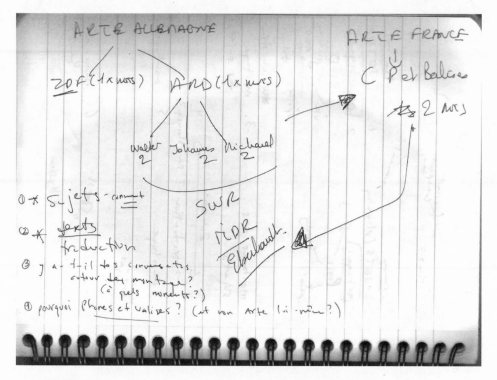

Figure 1.3 Another producer sketches production responsibilities, showing author's annotated questions in the lower left-hand corner. (From author's notebook)

alternation, and according to their relative size (roughly, by percentage of the ARD's overall budget). Hearing the details of this exquisite delegation of production responsibilities – amounting indeed to a mess of boxes and arrows – I expressed surprise. "So, wait, does this mean that the smaller channels have to supply ZOOM with, I don't know, maybe just 2 or 3 per cent of the program's reports?" She smiled sarcastically, but was nonchalant: "Welcome to ARTE," she said curtly. "*Bienvenue à ARTE.*"

By the end of my first months at ARTE's headquarters in Strasbourg, I would collect almost a dozen of these organigram sketches, each depicting some aspect of the channel's organization or production process and infrastructure. Some used boxes and arrows, some employed columns and charts, one department head even used multiple coloured markers to help make things clear for me. Seemingly lampooning

Figure 1.4 The cover of a brochure designed by artists invited to provide a week of art installations and participatory activities at ARTE's headquarters in Strasbourg; the text in bold translates as "a network beehive" or a "beehive of networks." (Credit Équipe d'artistes INTERIM, used with permission)

the unwieldiness and multidirectionality of ARTE's trans/national structures, a group of artists invited to ARTE's Strasbourg headquarters (as part of ARTE's artist residency program) played with the theme of arrows and boxes in a brochure introducing a week of activities the artists had planned, alluding on the brochure's cover to the labyrinthine assignation of responsibility at ARTE.

ARTE and the "trans/national"

These organograms – collections of boxes and arrows that provide ARTE staff with conceptual roadmaps and visual representations of how things get done at ARTE – illuminate a crucial element of ARTE's trans/national institutional culture. I use a slash between "trans" and "national" here and henceforth to indicate the dynamism, and equivocation, of social formations that both tether together, and move between, national and pluri- or supra-national jurisdictions. This slash means to explicitly disrupt the notion that the transnational or global is a *fait accompli,* and is meant as a reminder that, as this chapter will show, most trans/national organizations like ARTE's rest upon a complex set of compromises that have strung its work both *across* and *within* nation-states in ways that make trying to discern or "separate out" one from the other a difficult, if not fruitless, exercise.

Although ARTE is a joint project between France and Germany, and funded in the main by those countries' governments, the channel has recently begun receiving funding assistance from the European Union,[2] and also has a series of production agreements providing cooperation and film co-productions with public television channels throughout Europe (see Table 1.1). Twenty per cent of ARTE's documentary department's funding, for example, is specifically allocated for co-productions with Austria's ORF, Poland's TVP, or Belgium's RTBF public television channels. Whether these productions are to be understood as cooperations between European public broadcasters (what scholars of the European Union might refer to as "intergovernmental" arrangements) or as somehow emergently, supra-nationally "European," however, presents us with a complex set of considerations: How are films produced? In what nations are they broadcast, or distributed? Are their narratives somehow different from those usually encountered in "nationally" produced films? Who are their imagined audiences and "where" are they?

Table 1.1 European channels with varying degrees of cooperative agreements with ARTE (at the time of fieldwork)

"Contract of Association" (Accord d'association/Assoziierungsvertrag)
RTBF Belgium, signed in 1993 TVP Poland, signed in 2001
ORF Austria, signed in 2001
"In the framework of these contracts, associate members and ARTE have a reciprocal engagement to carry out a substantial amount of co-production; they deliver to one another an established volume of each channel's productions and associate members participate in deliberative meetings with a consultative voice."
"Contract of Cooperation" (Accord de coopération/Kooperationsvereinbarung)
SRG SSR Idée suisse Switzerland, signed in 1995
YLE (TV1) Finland, signed in 1991
ERT Greece, signed in 2009
"In the terms of these contracts, partner corporations and ARTE have principally the ambition to develop a substantial number of co-productions in all genres of audiovisual production."
"Contract of Co-production" (Accord de coproduction/
Koproduktionsabkommen)
BBC UK, signed in 2001
SVT Sweden, signed in 2002
"Contracts of co-production have opened a new, refocused way of co-producing without additional financial responsibilities."

This chapter argues that these sorts of questions, as I have articulated them above, and as they are often posed of "globalizing formations," are ultimately inadequate ways of approaching the partial, hybrid, even *un-localizable* structures borne out of global and trans/national processes. Anthropologists and other social scientists increasingly recognize that "either/or" questions oversimplify the complexities of global processes, presume their uni-directionality, and tend to be, as is evidenced by anthropology's theoretical shiftings over just the past decade or so, usually shortsighted.

Indeed, twenty-five years after Arjun Appadurai (1990) first theorized five "scapes" through which new kinds of transnational and global formations were supposedly undoing or remaking the hermetic logics and coherencies of national and other large-scale communities, we find ourselves at quite a different geopolitical and theoretical juncture. Whereas Appadurai boldly asserted in 1993, "We need to think ourselves beyond the nation" (1996, 158), he has written more recently, "Some critics saw my earlier effort to characterize the (then) emerging world of globalization ... as naively cheerful about the benefits of global flows. This essay ... addresses the darker sides of globalization" (2006, 3).

Similarly, Saskia Sassen's foundational work on global processes has shifted from an argument that "state sovereignty [and] nation-based citizenship ... are being destabilized and even transformed as a result of globalization and ... new technologies" (1996, xi–xii; cf. 2002), to a more nuanced and ambivalent account of global transformations in which she acknowledges that "the encounter between national and denation-alizing processes ... has multiple and variable outcomes," and that "the national [is] still alive and well" (2006, 2).

As I argued in my introduction, the history of ARTE (and the sentiments of those who work there) parallel the contours of shifting theoretical understandings of, and scholarly enthusiasm for, global-ism and globalization in quite an interesting way: indeed, the treaty establishing the channel was signed the very same year that Appadurai (1990) coined the now well-travelled neologism "mediascape." As if to directly implement Appadurai's thesis and bring to (institutional) life Benedict Anderson's pioneering theory that large-scale community and identities are held together because, "in the minds of each [community member] lives the image of their communion" (Anderson 1991, 6–7), the founders of ARTE believed they could construct a popular *imagina-tion* of Europe by *imaging* Europe in a new way.

In the heady days of the early 1990s, amidst intensive European inte-gration and institutional construction following the Single European Act (1986), ARTE seemed to symbolize Europe's imminent transcen-dence of its trade-treaty origins, confirming an emerging socio-cultural element marking the fruition of a united Europe dreamt about by Saint-Simon and Churchill,[3] a Europe that could offer a source of cultural identification and a sense of belonging akin to national identity. Indeed the literature on *"social Europe"* explodes in the early to mid-1990s, very quickly becoming a topic of debate and the object of theorization in policy circles (e.g., Leibfried and Pierson 1992; de Swaan 1994). The Maastricht Treaty aimed to ensconce emerging social and identitarian concerns in a document that stressed the *telos* of European integra-tion as an "ever closer union"[4] not of reified "nations" but, in a shift to socially charged language, of European "peoples" and "citizens."[5] This language exactly parallels that of ARTE's original founding treaty, which articulates its mission as the "bringing together" (*rapprochement*)[6] of the "peoples of Europe."

It is in this dual context, then – not only that of rapid *de facto* European integration but also a particular kind of policy zeitgeist assuming the European project could continue to prosper and expand through self-conscious social constructivism – that ARTE's first president, Jérôme

Clément, enthusiastically proclaimed in a 1992 *Le Monde* editorial that "ARTE is a European project ... What could be more important for Europe, now under construction, than to forge in common a memory, an imaginary, a common view of the world that surrounds us?"

A September 1992 issue of the left-leaning newspaper *Libération* featured photographs of French and German celebrities and public intellectuals with accompanying quotations explaining why they supported the launch of the European channel, and, implicitly, Europe. Régis Debray and Bernard-Henri Lévy (1989) even equated the stakes of the channel's success with the success of Europe as a whole:

> Will we write, one day, of the catastrophe named Europe? That depends today on some simple decisions. And these decisions are not played out on the terrain of quotas or coins – but on that of culture which alone can cement a common vision of the world and of oneself ... [ARTE] could become the location par excellence of creation and of discovery: of this Europe of word and idea which our country, mired in its provincial pride, always hears about, but to which it never gives figure. (n.p.; author's translation)

One detects in much of this early, enthusiastic discourse about ARTE – and in the enthusiasm for the potential of globalization to usher in a new global, post-national era – a fetishization, I would argue, of the ultra-mobile image perhaps best captured in the usual visualization of the "broadcast" as signals (sometimes lightning bolts) radiating outward and downward from the tip of an antenna.

ARTE, and globalization's *modus operandi*, seem to hinge on the imagination of media(tion) as unmoored from and unencumbered by national borders or sensibilities, since broadcasts – composed only of the immaterial fluidity of radio waves – could flow across and through national, cultural, ethnic and other kinds of borders, bringing to television and movie screens the same programs and narratives through which the shared "imagination" – equally evoked by Appadurai (1990), Anderson (1991), and ARTE's first president (1991) – might be cultivated and assembled. The belief that images-across-borders produce identities-across-borders (what I refer to in the introduction as "transcultural mediationism") may be less an insight into the actual mechanisms of global cultural processes (as these are assumed to hinge largely on flows of media) than indicative of the ways in which the concepts of *image* and *imagination* have been too cogently fused, and mutually constructed, as a result of linguistic semblance.

Indeed let us reconsider the etymological relationship between *images* and *imagination*. Appadurai (1990) writes in "Disjuncture and Difference in the Global Cultural Economy":

> The world we live in today is characterized by a new role for the imagination in social life. To grasp this new role, we need to bring together the old idea of images, especially mechanically produced images (in the Frankfurt School sense); the idea of the imagined community (in Anderson's sense); and the French idea of the imaginary *(imaginaire)* as a constructed landscape of collective aspirations, which is no more and no less real that the collective representations of Émile Durkheim, now mediated through the complex prism of modern media ... The image, the imagined, the imaginary – these are all terms that direct us to something critical and new in global cultural processes: *the imagination as social practice*. (31)

To understand the "new role of the imagination in social life," Appadurai (1990) argues for three distinct meanings that imagination must comprise: images, imagined community, and the *imaginaire*. New circulations of images (as "ideoscapes" and "mediascapes") (35–6) constitute "repertoires" and "narrative-based accounts of strips of reality" ("the old idea of images") which comprise "landscapes ... navigated by agents who both experience and constitute larger formations, in part form their own sense of what these landscapes have to offer" (i.e., imagined community). Images (media), then, are at once distinct from the imagination (it is their newly global circulations and centrality to social life that *gives rise* to new forms of mobility and agency), but also already constitutive of imagination.

Imagination here functions *through* images – and because it is partly predicated upon Anderson's (1991) "imagined communities," it does so doubly (or recursively), since Anderson's "community" itself hinges on communicative practices. That is, when Appadurai (1990) argues that, in the United States, "the issue is no longer of nostalgia but of a social *imaginaire* built largely around reruns ... The drug wars in Colombia recapitulate the tropical sweat of Vietnam ... Jimmy Stewart concealing John Wayne concealing Spiro Agnew" (30), imagination simultaneously denotes (1) a "social *imaginaire*" consisting of a kind of palimpsest of American image-memories of war; (2) mass media texts themselves, including John Wayne movies and television news reports; and (3) an *imagined* community of Americans who collectively watch and engage with these media, and for whom these media constitute the reality of national belonging.

The problem with this rendering of "imagination" is that, though it argues for a weaving-together or synthesis of image-texts, each of these discursive-theoretical "pieces" of imagination operate in quite distinct ways in located (ethnographic) worlds of social action: the "global" circulation of Hollywood films is not, in fact, synonymous with desire for mobility or travel; nor do these films merely or automatically "give rise to" imagined communities, be they local, national, or trans/national.

Only after over two decades of prolific attention to "globalization" are we able to better perceive the ways in which "globalization" has *itself* been constructed and reified through disproportionate attention to the mobility of images, imaginaries, and imaginings. Globalization and transnationalism have so earnestly drawn on tropes of "image" and "imagination" to constitute their meaning and analytics that we might wonder if the "global" has come to be primarily "imag-ined" as a fusing together of moving pictures – a kind of montage – rather than as an unwieldy sticking-and-tethering-together of legal contracts and budget documents; cross-border administrators and staff; rented office space and constructed buildings; and a palimpsest of arrangements for the moving of people, things, and media across national borders.

ARTE: a history of compromises and a compromising history

ARTE was partly the outgrowth of a French project initiated by Prime Minister Laurent Fabius in 1985 called "LA SEPT," which was more or less a pool of production funds meant to encourage the production of high-quality film and documentary to supplement the more mainstream programming of the major French networks. François Mitterand's socialist administration introduced LA SEPT, which refers to cinema – in French, cinema is *la septième art*, "the seventh art" – as a means of balancing the ongoing privatization, and *de facto* Americanization, of French media markets (Regourd 2004). LA SEPT's programming was first available only by satellite, then cable, and finally between 3 p.m. and midnight on the national channel France 5.

The idea for a French-German cultural television channel was first envisioned, however, by a German working group – composed of three regional minister-presidents – that brought the idea for a cultural television channel, initially French-German but expected to eventually expand to become a more broadly European channel, to the French government in early 1988. In November of that year French and German governments announced that the project was under consideration, and in France it was soon understood that LA SEPT might already provide the basic structures, on the French side of things, to accommodate this new European channel. It was the support of President François Mitterand and his counterpart Chancellor Helmut Kohl that perhaps most guaranteed a still-inchoate and visionary project the visibility and political legitimacy it required to move beyond ideas on paper. Indeed, the President and Chancellor's friendship has become something of an origin myth in the halls of ARTE, where I was told again and again that the channel would never have seen the light of day were it not for "these two men," "because Mitterand and Kohl understood the importance of sharing culture," and because "Kohl and Mitterand were very close, and made ARTE a symbol of their friendship and French-German reconciliation." On 2 October 1990, the evening of German reunification, the French government and the eleven regional governments of Germany signed the international treaty that established the foundations of ARTE, Association Rélative aux Télévisions Européennes (Association for European Television).

As the project moved forward, however, the architects of the world's first self-avowedly transnational and supranational television channel, who only months earlier had enthusiastically written about ARTE as a new kind of "television without borders" (*La Croix* 1992) that would disseminate "a living [Europe] by and through images" (Debray and Lévy 1989) found themselves wondering whether the project would ever even get off the ground. Nahima Vianna (2000) notes in her thesis on ARTE's institutional history that when French and Germans came together to discuss what form ARTE would practically take, Germans came quite close to quitting the negotiations and abandoning the project altogether. At issue was the very basic question: How would this bi-national and "European" channel be structurally organized?

"The French didn't understand that we have a very different, federal system in Germany," a German documentarian explained to me one day at lunch. "They *still* don't really understand this," she joked. "We have no centralized media in Germany because of our history. The Nazis used media so effectively in their propaganda that after the war the government broke up the media and put it in the hands of the German states [Länder] to prevent any centralized government from using the media for its own politics. Germans feel very strongly about this ... about the risks of centralized media." Indeed, German radio and television were decentralized after the Second World War, and in 1952 the main German public channel, the ARD (popularly referred to as *das Erste*, "the first" channel) began producing and broadcasting from what would eventually total nine antennae dispersed throughout Germany's federal states.

Many of the French negotiators wanted a strongly centralized ARTE, an administrative headquarters in Strasbourg that would firmly establish ARTE's identity as a transnational television channel, a television channel whose headquarters in a cultural borderlands would make all important production decisions, with French and German poles responsible merely for coordinating intra-national production studios, acting at its behest. Germans were strongly opposed to this centralized model, pointing to German law that prohibits the German government from establishing such a centralized broadcasting structure, and wondered at how the French could be so ignorant of their concerns and the more general risks of conflating media and government in such a configuration.

There was a second, parallel contention: because ARTE France, ARTE's French national office, would inhabit the buildings and structures already established for LA SEPT in Paris, French negotiators felt strongly that Germans should set up a German national office for ARTE that would mirror ARTE France's centralized structure. Berlin was suggested as an appropriate location, imagined to be roughly homologous to Paris in its television production capacities.[7] Germans again objected: German public television has not, since the Second World War, been centralized in Berlin, and ARTE could hardly ignore the legal, not to mention cultural-historical, aversion that Germans are likely to have to a centralized television station in Berlin; indeed, this history was vividly present, as Germans were in the throes of reunification and all its attendant reminders of the war.

ARTE's structure, it was eventually decided to the dismay of the French negotiators and advisees, would be centralized in France at ARTE France but, to avoid German legal complications, would be organized in Germany at and through the two existing major German public channels, the ARD and the ZDF. ARTE France and ARTE Deutschland (the ARD and ZDF) would each produce 40 per cent of ARTE's programming, with the remaining 20 per cent produced by ARTE's co-production partners. French-side production would be managed by staff housed in Paris. In Germany, half of the production would be produced by the ZDF, located for the most part in Mainz, and half would be produced by the nine regional stations of the ARD. ARTE's headquarters in Strasbourg (referred to as ARTE GEIE) would be responsible for the governance

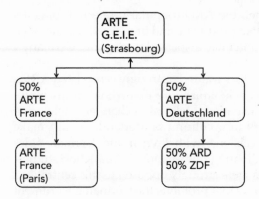

Figure 1.5 Organigram of ARTE's organizational compromise. (Graphic by author)

and programming of the channel, some of its marketing and publicity efforts (mainly for German press), and would house all the technical aspects of the channel including the antennae which would simulcast the channel's broadcasts to French and German audiences. ARTE GEIE also has a small budget to purchase or produce programs directly, without resorting to proposals from France, Germany, or co-producing channels.

The turbulent and sometimes acrimonious negotiations over what ARTE's structure would look like, and how its television production would be practically organized, came as a rude awakening for a channel that was originally envisioned as borderless, transnational, and European in spirit. The founders and early staff at ARTE found themselves not so much "imagining Europe together," as its first president had heralded the channel's mission, but mired, instead, in national-legal frameworks and clashing beliefs about whether centralized media lend themselves to political appropriation and propaganda. As production work began and ARTE began broadcasting at the end of May 1992, it was clear that imagination would have to embrace a number of compromises that were slowly contorting and convoluting the channel's work flow and bureaucratic structure: the channel wouldn't have as strong a central headquarters as France had wanted; ARTE Germany would be nearly non-existent, housed instead in the national public channels; the Germans wanted to establish a set of standard reimbursement rates for the regional channels' production work, while some French found the reimbursement rates to be too generous; and no one wanted to take a stand on the issue of language, which some felt should require all ARTE staff to speak fluent French and German, about which the French, who were less likely to speak German, tended to be somewhat apathetic.

The channel's governing structures were eventually established, but ultimately stretched among a governing committee, the administration in Strasbourg, and the administrations in Paris and Baden-Baden, resulting in a sometimes elaborate back-and-forth protocol for reaching important decisions about the channel. A complex system was eventually negotiated whereby these various administrating bodies would meet once a month in Strasbourg, but also, on a rotating basis, in cities in France or Germany.

Production work would be split between French and German production studios, but whereas ARTE France housed all the producers and programmers responsible for providing Strasbourg with the French half of the programming, in Germany the production responsibilities of the ARD were fractioned roughly according to regional station size (see Table 1.2).

Because of differing technological histories of television in the two countries, ARTE would have a terrestrial signal accessible on one of the five major networks in France, and in Germany it would be one of two dozen cable channels. As a consequence, German audiences would be about a quarter of the size of French audiences.

Table 1.2 Production quotas for the ARD, accounting for one half of ARTE's German-side production

WDR, Westdeutscher Rundfunk (Cologne) 22%
SWR, Südwestrundfunk (Stuttgart) 16.75%
NDR, Norddeutscher Rundfunk (Hamburg) 16.25%
BR, Bayerischer Rundfunk (Munich) 14.50%
MDR, Mitteldeutscher Rundfunk (Leipzig) 10.5%
HR, Hessischer Rundfunk (Frankfurt) 7%
SFB, Sender Freies Berlin (Berlin) 5.5%
ORB, Ostdeutscher Rundfunk Brandenberg (Potsdam) 2.5%
RB, Radio Bremen (Bremen) 2.5%
SR, Saarländischer Rundfunk (Sarrebrück) 2.5%
TOTAL ARD 100%

In the first months that I worked in development at ARTE France, I grappled firsthand with one of the most fundamental and difficult aspects of ARTE's day-to-day functioning, one which made clear to me the constantly negotiated nature of the channel's transnational production work: distribution rights. As I sought to make a list of programming that we could make available to U.S. universities, or which we might be able to eventually stream on ARTE's soon-to-be updated website, I was informed that about a third of the films I had selected – documentaries about Hitler, a series about architecture, a program about geography – could not be distributed to, or broadcast in, the U.S. At the time a production contract is produced, ARTE negotiates purchase prices with producers and production companies. It is generally more expensive to buy various rights – first broadcast, rebroadcast, distribution as DVDs, and so on – for more than one country. Although most of ARTE's contracts grant rights in both France and Germany, not all did, so sometimes DVDs could be sold to viewers in France but not in Germany. Buying rights for trans-European distribution was more expensive, and exclusive global redistribution rights often prohibitively so.

What's more, France and Germany have different laws regarding distribution and broadcast of online media – as streamed video, for example – and while I was working in ARTE's development department, German laws prohibited ARTE from showing some video that was available on its mirrored French website. So an ARTE documentary might have French-German initial broadcast rights, rebroadcast rights only in Germany, video streaming rights only in France, DVD distribution rights throughout Europe, but no distribution rights in the United States or the rest of the world. Establishing, adhering to, and sometimes renegotiating rights was the full-time business of about twenty staff members, and the part-time business of nearly everyone else.

from the channel of "imagination" to the *Mengengerüst*

"At the beginning, working at ARTE was really exciting," a French secretary in the programming department told me one day after she asked me what an American was doing at ARTE. "Everything was new, and we came to work every day, and we were working with Germans!" She smiled. "And we used to joke all the time and at the end of the day, no one wanted to go home! It was really this feeling that we were doing something special. And ARTE was much smaller, and people from ARTE would go out together after work all together ..."

"It seems like now it's bigger, more bureaucracy," I said.

"Yes it's bigger, there is more bureaucracy, but yes ... I don't know ... in the beginning we always said that it would get easier as time went on but it just sometimes seems like things have gotten harder, not easier."

Just a few months after ARTE began broadcasting, *Le Nouvel Observateur* published an article entitled "ARTE: La Guerre des Cultures" (Soula 1992, 19–21), in which the prominent news magazine reported on an argument that French and German staff at ARTE were having over whether or not to measure audiences. This article revealed a deeper set of disagreements about whether ARTE was meant to ignore whether its programs were popular (said "the Germans") or worry if people were watching (thought "the French").[8]

Figure 1.6 "ARTE: The War of Cultures." *Le Nouvel Observateur* newspaper article published in 1992 about emerging conflicts between the French and Germans over the administration of ARTE. (Used with permission, *Le Nouvel Observateur*, 9 August 1992)

The headline "ARTE: Television Without Borders" was superseded by "ARTE: The War of Cultures" in a matter of months. To the surprise and dismay of ARTE's architects and staff, the channel's organization grew ever more complex, compromises and negotiations that materialized into even more protocol and paperwork: tables of phone numbers; packets of contact people; flow-charts; spreadsheets; paragraphs explaining when to contact ARD stations and when to contact the office in Baden-Baden; and meetings upon meetings about the programming decision-making process chain between Strasbourg and the French and German poles.

The many flow-charts, organigrams, and Post-it Notes that covered ARTE staff's desks, and which could be instantly reproduced for me from memory (and often were, spontaneously, in lieu of lengthy explanation), indicate something crucial about the makeshift, heterogeneous assemblages produced at the places where seemingly diaphanous transnational and supra-national ideas (and images) meet up with the on-the-ground limitations of national technological networks; encoded national legal frameworks; a cyclically reappropriated budget; disparate educational and technical training; ideas about the meanings of French and German history (see chapter 3); and deeply held beliefs about French and German "working styles" and attitudes towards authority.

These notes and charts render evidence, and are the precipitate, of the frictions that inhere in global processes of integration (and disintegration), reflecting the myriad ways that trans/nationalization is literally held together and made understandable and navigable on a daily basis by those who experience the structures of its interstices. These notes and sketches reflect and anchor the multiple protocols and assignations of competencies and responsibilities; maybe it is their very materiality – arrows upon arrows, Post-its upon Post-its, piles of paper – that amounts to a kind of heaviness, an accumulation of processes and protocols that are ultimately, literally too heavy/*lourd*/*schwer* to remember, manage, and practise—but which nonetheless hold the thing together.

Identifying the importance of friction to understanding transnational and global aspirations, Anna Tsing (2005) emphasizes the importance of understanding "how knowledge moves" in places of trans/national collaboration: "It is important to learn about the collaborations through which knowledge is made and maintained ... Through the frictions of ... collaborations, [global projects] gain their shape" (13). She continues, "Collaboration is not a simple sharing of information. There is no reason to assume collaborators share common goals. In transnational collaborations, overlapping but discrepant forms of cosmopolitanism may inform contributors, allowing them to converse – but across difference" (13). As Tsing puts it, "This is not because the force of global connections has disappeared – but it no longer looks so neat ... Now it is time to turn attention ... to discontinuity and awkward connection" (11). Fifteen years after ARTE's president spoke of ARTE as a means of constructing the European imagination that, beyond common coinage or legal directives, would endow Europe with a common spirit and "way of seeing the world," at ARTE today it is the *Mengengerüst* (a word used both by French and German staff) that perhaps best embodies the frictions and structural emplacements that have ensued as ARTE's halcyon predictions of transnational and global connectivity, and social theory alike, have met with realities "on the ground."

The *Mengengerüst* is a sort of multi-page spreadsheet, a crucial tool for nearly all ARTE staff, identifying exactly what each ARD station is required to produce, how many episodes of which program, how many episodes ARTE France needs to provide, and how the budget has been allocated per program and per episode. When a question arises about a program, it is immediately to the *Mengengerüst* that a secretary or director of production must turn to gain his/her bearings in an organization that splits its production activities to the quarter of a per cent; where no one would otherwise know who is responsible for what; and in which even longtime members of the documentary unit couldn't quite explain to me exactly what happens to a program proposal after it enters the building. The *Mengengerüst* clarifies all this with its spreadsheet and percentages, but also demonstrates how far ARTE has evolved from the simple idea of a European cultural television channel to a media organization that holds ARTE France and ARTE Germany – and their partners – together with rope and string.

Mengengerüst, generally translated as "accounting" or "structure of costs," is more interestingly translated through its root words of *mengen*, "to blend," and *Gerüst*, "structure." Rather than through tropes of imagination and imaginaries, bridges and bridgings, or fusings and flowings, ARTE and transnational organizations and processes must be understood as structures of meaning that come to be welded together at odd angles, with odds and ends that hang off the sides, which must sometimes be tacked on or snipped off. In addition to retheorizations of the transnational and global that have now turned to metaphors of assemblage and friction, the *Mengengerüst* – colour-coded and omnipresent – suggests we should also pay further attention to the ways in which such trans-border projects are not merely smushings-together,

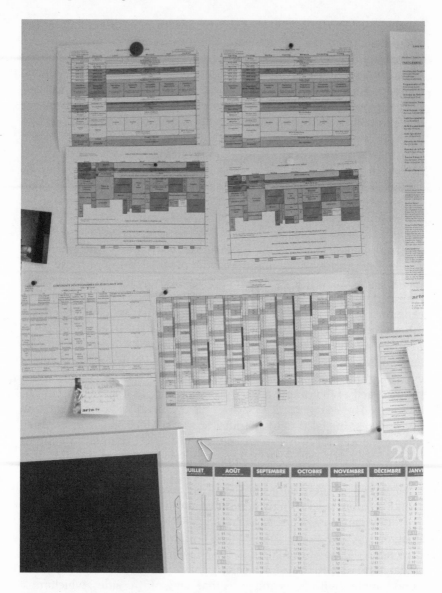

Figure 1.7 A typical workspace at ARTE's headquarters, with programming schedules in French and German, a protocol explaining the institutional route programs take during evaluation, and a *Mengengerüst*, which identifies the production responsibilities by program type and episode, assigned to ARTE France, the ARD, and the ZDF. (Photo by author)

or semi-hybrids, of pre-existing frameworks and practices (what Marshall Sahlins [1985] might call the "structure of the conjuncture"), but ones that must be rendered objective, knowable, and visible for those who work in these settings. If E.P. Thompson (1967) identified the visibility and ubiquity of the clock as marking the onset of a capitalist modernity, we might wonder if *Mengengerüste* – spreadsheets, percentages, allocations, and alternating (rather than merely "shared") functional responsibilities – are something like the preferred instrument – temporal, but also spatial – of a trans/national modernity.

The "actual global" – as Aihwa Ong and Stephen J. Collier (2005) explain in the introduction to their influential volume on global assemblages – suggests "inherent tensions" (12) and contradictions which cannot avail themselves to "grand diagnoses" either as "celebratory proclamations" or "visions of cataclysm" (15). In the quotidian ethnography of trans/national and "global" settings, the frictions and "inherent tensions" of transnational and global processes – as people from different places come together to work or play together – come to take banal material forms: notes, lists, phone numbers, how-to guides, manuals, organigrams. These, I would argue, more often than collective aspirations or shared "imagination," are the glue that keeps the trans/national pieced together.

2

producing trans/national media

For all the talk of transnational and global media, there has been surprisingly little ethnographic attention to their production. Part of the reason for this, of course, is that media industries remain highly nationalized. As Benedict Anderson (1991) argued, the origin of "audiences" substantially corresponds to the co-emergence of linguistic vernaculars and the print, which together rendered possible the widespread circulation of shared texts, and thus readerships. While media have dramatically changed over several centuries, vernacular languages have, despite our "electronic age," remained mostly locally and nationally bound (cf. Ginsburg 2008). Books, film, television, and electronic media, when produced in foreign languages, must, for all our technological know-how, still be painstakingly dubbed, translated, and otherwise adapted by national or local media outlets before they can be widely accessed. As Brian Larkin (2004, 2008) has elucidated in his ethnography of the Nigerian film industry, the movements of media can be often traced in the audiovisual distortions (fuzzy images, muffled sound) that translation, subtitles, dubbing, or copying materially impart on films, whether celluloid or digital.

Undoing mediated borders is hardly just a matter of translating, copying, or reformatting a DVD to a different regional code, however; indeed, the power of Anderson's (1991) linguistic theory is the way in which it captures how readerships and language communities – much more than just *enabling* shared communication by providing a common code – come to increasingly diverge into assemblings of shared narratives which, reciprocally, circularly, shape and deepen the relevance of a shared linguistic community. Anderson's argument presumes a kind of self-fulfilling self-reflexivity: much more than simply defining a linguistic community – that abstract collectivity known as "readers of French" – such collectivities eventually come to confirm and reproduce the existence of these communities – "the French" – through cumulative narrative iterations and interpellations (cf. Warner 2002). While at first it may have only mattered that a story was written in French (as indeed was the case in the first vernacular translations of the Bible [Anderson 1991, 38–9]), over time it matters less that these stories are in French and more that these stories are about what it *means* to be "French." Language per se matters less than the portrayal of national character and the ways these stories increasingly help "us" to understand who "we" are, argues Anderson (1991). Thus, understanding what Proust's *Remembrance of Things Past* ([1913–1927] 1982) means for some readers in France (and I would emphasize "some") thus requires *more* than just being able to read the volumes in French. The doubleness of the Andersonian linguistic community, to put it another way, is first about a linguistic *we,* but over time, increasingly, about *what* "we" means.

This chapter offers a thick description and analysis of production work at ARTE, demonstrating the semantically and symbolically "thick conjunctures" at which various scalings of media – local, national, international, transnational, and global – intersect and entangle. I argue that the production decisions of ARTE staff must be understood vis-à-vis the limited resources, and the finite sensibilities and training, of producers (cf. Mayer, Banks, and Caldwell 2009), as well as the up-close (local) settings in which they are producing media, rather than presuming an emergent "transnational production space" resembling the intersection of a Venn diagram. In these trans/national spaces, a variety of strategies are employed, sometimes as people worry about audience numbers, sometimes because production time is tight, sometimes in order to argue for what a politics of Europe should entail – and often several of these at once. Nonetheless, the solutions, compromises, failures, and success of cross-border production at ARTE sheds light on the multiplicity of mechanisms and strategies through which trans/national and global media are planned, produced, and disseminated. On a daily basis, filmmakers, programmers, editors, journalists and others who work for ARTE encounter, and must resolve, myriad problems – technical, linguistic, legal, logistical, aesthetic, political – incurred by ARTE's reachings beyond well-established national production contexts, communities, and infrastructures.

This chapter is organized into two parts: I begin by outlining the production process at ARTE – its dynamics must be understood in order to comprehend ARTE's programming. I highlight the importance of understanding production at ARTE as the circulation of audiovisual texts through a series of production stages and loci. In the second, longer half of the chapter, I consider four production contexts at length in order to examine the multiplicity of strategies deployed by ARTE staff as they go about producing trans/national television.

part I: production work at ARTE

During my first weeks at ARTE in Paris, then at its headquarters in Strasbourg (ARTE GEIE), I wondered if I was actually working at a television station. Where were the cameras? The studios? The editing stations? At first I would peep around corners or squint through blinded windows hoping to catch a glance of equipment or one of the many make-upped presenters that introduce and moderate *ARTE*'s weekly series. And then I started asking around. "Oh no, we don't do any of the editing here!" I was told. "This program is produced by *Doc en Stock*," or "That's produced at ARTE *Laboratoire* in the nineteenth arrondissement," or "That's made in Berlin."

The technical production of ARTE's programming (filming, editing) is for the most part outsourced, as is the case with nearly all television channels these days (see Lawrence and Phillips 2000), to a variety of external production companies, which may in turn delegate various parts of the production process (voiceover, for example, or graphic art design) to further specialized production studios. ARTE-produced films,[1] when they are not purchased, are assembled by filmmakers and production companies, which may in turn work with several co-producing partners in divvying up various parts of the filmmaking and editing process. Regularly appearing programs – news magazine programs, weekly series about contemporary design, or about cooking – are produced by television production studios, which tend to manage most of the production process in-house or near their studios.

Production for ARTE is therefore organized into a complex set of branching processes, and subprocesses, of which no one has full purview or knowledge. Indeed, when I first began asking about the production process in order to decipher where and how I might get involved, many of those who worked at ARTE themselves couldn't explain to me exactly how production worked beyond the one or two steps in which they were directly involved. "Nobody understands the whole process," one administrative assistant told me. "Well, except maybe Mr. Suard [then director of programming]. He has a brain like a computer. He may honestly be the only one who always knows exactly where things are going and when."

If Mr. Suard's brain is like a computer, perhaps it operated like the software program APIOS. During my research, APIOS was something like the nervous system of ARTE, essentially a searchable database and series of pull-down menus and tabs, which organizes the production process into proposals, comments, transcripts, budgets, calendars, and digitalized, streamable versions of rough cuts and final cuts. The whole system was bilingual, though information about a program tends to be in the original language for the preliminary stages of production, and comments were usually entered in French or German, but not both. APIOS essentially allowed ARTE staff, wherever they were, to monitor production and communicate with producers; it is one of the reasons why one can work at ARTE for years and only infrequently see a camera or the inside of an actual studio. The "outside" directors of production at the various television production studios that work with ARTE each had a staff member or two networked to APIOS, who would upload clips of work in progress, fill in production calendars, and otherwise coordinate production with ARTE staff in Paris, Strasbourg, or Baden-Baden.

The production process at ARTE was held together by APIOS, abundant phone calls, and scheduled production meetings (which ARTE producers are regularly required to attend at one of ARTE's offices), yet remains byzantine. In this section I mean to provide a sense of how ARTE's programming arrives at and trickles through ARTE. The goal here is, initially, to map out contemporary (trans-border) media production processes, providing orientation to the ways in which the assembling of audiovisual programming today is ever more complex in its organization through concatenated production places and activities. "Authorship" of ARTE's audiovisual texts, we will see, is a multivocal, complex matter.

the (relative) semantic stability of editorial lines

Until I eventually pieced together the production process at ARTE, it was difficult to understand the motivating logics or production values mobilizing ARTE's programming; for months ARTE seemed a disparate set of films arriving from a large number of production contexts, seemingly without rhyme or reason. Over time, I began not so much to see the "big picture" as to catch glimpses of the ways in which certain pieces of production fit together.

While working with ARTE's documentary department in Strasbourg, I began to follow the production process from the proposal stage to post-production through email, programming meetings, and production meetings. Weekly departmental meetings provide a sort of backbone through which members of the unit keep abreast of production. They are also critical in deciding what ARTE purchases and produces. Unsolicited proposals for programming, which fill the mailboxes and inboxes of documentary staff, are also evaluated and discussed at these meetings. More or less informal "calls for programming" are also coordinated through these meetings. ARTE's directors might decide that the channel needs more programming about the Cold War, or about new media. Such requests are passed down through heads of departments, who ask their staff to disseminate requests to producers and filmmakers with whom they've worked before and who might be interested in submitting a proposal. Members of departments themselves often filter proposals according to various upcoming anniversaries or commemorations for which they might propose a special night of programming: the fiftieth anniversary of the liberation of Auschwitz, the Louvre's two-hundredth anniversary, artist Louise Bourgeois's ninetieth birthday, 150 years since the birth of the baguette (in Vienna, it turns out, not France). One of my tasks at ARTE was compiling lists of such anniversaries, birthdays, and "years since" that might lend themselves to nights, weeks, or months of programming that would feature multiple films, sometimes a blending of fictional and non-fictional, grouped around a theme.

The real bread-and-butter of ARTE's regular programming, however, is provided by the *lignes éditoriales* (editorial lines, almost always referred to in French). These paragraph-long descriptions of programming stipulate the content of ARTE's scheduled blocks of programming; they provide guidelines for departmental programmers, and producers, about the particular genre, perspective, and format a scheduled slot of programming should provide. Each programmer in the documentary

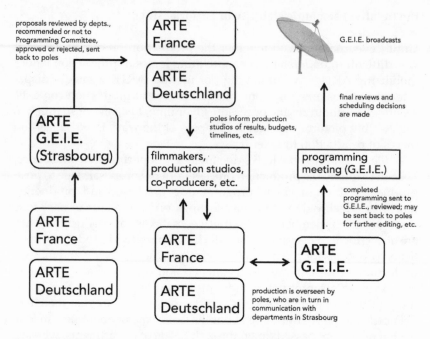

Figure 2.1 A generalized overview of the production process at ARTE; there are many contingencies that might complicate the production process, but this schematic provides a broad sense of how programs tend to circulate. (Graphic by author)

department at ARTE GEIE was responsible for soliciting, reviewing, and overseeing (and assisting with) production for one or two editorial lines. The blocks of ARTE's thematically colour-coded schedule may correspond to films that fit a format or genre (e.g., classic cinema), or may be a series that is produced by and for ARTE (e.g., *Tracks*, ARTE's series about trends in popular music). Producers and filmmakers whose proposals to ARTE were successful tended to specifically hone their film treatments and proposals to ARTE's *lignes éditoriales*; in the case of long-format films, this was less often the case, however, since these formats tended to require more funding and therefore more production funding spread among more channels and studios (and so would need to partly satisfy several editorial lines).

Editorial lines were themselves shuffled around various ARTE departments and offices at ARTE's headquarters and its poles, written by programming departments in conjunction with coordinating staff at

ARTE France and Germany, but edited (or sent back for specific revision) by the programming department and administrators. They were regularly revised through quarterly reviews, though the most established programs saw little change in their paragraph-sized descriptions of content; rather than seeing their editorial line radically revised, programmers more often saw the allotted programming length increased or decreased, or their place in the programming grid altered.

Matthew Hull (2012) has argued for restoring "the visibility of documents, to look at rather than through them ... to treat them as mediators ... not as neutral purveyors of discourse, but as mediators that shape the significance of the signs inscribed on them and their relations with the objects they refer to" (253). The importance of the *lignes éditoriales* cannot be overstated; they are the standards by which every ARTE staff member evaluates the appropriateness of a program for ARTE and the texts with which programs are debated, fought for, or railed against.

As the building blocks of ARTE's programming and its identity as a channel, the *lignes éditoriales* are also the points of friction at which French, German, and transnational interests and interpretations of ARTE's mission are articulated. The purpose and direction of the channel are rarely debated in abstract terms, but rather through the composition of the programming grid and, more importantly, in these descriptions of content that scheduling blocks are intended to reflect and embody.[2] Editorial lines tend to be the smallest bits of condensed content that are regularly circulated to anyone producing for ARTE and whose meanings – so crucial to the everyday work of ARTE – must be self-consciously consistent across a large number of transnational, trans-linguistic, and trans-contextual sites. Because they are so frequently discussed, clarified, and compared across space, they are likely among the most stable discursive elements of ARTE's multilocal, multivocal production contexts. Most every ARTE producer and staff has departmental *lignes éditoriales* hung at his/her desk. But many programmers can furthermore recite them by heart, and know exactly which parts of the paragraph matter most in determining if a program is appropriate. While reviewing a documentary about China with a programmer, for example, I was told that, while the film was really compelling, "unfortunately ... it just doesn't fit into one of *les cases* [boxes, slots] – it's too short for the long format, but not really 'historical' enough for the Wednesday history block." What about for the *La Lucarne* slot, I asked? "It's not really 'poetic' enough," the programmer responded without blinking. "[The *La Lucarne* slot] asks for more original, *poetic* kinds of

Table 2.1 Two editorial lines from ARTE's documentary department

---

– Wednesdays at 8:35 p.m., in the *History Wednesdays* slot: Produced in a 90-minute format or 2 × 52 minutes, the department privileges for *History Wednesdays* programs which move away from foreclosed histories and which look to the past for keys to put into perspective the big questions of today. This means ambitious documentaries, rooted in the world's largest archival resources, validated by renowned historians, and co-produced internationally.

– Sundays at midnight, in the *La Lucarne* [Skylight] slot: Off the beaten path, this midnight rendez-vous offers the discovery of rare pearls of independent productions worldwide. Strong works singular, poetic, which propose a different and original perspective on society, brought by filmmakers such as Naomi Kawasé, Claudio Pazienza, Lech Kowalski, Alain Cavalier, and many other lesser-known filmmakers.

---

films." The programmer was borrowing directly from the text of *La Lucarne*'s editorial line. (See Table 2.1 for an example of editorial lines.)

While a programmer's opinion about whether a film is "poetic" enough for the *La Lucarne* spot is of course highly subjective, I was surprised by the consistency with which producers and programmers employed particular pieces of the *lignes éditoriales* in their evaluations. The programmers with whom I worked seemed to have a "feel" for what a particular spot on ARTE's grid called for, and certain words or phrases of the editorial line were ones that they seemed to specifically look for when they scanned a proposal or watched a screener (a DVD or film that is provided for evaluation). For a history programmer, the mention of "archives" was crucial; for one of the long-format documentary programmers, the need for a film to be "narrative" was central to her assessments – this meant, she explained to me, a *personal* perspective that told a meaningful story from the filmmaker's point of view.

I found that other documentary programmers, in a fairly uniform way, also knew to equate "narrative" with a first-person "auteur" perspective. I realized, in hindsight, that this uniform understanding of the *lignes éditoriales* could likely be ascribed to the training that staff receive when they arrive at ARTE. As an intern, I was encouraged to evaluate screeners and proposals with a view to the language of the *lignes éditoriales* – and to memorize particular words and phrases that were crucial to each. After watching a documentary about poverty in Lima, Peru, one of the documentary staff, Katrin, quizzed me:

K: What do you think about the perspective of the film?
DS: It's beautiful … it feels very intimate.
K: Intimate? What do you mean by that?

DS: That the filmmaker seems close to the material, has a good sense of the city.

K: Do you mean she has a *personal* "perspective"?

DS: Yes. It seems quite personal. We hear the filmmaker's narration, her voice.

K: Okay, so is it appropriate for *La Lucarne*?

DS: Yes, I think so.

K: Why?

DS: Because it has a narrative, a story but from the perspective of the filmmaker.

K: Yes. *Voilà*.

Producers and programmers distill and apply these descriptives so that they are able to draw upon and negotiate these criteria in meetings with departmental colleagues, administrators, or producers from a co-producing country; the *lignes éditoriales* are the lingua franca of ARTE, which, like a code of law, are stably interpretable.

trans/national "production-circulation"

Compared with the relative stability of the editorial lines, the many sites of production through which these *lignes éditoriales* travel can be dizzying. While ARTE provides a concrete set of buildings and offices that function as nodes through which its programs must move, ARTE programs might arrive at the desks of its documentary department in a variety of ways, through a variety of circuits, with a range of funding types, and already having been assembled, in whole or in part, in another part of Europe or of the world. Within ARTE's walls programs are evaluated against standards, production is overseen and tracked, and budgets are managed. But I soon learned to understand production at ARTE as synonymous with circulation; a bit like Heisenberg's Uncertainty Principle, a particular program can be impossible to fully locate, though we might at certain points in time obtain a snapshot of where it is going, or where it has been. Understanding the manufacture of media at ARTE as "production-circulation" emphasizes how pieces of programming appear (literally, for example, as a new video clip in a program's APIOS file) and move across spaces of (trans-border) production – pushing against accounts of production that have often emphasized hierarchy, consensus, or other forms of collective (under-the-same-roof) negotiation (cf., e.g., Mahon 2000, 468–71).

Classic studies of the television production process – from Roger Silverstone's (1985) excellent but relatively obscure study of the production of a BBC science documentary to Todd Gitlin's *Inside Prime Time* (2000) and Barry Dornfeld's (1998) ethnography of the creation of a PBS documentary – have all been situated within national borders and singular sites of production (though see Ganti 2012 for a more complicated intra-national account). Even Georgina Born's (2004) more recent examination of corporatization and neoliberalization of the BBC focuses on the specific historical trajectories of the BBC in its relationship to the British state (although Born connects the BBC to broader contexts of neoliberalization).

At ARTE, circuits of production and distribution are untied and loosened, if not altogether, from national localizations and coherencies:[3] Dornfeld (1998), Gitlin (2000), and Born (2004) argue for the centrality of the various cultural industries they study to the production of public and national culture. The various pieces of what is eventually broadcast by ARTE, by contrast, circulate in and across multiple public spheres and "regimes of value" (Myers 2001) about what the "public" is, and about how media should interpellate publics.[4] Production studies tend to invoke a *singular* "public" or national culture, even if this work tends to acknowledge the ways in which co-national producers struggle over the semantic content and intentionality of their work (Dornfeld 1998, 69; Mahon 2000, 474). A theory of cultural production for a trans/national era of media cannot merely broaden or "scale up" presumptions about constructions of national public culture to, in this case, "France-Germany" or "Europe" – but must account for the fragmented, partial ways in which national-linguistic production practices and sensibilities overlap, intersect, or diverge. The mechanisms by which trans/national "publics" hold together do not align, I maintain, with those of national imagined communities (not least because of the dramatic multiplication and fragmentation of audience, national and otherwise, over two decades; see chapter 6).

A concrete example may elucidate why "production-circulation" more accurately describes the partiality and dynamism of trans/national and trans-border media work. At a meeting of ARTE department heads and programming officials, someone brought up the extraordinary success of Ken Burns's *The War* (PBS, 2007), which ARTE purchased in 2008 and broadcast to unusually high audience shares in both France and Germany. "Why don't we produce a European version of *The War*?" asked a member of the documentary department. "Instead of the Second World War, we could focus on the 1980s, the fall of communism and its aftermath in various European countries – but keep *The War*'s format of following particular people and their fate across the decade." The programming meeting brought together staff from ARTE France, ARTE GEIE in Strasbourg, and ARTE Germany, but it was decided that ARTE France should manage the proposal – ARTE France would co-produce the series with GEIE, which would contribute from its own small production monies (20 per cent of ARTE's total budget). After some weeks of pre-production deliberation, ARTE GEIE staff began participating in discussions about ARTE France's proposal, which would be produced by a French filmmaker who had already produced several historical documentaries for ARTE. They didn't like what they were hearing. A member of the documentary unit later somewhat vaguely explained to me, "We've had problems in the past with ARTE France-produced films about Eastern Europe." There was a kind of sensibility, or sensitivity, that producers in France seemed to lack in the way they "treat" (*traiter*) Eastern Europe: "The Germans tend to do a better job with this history," explained the programmer. It was decided that the proposal would shift to Strasbourg (ARTE GEIE), which would manage production with ARTE France, also bringing German channels into the co-production mix.

Weeks later, while phone calls and emails were still being exchanged about exactly how to distribute production among staff at ARTE France, ARTE GEIE, and ARTE Germany, someone at GEIE headquarters asked why ARTE wouldn't include Eastern European channels in production of at least some of the series' episodes. TVP Poland (with which ARTE holds a co-production/programming sharing agreement) should certainly contribute, and might the Greeks or Finns be able to provide another perspective? ARTE's partners were contacted and shares of production were redistributed in terms of the number and production share of total episodes. On the one hand, people told me they were excited to see such trans-border collaboration, which was "very ARTE." ARTE had the capacity to both mobilize these various producers and, especially its Strasbourg's bi-national staff, could ensure some balance of historical perspective. On the other hand, people were sceptical of too many cooks spoiling the broth – would such a series be coherent with this many producing partners? Who would have editorial control in the end? The balance sought in the project – a problem specific to trans/national production-circulation – was between the coherence of narrative and production style, and the inclusion of multiple partners, sources of funding, and cultural sensibilities as these stretch across borders.

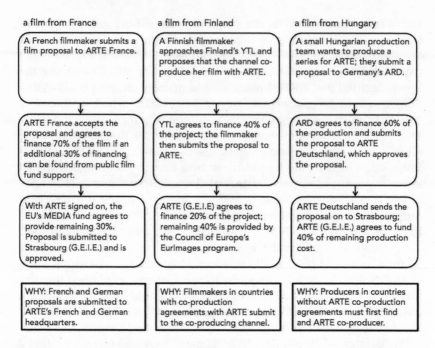

a film from France	a film from Finland	a film from Hungary
A French filmmaker submits a film proposal to ARTE France.	A Finnish filmmaker approaches Finland's YTL and proposes that the channel co-produce her film with ARTE.	A small Hungarian production team wants to produce a series for ARTE; they submit a proposal to Germany's ARD.
ARTE France accepts the proposal and agrees to finance 70% of the film if an additional 30% of financing can be found from public film fund support.	YTL agrees to finance 40% of the project; the filmmaker then submits the proposal to ARTE.	ARD agrees to finance 60% of the production and submits the proposal to ARTE Deutschland, which approves the proposal.
With ARTE signed on, the EU's MEDIA fund agrees to provide remaining 30%. Proposal is submitted to Strasbourg (G.E.I.E.) and is approved.	ARTE (G.E.I.E) agrees to finance 20% of the project; remaining 40% is provided by the Council of Europe's EurImages program.	ARTE Deutschland sends the proposal on to Strasbourg; ARTE (G.E.I.E.) agrees to fund 40% of remaining production cost.
WHY: French and German proposals are submitted to ARTE's French and German headquarters.	WHY: Filmmakers in countries with co-production agreements with ARTE submit to the co-producing channel.	WHY: Producers in countries without ARTE co-production agreements must first find and ARTE co-producer.

Figure 2.2 Three scenarios for a film or series to be produced by ARTE. (Graphic by author)

Many of ARTE's programs are produced through this kind of elaborate partnership and budget management (organized, to recall, into pages of grids of *Mengengerüst* spreadsheets [see chapter 1]), which evolve organically and often informally, through the personal networking and communications of ARTE staff (who are distributed throughout its trans-border offices) and external producers. ARTE producers allow programs to head out towards various filmmakers and studios, thereby diffusing and fragmenting production decisions until they are called in for some later moment of review or revision, which would provide a snapshot of how the production process was interlocking co-producing partners, often concretized through spreadsheets and organigrams clarifying, and temporarily reifying, an otherwise diffuse, in-motion, amorphous process.

Production-circulation at ARTE means that, although there are patterns to production protocols and processes, authorship and editorial control must be understood as an accruing set of intra-border and trans-border inputs and decisions – resulting in what we might think of as audiovisual palimpsests. Budget allocations and ARTE's evaluative procedures tend to be substantially more extensive – elongated both spatially and temporally – than those travelling *within* national borders, because national production work generally demands less circuitous routes of trans-linguistic and trans-cultural production, and requires fewer layers of depersonalized kinds of communication (emails, phone calls, and faxes in lieu of meetings) necessary to bridge numerous production personnel across multiple borders.

Several examples of the contexts in which these media are produced will provide a deeper sense of the entanglements and tyings-together of production ideologies and micro-practices that more immediately inform what ARTE's programs look like. I have selected contexts of production that demonstrate a range and continuum of strategies, sensibilities, and scalings that I found at ARTE – from a series about philosophy, which aims to transcend borders through attention to ostensibly universal human experience; to the program *Karambolage*, which aims to construct a Europe through French and German national mutual understanding; *ARTE Info* which works at the intersections of French/German knowledge and production practices; to *ZOOM Europa*, which attempts to present explicitly European topics in a way that is broadly accessible and which are understood to be relatively free from national bias and "inside" cultural knowledge. Together, these production contexts demonstrate that ARTE producers rely on no single understanding or coherent vision of how nation, Europe, and world might be fit together, but come to juxtapose, overlay, and conflate these idioms of belonging in a variety of ways as they conceptualize and produce transborder media.

part II: production contexts

1. (mis)translating *Philosophie*

Philosophie, launched in 2007 during my time at ARTE, was a project initiated by ARTE France partly because previously philosophy-oriented programs had done well in France and on ARTE. "It's a good program for ARTE," explained a woman in ARTE France development, "because philosophy is obviously of interest to French and Germans, [to] Europeans. There are French philosophers, German philosophers ... each program discusses a broad philosophical issue ... 'what is truth,' and so on – the universal questions of philosophy." I heard rumours around ARTE France that the launch party for the series was quite a hot ticket, not least because the handsome moderator of the series, Raphaël Enthoven, was the ex-husband of the former French president Nicolas Sarkozy's then-still-new wife Carla Bruni. "I'm a little bit worried this isn't going to win ARTE much favour with the president," joked a woman at ARTE France. There were, in fact, personal politics between ARTE administrators and state officials that sometimes played out at ARTE in exactly this kind of way, but in this case, Professor Enthoven was more likely chosen for his status as a high-profile, charismatic public intellectual.

The episodes of *Philosophie* each consist essentially of a conversation between the host, Enthoven, and another eminent philosopher, who walk around a tastefully decorated, light-filled Paris loft together discussing "classic" philosophical themes or problems.[5] Episodes have focused, for example, on power (*pouvoir/Macht*), melancholy (*mélancholie/Melancholie*), ugliness (*laideur/Hässlichkeit*), the body (*corps/Körper*), love (*amour/Liebe*), and stupidity (*bêtise/Dummheit*). As the interlocuteurs meander through the studio space, they stop at various photos or objects, each of which help to facilitate discussion or to illustrate some aspect of the philosophical problem at hand.

Months after the series had been announced and several of the episodes already filmed in Paris, I sat in front of a computer at ARTE's headquarters, in Strasbourg, with a list of the textual citations that would be used in the series, trying to match French and German philosophical sources – books, treatises, and so on. The woman responsible for the program at ARTE GEIE, in the documentary unit, explained that we needed to find German equivalents for book titles that would appear as on-screen text as Enthoven mentioned them. (The text titling work had already been completed for several of the French-language episodes.) We also needed the equivalent German source texts for a bibliography for the program's website and, most importantly, so that particular words or excerpts could be used in the German voiceover that most closely matched the French version.

ARTE France had sent along transcripts of the French-version episodes, and when possible, had provided German translations of key passages that would be cited or quoted at length in the episodes. Yet many passages had been left untranslated, or else the producers had provided instead an English translation, or provided a translation that was accompanied by a question mark. In sifting through the German-language voiceover script for the "Melancholy" episode, Beate – the producer in Strasbourg – and I soon realized that the problem was that certain books that had been cited simply did not exist in German translation. The French production team had in many cases improvised, sometimes providing their own German translation of texts that existed only in French or English.

One example, from the "Melancholy" episode, was the *The Life of Adam (La Vie d'Adam)*, a Venetian biblical exegesis written in the seventeenth century by Giovanni Francesco Loredano. While the small book was translated into French and published in Paris in 1695, it exists only in only partial translation, in an obscure literary journal, *Allgemeine Literatur-Zeitung*, published in 1790 (*Das Leben Adams*). The guest philosopher, Frédéric Gabriel, quotes from the book at length. In Strasbourg, unable to locate a full German translation, producers decided to just translate the few lines of French that appear in the transcript. More important than the issue of translation (or translatability) per se, our research revealed how certain books, texts, and literary references were more or less present in – more or less relevant to – particular national-linguistic philosophical traditions. During the recording of the voiceover for the German-language "Melancholy" episode, Beate sat staring at the script wondering if they shouldn't somehow include more context, or else find the original text to provide a more faithful translation. "Did you find online a version of the original text, in Italian?" she asked me, swiveling in her chair to face me. "No, just the French," I replied. She shrugged, pushing a button and saying into the microphone, "Okay, well let's move on" (*Dann … gehen wir weiter*). In the recording booth that faced us, the actors flipped a page.

But these moments multiplied as we continued to work through a German version of the episode. Hippocrates's "complete works" were translated by the French lexicographer Emile Littré in the mid-nineteenth century and published as a *livre de poche* – an inexpensive paperback series that is likely to have circulated widely in France – and we were able to find several books online reproducing the section of text cited in the episode. But we could not easily locate the original passage quoted in the program in German, save on a website for a medical conference for which a small section of the passage had been translated. This cut-and-pasted website translation is what we gave to the German voiceover actor to read as we recorded the German version of "Melancholy." Again, it is not merely whether or not a certain text exists in both French and German, but also about its presence in wider discourse, the ways in which it has or has not circulated, and whether it has therefore been available (or unavailable) for consideration by philosophers and others. If Kant's *Critique of Pure Reason* had not been translated into

French, for example, it is likely that French philosophical engagements and understandings of knowledge and logic would be inflected away from a philosophy of knowledge that both German and French scholars would recognize. These uneven textual circulations result in various imbalances (or incongruences) in how various texts are translated and (unequally) trans/nationalized at ARTE — but they also implicitly limit the semantic traction and relevance that a given program or film can have across borders. With every approximate or off-the-cuff translation, the parallel meanings of the program in France and Germany were set askew.

The micro-decisions about translations accumulate in ways that might go mostly unnoticed by audiences, but there were also broader thematic questions that were mistranslated, or were untranslatable, as we worked to make an episode about *mélancholie* into a program about *Melancholie*; indeed, we even debated whether the title of the program should be rendered as *Melancholie* or as *Schwermut*; the former was more clearly a cognate of the French, but the latter perhaps a more familiar, quotidian way of conveying the intended meaning.

In the weeks I spent assisting with the production of three German episodes of *Philosophie,* a key moment came during a segment of the "Melancholy" program in which Enthoven and his guest, Frédéric Gabriel, meander over to a blown-up photograph of Ivry-sur-Seine, located just outside of Paris. Enthoven explains that the black-and-white photograph is well-known, taken by Raymond Depardon in 1992. How does the photograph reflect, or help us to understand, the philosophical nature of melancholy? "It's not totally a desert, but almost," explains Enthoven. "Since the twentieth century [marks] the invention of industrial deserts."

"In what way can we say that this landscape, Frédéric Gabriel, is objectively melancholic? Is it objectively melancholic, or is it in the eye of the beholder [*ou est-ce qu'il l'est uniquement par l'oeil de celui qui regarde*]?" His guest replies, "I think we can say that it is objectively melancholic with this quality that it has, of being manmade [*avec cette ... qualité qu'il a d'être construit par l'homme*] ... There's a long history of melancholic landscapes ... and there [*là*], this is a new melancholic landscape, objectively melancholic ... a sort of suburb, but in this way also a non-place [*une sorte de banlieue, mais justement une sorte de non-lieu*]."

The philosophers focus on the ways in which the photograph of the Parisian suburb is "objectively" melancholic, concluding that is so because it is a manmade place and also a "non-place." But when the sound technician paused the recording after we ran through this bit of the program, the Germans sat dumbfounded. How to translate *banlieue*, which in French was understood to "objectively" convey melancholy, but which in German would have to be translated, it was decided after some debate, as *Vorort*, which would convey something totally different?

"This isn't going to translate at all," said Beate, with furrowed brows. The voiceover actors, one of which had grown up in both France and Germany, and so spoke both fluently, agreed. "Why would they pick a photo of the *banlieue*?" he asked. On the one hand, Ivry-sur-Seine in particular, for many French and especially those living in Paris, references the Communist Party, of which the suburb has been something of a local political bastion. On the other hand, the town has been notorious as the site of one the largest garbage incinerators in the greater Paris metropolitan area, and is also popularly known as partly synonymous with Chinatown, which has expanded out from the thirteenth arrondissement. Furthermore, while the word *banlieue* might also connote, to viewers in France, decades of polarizing debates about poverty, race, and urban planning (Beriss 2004; Rey 1996), German cities are often circumscribed by tranquil bedroom communities, often with their own town centres. Whether or not German audiences would understand the meaning of this part of the program, thought the production team, would likely be contingent on whether or not they were familiar with the context and debates of the *banlieue* and modernization in France; the program's translation (implying that a *Vorort* conveys *Melancholie*) was likely to not make much sense to most Germans (cf. Kastoryano 2002, 68–74).

The (mis)translation seems to indicate that the photograph of the *banlieue* may be less "objectively" melancholic than the philosophers in the program imply. Indeed, although "melancholy" as an affective state or quality is presented by the program as something of a universal philosophical state or arena of human experience – like "stupidity" or "ugliness (i.e., beauty)," which are the subject of other episodes, the *in situ* production and translation of these episodes reveals the linguistic and semantic frays and snaps that seem to render the program's interpretation and representation of "melancholy" predominantly French (if not more narrowly Parisian). After production of the melancholy episode, I was researching texts and images that appear in the *Philosophie* episode on "power." One of the central images in the episode is Louis XIV, used to illustrate the notion of monarchy more generally. "This seems really French to me as an example," I mentioned to Beate. "Does this seem really French to you – the example of the court, and so on?" "Of course," Beate replied, almost unthinkingly. "The entire series is very, very French. But we do our best to make it accessible."

And yet the series was partly conceived and concocted by ARTE France because of the perceived trans-border mobility and transparency of broad philosophical themes like "melancholy" and "power," which are generally understood, to a greater or lesser degree, as universal human categories. Indeed this is the very basis and meaning of "philosophy" as an epistemological system: the ability to discuss the meaning of "power" or "friendship" in ways that are detached from local or national inflections, predicated instead on generalized and generalizable human experience. (Otherwise, what happens to "theory"?)[6]

The production process of *Philosophie* reveals the micro-practices through which translations and traffickings of meaning across borders are necessarily imperfect, approximate, erosive. The series is particularly illuminating in this regard because the show's principal strategy, and basis of legitimacy as a transnational television program, is its claim to universality through the abstracted domain of philosophy, presumed to more easily traverse borders than programs about more nationally specific themes or referents. As Anna Tsing (2005) has put it, however, "universals ... include contrasting sources of knowledge and define varied kinds of participants in the knowledge-making process" (111). Tsing evokes the "quiet exclusions" through which a "universal" category of knowledge both "facilitates and obscures" collaboration (111). Universals, or rather claims to universal meaning, raise a "disturbing" question, writes Tsing: "How can universals be so effective in forging global connections if they posit an already united world in which the work of connection is unnecessary?" (7) The question points to a paradox at the heart of *Philosophie*, and to some extent, of all ARTE programming: If there were truly transparent categories of "truth," "beauty," and "power" across borders, the need for a program like *Philosophie*, or a channel like ARTE – which exists to further trans-border understanding of exactly such categories – would be obviated. And so (and yet), *Philosophie* continues, through the "quiet exclusions" which accumulate during the production process, reproducing and effecting deviations in "universal" ideas like what "melancholy" means as a human emotion, or how "power" is instantiated by the state – even as it strives to construct and disseminate shared meanings.

2. *Karambolage* and idealizations of national *habitus*

It could be argued that it is exactly the incurred "quiet exclusions" of programs like *Philosophie* that leads some ARTE producers and programmers to adopt something of a converse strategy: to directly confront and

les rubriques	die Rubriken
l'objet ◀▶	der Gegenstand
le quotidien ◀▶	der Alltag
la coutume ◀▶	der Brauch
le mot ◀▶	das Wort
le symbole ◀▶	das Symbol
l'analyse d'image ◀▶	die Bildanalyse
l'onomatopée ◀▶	die Lautmalerei

Figure 2.3 The "rubrics" that organize the brief didactic segments of *Karambolage*, from the *Karambolage* DVD, Season 2; they translate as "the object," "the everyday," "the custom," "the word," "the symbol," "image analysis," and "onomatopoeia."

engage with (perceptions of) national difference. *Karambolage*, one of ARTE's most popular and established programs, seeks to forge French-German cultural understanding by highlighting various aspects of French and German social life and society. Now in its sixteenth season, the show attracts, according to ARTE audience data, as many as 300,000 households each week.[7] Its episodes last just twelve minutes, broken into "rubrics" that organize the show into a series of short vignettes, linguistic analyses, explications, demonstrations, and "just-so" stories. The show aims, in these three or four minute segments, to help non-German audiences to understand Germans and life in Germany, and non-French audiences to better understand French people and life in France. The show is explicitly didactic; these are lessons, demonstrations, and illustrated guides to everyday life in France and Germany. But as I often heard from viewers I encountered during my fieldwork, viewers enjoy the show because it's *funny*. One of my German tutors told me, "You know, I love *Karambolage* because it just gets it *so* right. And when you think, 'Yes, German people *are* like that,' it makes you laugh."

In one segment of *Karambolage*, for example, we watch a man demonstrate how to make *Bleigießen*, a New Year's custom in Germany that involves dropping pieces of molten lead into water where they take the form of objects that are said to predict a person's fortunes for the coming year. In another, we are taught the history and long-held traditions of the esteemed Académie française. We learn how Germans use a *Schnippelbohnenmaschine* to cut up green beans. We are taught the differences in how French and German toilets work. Children in France and Germany demonstrate the different sounds that a bird makes in each country (in France, "meeeeep meeep" but in Germany, "beeep beeep"). We watch a five-minute history of Parisian water fountains, learn about some of the stereotypes that Germans have of Bavarians, and learn the different origins for the French and German words for "to work," *travailler* and *arbeiten*. *Karambolage* is filled with colourful, well-designed graphics and its tone is often tongue-in-cheek, which endears it to viewers.

One four-minute segment of *Karambolage* begins by observing that if we go to hotels in France and Germany, we'll find an important difference: in 80 per cent of hotel rooms in Germany we'll find Bibles, but we'll find very few in French hotels.[8] Why? With a series of graphics, the segment goes on to explain that the Bible helps us to understand something about the difference in the relationship between religion and the state in each country: "In France, you may know, one of the fundamental principles of the Constitution resides in its *laïcité*, and that's why you will only very rarely find a Bible in a hotel room. Otherwise it would be necessary, in respecting the equality of religions, to also make available the Koran, the Torah, etc., etc." The voiceover continues, "In Germany, the intrusion of religion into society is much more accepted. What's more, Protestantism, a religion – as we know – which is deeply rooted [*très implantée*] in Germany, places much importance on Holy Scripture."[9]

"You have to start with the *every day*, the particular, the concrete," Claire Doutriaux, the show's creator, explained to me. "You can't start with the behavioral [*comportementale*]. You have to start with very small, concrete things…a word, an object, the tangible. You *can't* do it any other way." In this example, it is the specific, concrete phenomenon of Bibles in hotel rooms through which a discussion of religion in France and Germany is broached. The segment goes on to explain that Gideons International, an evangelical Christian association founded in Wisconsin in 1899, has attempted to distribute free Bibles to hotels, hospitals, prisons, schools, and military bases. The German branch of Gideons is "particularly prosperous," says the voiceover, with 3,900 members, but in France there are far fewer Gideons because there they are "much less accepted by the population and are sometimes compared to a sect."

I was able to work with the *Karambolage* production team at their offices and studio in Paris during which time we completed production on a segment about the different ways that French people eat and store camembert cheese.

   To prepare for the segment, two interns and I headed to a Franprix grocery store near the *Karambolage* offices and studios in the sixteenth arrondissement of Paris. We bought grapes, then deliberated about which bottle of wine to buy – "a Bordeaux, I think Claire said, and she wanted a bottle that looks nice," said one of the interns. We also bought several round boxes of camembert cheese – matching a brand of camembert cheese Claire had already chosen – and a few small tangerines. We then stopped at a quaint boulangerie and picked up some little cookies and three or four traditional baguettes. Back at the *Karambolage* offices, we picked up a bag of yet more camemberts that had been bought the day before – but left out so that they would be gooey – a cheese knife, and a box of *verres ballons* – small, round wine glasses found in many Parisian cafés. Along with some dry cleaning and other miscellanea, we walked over to *ARTE*'s Paris production studios, a ten-minute walk or so from the building housing the *Karambolage* offices.

   On the *plateau* – the actual set – final preparations were unfolding. Technicians set up monitors, the cookies and fruit were set out as snacks for the production staff, two wine glasses were taken out of their packaging and rubbed shiny with a cloth. Claire arrived, deposited her coat on a chair, said hellos, and then announced that the actor was sick. "I don't know if we'll be able to shoot today," she said to me, aside, as she got settled. Nonetheless, everyone scurried to get ready for the shoot. "Let's get one of the table cloths on the table and wipe it down," directed Claire, adjusting the camera monitor. "We need another monitor for the other camera," she told the cameraman, who deferred the order to a young technician, who set up another monitor next to the first. Claire toyed with the colour on one of the monitors. The cameraman was now making final preparations, framing the table with each of the two cameras, the one wide, the other in close. The actor, Jacques, walked in, already made-up and wearing one of the dry-cleaned shirts we had brought down, looking as if he might have a cold (he was sniffling). There was a conversation about whether he was okay to film. "You'll be under the lights for six hours, Jacques, so you tell me if you can't do it," said Claire. "Well, I think I can try it," he replied, squinting at an overhead spotlight. "If you're too sick, tell me." Claire dispatched an intern to search for some aspirin. "I should be okay," said Jacques, before coughing.

   The red tablecloth was carefully laid over the table and wiped down. Camemberts were inspected and one chosen and set on the table. Half of a carefully selected demi-baguette was decided upon – it needed to be "crusty," said Claire. (Claire wanted the baguettes to be cut precisely into halves rather than ripped or otherwise cut, so the baguettes had to been taken back to the boulangerie by an intern to be cut, by the boulangère herself, into six perfect demi-baguettes.) Placed on the table, the half-baguette was moved around and rotated, its angle adjusted fifteen degrees here, then there, until just so. A butter knife was set next to it to one side, the wine glass to the other side, now half full of deep red liquid. We all peered at the monitor to check how it all looked on camera. There was further debate about how to compose the objects – the knife was turned so that it would face Jacques. It was moved to the other side of the table. It was flipped, at Claire's request, with the blade facing inward. The box of camembert was moved forward, then back, to centre it properly. The bread was once more re-angled, and the wine glass brought closer to the table's centre.

With a "*Ça tourne!*" we began filming. Claire began reading the voiceover script as Jacques went through the narrated motions (although the actual voiceover would be recorded later in a sound studio). Since the segment would actually be a split-screen comparison of the two different ways a Frenchman might eat his camembert, we would film Jacques twice, in two different shirts, with two different tablecloths; the two "Jacques" eating cheese two different ways would then be juxtaposed in editing.

"This monsieur whom you recognize is of course a French monsieur," began Claire, in the lilted speech characteristic of the series, "but this monsieur here, yes, whom you also know well, is also a French monsieur …[10] Both are in their French kitchens, both are a little hungry. They are getting ready to taste a delicious snack: So here therefore is a very crusty baguette, a good camembert from Normandy, and, of course, a little *ballon* of red wine."[11]

Jacques holds up the camembert, the baguette, and the glass of wine as they are named, then goes on to demonstrate two ways to eat and store the cheese. Some French, the voiceover explains, allow their camembert to melt when it is replaced in its original box. Others (Jacques demonstrates) use a special plastic "camembert box" (*boîte à camembert*), which suspends the cheese so as to prevent its insides from melting out – its shape is perfectly retained. As we filmed the segment, mistakes were made, of course, and we discarded camembert after camembert since the actor would often cut into the cheese before we had to cut and refilm.

At some point during the segment, I began to appreciate the extent to which the performance was being narrated and choreographed. At several moments, for example, Claire exhorted Jacques to be more

Figure 2.4 A table with props from the *Karambolage* camembert segment.
(Photo by author)

convincing in his facial expressions: "You *really* love the cheese," she
would direct him. "Yum, yum … yes… delicious!" (Jacques would try
to emulate eating a delicious camembert, but his efforts to be convincing were complicated by the fact that he felt sick, and didn't particularly
want to be eating knife-full after knife-full of cheese and sipping red
wine.) "Mmmm," Claire would say, encouraging him to smile, then to
take a sip of wine. "Yes, it's a good wine. Now smile, Jacques, yes …
gooood."

It wasn't just how the segment was choreographed – it was, I eventually realized, *what* was being choreographed and, ultimately, produced.
"Idealizations," in Goffman's (1959) performative sense (30–4; cf. 1974),
abound here, and at several levels: what this "French" man looks like,
how he goes about bodily interacting with the materials in his performance of the activity, his affective reactions to the food, right down to
the selection of wine and cheese itself. In effect, the segment moves to
visually demonstrate, if not to teach, an audiovisualized ideal type of
"French-ness."

The process through which the show arrives at such an idealized performance is marked by efforts to find a perfect-looking camembert, the "right" kind of baguette, a "typical" bottle of French wine, or a wine glass of the kind that is found in Parisian cafés – items that literally object-ify a particular version of French-ness. The performance is also produced through a scripting, and Claire's elicitation, of embodied affect that presumes to reference (primarily for "French" audiences), and demonstrate (primarily for "German" audiences), several kinds of identity roles: this is a French person, but this is also a French person of a certain apparent race, class, a certain gender, all of which are being performed and displayed. The segment draws attention to its own conceit – seems to play with its artificiality, to ironically frame its own framing with self-conscious attention to the plainness of its representation. It is for this reason that the actor has to add flair, exaggerated personality, and affect – he must convey, alongside the task he performs, that this is all a bit light-hearted.

And yet as *Karambolage* traffics in what are presumably "French" and "German" comportments, it also necessarily fixes and reifies these as "standard" kinds of French and German people and practices, thereby "iconizing" French-ness and German-ness (Irvine and Gal 2000). In its didacticism, the program strives to move beyond stereotype – indeed as Claire explains it, the show's purpose is precisely to counteract the simplistic and often inaccurate ideas that French and Germans have about each other. Yet the camembert example, I would argue, suggests that the show may ultimately offset or replace stereotype with still-reductive characterizations of "French" and "German" people and ways of life.

We might reconsider the *Karambolage* segment on Bibles in hotel rooms in France and Germany. While the segment sheds light on the different relationships of state and religion in the two countries, it largely mischaracterizes Protestantism in Germany and *laïcité* in France; in fact, there are likely more practising Catholics than Protestants in Germany,[12] and *laïcité*, as countless scholars of France have shown, is a highly fraught notion that does not, though the segment implies otherwise, guarantee a secular public sphere in which religions are equally kept at bay (Bowen 2007, 2009; Auslander 2000).

But what is perhaps most problematic is that in the show's highly self-conscious attention to national character and difference, it may distance viewers who do not see their sense of what it means to be French or German represented in the graphics, objects, rites, and analyses of *Karambolage*. It isn't merely that camembert isn't uniformly the snack cheese of choice across France (in Strasbourg, I found, someone was as likely to pull out a chunk of Muenster cheese), it is also that the dynamism of what it means to be "French" or "German" in Europe today is lost in these abstracted visualizations and objectifications, which often lock into time (perhaps because steeped in nostalgia) a particular version of French-ness and German-ness. At a *Karambolage* event I attended outside of Paris held at the Heinrich Heine House of the Cité Universitaire, a member of the audience asked why Germans of Turkish origins were not featured in the show, or French people who had emigrated from Morocco. "Right now," replied Claire, "we're having enough difficulty just trying to get things right for the larger part of the French and German population." Then she added, "But it's something to think about."

How are "normal French" practices and "taste" defined? Pierre Bourdieu found in his very widely read *Distinction* (1984) that class, among other social categories, is central to imparting the natural-seeming ideas that we hold about what people eat, how people eat, what kinds of objects people have in their homes, or how people engage with the aestheticism of objects (cf. Balibar and Wallerstein 1991). ARTE's self-conscious representations of what it means to be French or German (or European, for that matter) must be understood as positioned within fields of ordinary experience through which "social identity is defined and asserted through difference" (Bourdieu 1984, 169, 171); eating and drinking, observed Bourdieu (1984), are especially marked by *habitus* and learned bodily practices through which one's social position is asserted and reproduced (177–99).[13] It isn't simply the case that eating camembert cheese with a *ballon* of red wine is "French"; rather, such practices must be located within class-oriented and other dispositions, which unevenly striate, and internally differentiate, the "nation." Strategies like that of *Karambolage*, to disseminate knowledge about "national" groups in order to foster and build trans/national and European sensibilities, tend to flatten the "national" as a category of difference and community of practice, when there are important, and politically salient, distinctions within the social realities represented by "France" and "Germany" – which the "French" or the "German" can stand in for, but which they cannot fully represent.

Interestingly, these terms have, in some ways, begun to change or disintegrate as the program continues past its 200th episode: today *Karambolage* increasingly takes on segments that engage with both regional and migrant cultures and practices. Segments from recent episodes have explored Polish German traditions, how German Turks read tea leaves, why some Algerian last names have been mistransliterated into

French, and why *Deutschland einig Vaterland* (Germany one Fatherland) has very different connotations for Germans in eastern Germany than for other "Germans."[14] In one such segment, a man explains in German how attached he is to his Tesbih prayer beads and how the beads are similar to and different from the Catholic rosary. In another, a woman who has immigrated to France from West Africa explains the importance of the Cube Maggi (a bouillon cube) to African cuisine, explaining its importance to the Cameroonian *ndolé* dish, the *sauce graine* of the Ivory Coast, and the Sengalese *tiebboudienne*, also explaining how the spice mixture reached West Africa via the French colonial entrepreneur Julius Maggi. This inclusion and recognition of a variety of French and German voices – although not fully disentangled from notions of bounded culture – has begun to acknowledge the dynamism and complexity of what it means to be "French" or "German" today, and what a "typically" French or German person is likely to look like, to dress like, or to eat.

3. making news at ARTE

Some of ARTE's programs attempt to tack between national and trans/national or European perspectives and production practices. During the month that I spent with ARTE's news bureau (ARTE *Info*), located on the ground floor of the channel's Strasbourg headquarters, I came to understand that at *Info*, there was a daily negotiation of what kinds of news stories to report – national, European, or global (often categorized explicitly in these terms) – as ARTE journalists weighed the relevance of stories both against some abstract sense of "what matters in the world today," and the channel's mission and editorial line encouraging the privileging of a more particularly trans/national and European perspective.

The then-director of ARTE's news department, Pascale Guimier, explained:

> In sixteen minutes – half as much time as the news programs of TF1 or M6, and with €100,000 less money, we can only offer a sort of complement – our own perspective – in our own way, with our resources. Our editorial line … it's to turn a critical eye abroad, and to Europe in particular … not necessarily to the European Union, [but] to a Europe that includes forty-nine countries. We ask how different countries are responding to problems that face everyone, but each of which has its own answer to these problems.

The director offered globalization, immigration, and purchasing power (*pouvoir d'achat*) as examples. "Don't most news programs, on French and German national channels, also offer a somewhat 'international' perspective," I asked? "No," replied Pascale. "The war in Iraq? [For national channels] it's not about what's happening abroad [*C'est pas l'étranger*]. It's about *France* and its relationship to Germany and the U.S. ... Terrorism in London? [In French media] it's about possible risks for France, or a comparison of Muslims in London to those in France." A truly "European" and "international" perspective, he explained, is one that has no hidden national agenda but points out the relevance of a story beyond national borders, raising them to the level of French-German and European regional relevance in a comparative perspective, at least, if not also emphasizing the universal and humanist dimensions of particular issues.

I would begin my work with the news department at about 10:45 a.m. with a meeting called (by Germans and French alike) the *qui fait quoi* (who does what). Such meetings were frequent and informal, full of humour and exchanged jibes, but these meetings of fifteen or so journalists and production staff were critical to determining what news stories would be covered, by whom, and often, how.

Photocopies of the tentative agenda for the day's news programming are passed out – which list the various types of stories, from the twenty-second-long "fax," to "desks," more in-depth reports of two and one-half minutes, and next to them a title referring to what would be slotted for each of the three faxes and three desks.[15] Journalists in the room scan the stories, most of which are already being assembled for ARTE's midday 12:30 news broadcast; many of the stories will carry over into that evening's 7:45 p.m. broadcast, with only a limited amount of editing and updating. (A "morning" shift of reporters, translators, and production staff has already been putting together the midday broadcast and do not attend the 11 a.m. meeting, as they are busy finalizing their stories and voiceovers.)

Johannes, the editor-in-chief this week, begins the meeting casually, immediately launching into the list of topics, and confirming those that would roll over into the evening broadcast: an attack in Libya, an EU summit in Marseille, a report about elections in Germany that ARTE journalists had assembled after returning from Berlin. The reports add up to too much time, however, says Johannes, and so he proposes they drop a story about non-democratic elections in Belarus, choosing to keep another about hostages being freed in Egypt. "There are not only French hostages being released, but also some Germans." One of the

Figure 2.5 The ARTE newsroom. (Photo by author)

journalists asks why the Egypt story shouldn't be dropped instead. "The Belarus story seems more worthwhile to me," he says. Johannes replies that they have been following the Egypt story for three days. "So we should have the conclusion of the story we've been following …" The journalist counters, "Well we've had two stories about the elections in Belarus, so I don't really see the difference." But the hostage story is kept, the Belarus story dropped.

The day's most important story, however, would be the financial crisis in the United States that had begun two weeks earlier and was still fast unfolding. A bailout plan would soon be announced, and banks around the world were reeling in response to a series of financial shockwaves. How would ARTE cover the crisis and a plan to bailout banks? ARTE's angle was introduced by two of ARTE's editors in chief; the editors in chief meet before the *qui fait quoi*, and so often already have a sense of what stories they would like to report about, and how they'd like these stories reported (often conveyed through a series of "suggested" investigative questions).

"We'll continue to cover what's happening in Washington, but I'm not sure we'll have much time since with the time difference we probably won't have much information before 4 or 5 p.m. But the question is, is Europe going to do something? Is everyone just going to deal with their own stuff [*est-ce que chacun fait son sauce*] or ... are we going to do something at the level of Europe?" Another editor-in-chief, who was German, mentioned that a German newspaper editorial argued that European Commission should have a porte-parole so that Europe can speak with "one voice" – "*parler avec un voix ...* [then in German] *mit einer Stimme spricht.*" We move to assigning stories as people around the room volunteer to take on one story or another. A younger French-speaking journalist claimed the story about the United States. A more senior German-speaking journalist said that she would report on the European response. I followed them as the meeting broke and they began to assemble their stories.

ARTE's coverage of the crisis in the United States had begun two weeks before with the failure of Lehman Brothers and a plunging stock market. Today's story would cover the plan to bailout banks – an agreement had been reached and would be announced later during the day. The journalist who agreed to allow me to watch her construct her report, Paulette, went first to her computer and read several articles that had appeared about the bailout plan that had appeared that morning in national media – *Le Monde, Libération, Agence France-Presse.* She searched the electronic news wire service, INEWS, on her computer and scrolled through several *dépêches* about the crisis and bailout. INEWS stories came from news services around the world – the Associated Press, Agence France Presse, Deutsche Welle, and Reuters, among others – but Paulette mainly read those that were written in French. She printed out several, and I fetched them from the printer as she reviewed the television news stories about the bailout that had appeared that morning on TF1 and *EuroNews,* viewable on a monitor that provided specialized access to other news-producing channels in France and Germany. Paulette explained that all this was made available via subscription. "I'm pretty sure it costs a fortune," she said.

Little by little, she assembled together the story's narration, partly by cutting and pasting from pre-existing news wire blurbs, partly by adding her own phrases and sentences. She finished reading a *Le Monde* newspaper article, sat silently for a few minutes, then added a sentence about the probable size of the bailout. I detected, however, through her asides and comments, that Paulette had her own thesis for the story: that it was everyday American people would pay for Wall Street's mistakes. This shaped the first sentences of her report, which asserted that the "golden age" of CEOs' salaries was coming to an end. After writing two paragraphs – about 300 words – she contacted, via intercom, the news footage manager, whose job it was to locate and download available footage for the story from a large database of news footage, some of which had been acquired by ARTE-hired contractors and stringers, some shot by ARTE's own news teams, if they had been covering a story on location.

"Hi Frank, it's Paulette."

"Hi Paulette."

"I need some images of financial stuff, Wall Street, if we have some *trattoirs* [street interviews] ..."

"Okay, give me fifteen minutes."

After a coffee break, we moved to a small editing suite down the hall, where we began to work with an editor; they spoke together in French. He found the clips that Paulette had requested that had already been downloaded onto the suite's computer. Some already had accompanying narration (which could be eliminated), some were fixed shots and cutaways, some provided ambient sound – as, for example, one that featured the opening bell of Wall Street from the previous day. Frank had also downloaded several clips of politicians. One featured Nancy Pelosi declaring, "The party is over." "*La fête, c'est fini, c'est ça?*" Paulette verified the translation with me, smiled at how straightforward it seemed, and decided to begin her story with the Speaker's terse appraisal of Wall Street's demise. "We'll begin with that," she told the editor, who duly bookended the clip with "start" and "stop" cues in the Avid Pro editing program. "Okay, that's about seven seconds," said the editor, looking at the on-screen timeline. Paulette wanted next to cut to a clip of the New York Stock Exchange, then decided on the clip of the opening bell. Thirty seconds or so of the trading floor followed, with its ambient sound of shouting. The editor started from the beginning, and Paulette read from her in-progress script so as to see how her spoken narration would land on the images. We added five seconds here, deleted three seconds there, so that the breaks in the story would align with the changing clips.

After lunch, and a short follow-up meeting that everyone gathers for around 2 p.m., things in the ARTE newsroom began to accelerate, since by about 5 p.m. the story would have to be sent to the chief editors (who had to electronically approve the story in the computer system) and, finally, to translators. Between 6 and 7:30 p.m., French and German voiceovers would have to be recorded, and the broadcast as a whole edited and assembled.

Paulette and the editor continued to sift through footage; at about a minute and a half, the report was a little over half complete. "I would really like someone who says something like it's the people who are going to pay to rescue the banks," said Paulette off-handedly, more or less stating the thesis of her report. I helped to translate the *trattoirs* as we went through them, sometimes offering some additional context for a clip. A man in a suit on Wall Street explained that he was likely to get laid off, but couldn't agree with the principle of the bailout. The interview confused Paulette and the editor, even after I translated, and I explained that he was a trader, or banker, which apparently wasn't clear from the interview. They didn't use the clip, choosing instead another in which a man, not dressed in a suit, somewhere in New York, explains that he doesn't think it's fair that taxpayers should have to bail out banks. "I don't think we should have to pay to keep the banks in business," says the man, although the journalist and editor initially mistranslated his words as "we will have to pay." "*C'est bien* [That's

Figure 2.6 Editing a story about the financial crisis. (Photo by author)

good]," said Paulette, after the editor had dragged the clip onto the editing software's "timeline."

Intermittently, while Paulette and the editor worked, I visited another part of the newsroom, where things were progressing somewhat differently. Another journalist, Anja, was composing a report about the European response to the crisis, in German. She had jotted down a number of time codes that indexed pieces of available footage about the crisis of banks across Europe. She had also highlighted portions of the "dope sheets" – transcriptions of the stock footage available through a video wire service (to which ARTE also subscribes) – so that she already had a sense of exactly what quotes she wanted to use from the various clips. After lunch, she invited me to join her and her German editor in Cutting Room 3. Unlike Paulette and her editor, who discussed together at length which pieces of the clips they think they should use, Anja went down her list, naming clips by their reference numbers, and telling the editor where she wanted the "in" for the clip to begin: "Clip EV2205." The editor pulled it up on one of the monitors. "*Genau* [exactly], starting with, 'These banks won't survive …'" The editor cut from the beginning of the clip. "Ending with [*Mit der Endung*], 'a bailout plan that works for Europe [*reading the quotation in English*].'" Various clips were in German, English, and French, but Anja spoke nearly accent-less English when she read English text from the dope sheets. While the editor laid down the clips on the timeline, added transitions between clips, and adjusted sound levels, Anja worked on her own computer adding text that would accompany the accumulating footage. There were long periods during which the Anja and the editor didn't speak at all as each went about their work. As the story took shape, there were changes here and there, but the overall report tended to expand in sporadic intervals across the on-screen timeline rather than gradually. Anja considered footage of French president Nicolas Sarkozy criticizing the lack of a united European response to the crisis, but she decided against it in the end, framing the story more clearly around various bank failures in France, the UK, and Germany, and posing the question of a common European response without clearly positing a perspective on whether a "European bailout" would be a good or bad thing.

In contrast with Paulette's thesis-driven story, Anja's was oriented towards a stepwise assembling of images and audio clips in order to provide background and breadth. The audiovisual structure of the story was almost completely in place before Anja began typing the story's accompanying voiceover narration. Working with time codes, Anja and the editor calculated how long each of her voiceovers would have to be, and she wrote them while closely monitoring how much time she had for commentary between clips. Anja crafted the story out of available footage and sound bytes, while Paulette had moved roughly in the opposite direction, beginning with the story she wanted to tell, and dragging clips onto her timeline in order to fit the basic outline of what she had written. Anja and her editor finished their story around 5 p.m., while Paulette continued to edit and tweak her story until deadline, a little after 6 p.m. The day's team of editors in chief moved from editing room to editing room to review the "desks" and the three twenty-second faxes, which were assembled by the same journalist.

"I criticize almost every German story I see," the director of ARTE's news department told me. "They emphasize the facts, the accurateness and quality of the information, but there's often very little visual interest or polemic." Almost every journalist I spoke with at *Info* agreed that this was a key difference between French and German journalists: news was about a sense of "accuracy" or "information" for the Germans, but about the "human interest" and "polemic" for the French.

I did observe pronounced differences in the editing practices among French-speaking and German-speaking journalists – or rather, I will note, between journalists who had worked primarily at national media outlets in France or Germany before arriving at ARTE. One of the translators whom I spoke with at length put it this way: "German stories are a little bit 'harder,' a little bit heavier, sometimes. In French, stories are often a bit atmospheric [*atmosphérique*]," said the translator, himself from Germany, as he tried to find the right words. "Ambience [*L'ambiance*] is important in the French reports … there's more of the metaphorical, a figurative aspect." Was it difficult, I asked, to capture the tone of a story, to translate the "feeling" of a story? Yes, he nodded. "French stories tend to be lighter somehow. German stories, I don't know, more substantive [*substantive*]."

Other journalists described the difference in terms of the willingness of a journalist to imply a politics or opinion about a given topic. When I asked Anja about differences she noted in French and German journalistic "styles," she explained, "The French allow themselves to … lightly insert their opinion or commentary. Or sometimes they use words, the way they say something, that expresses their opinion, is a commentary." She switched to German. "For Germans, everything that is opinion [*Ansicht*] just won't pass [*geht's nicht*]." She stated this as a principle, chopping one of her hands for emphasis. "Germans are trained not to do this." I offered her an example from a story that I had watched edited with one of the French journalists, who used the word *bourgeois* in a story to describe bankers, in what seemed to me, a vaguely condescending way. "Exactly," replied Anja. "I don't think a German journalist would feel comfortable with that." In form and content, then, French and German journalists were understood, at ARTE, to clearly differ in editing style. As both the translator and Anja made clear, ARTE journalists and production staff have a sense of exactly what these differences are – and can describe, in pithy terms, what makes "French" journalism different from "German" news.

There is a distinction worth making and emphasizing here, however. While journalists at ARTE may understand "French" and "German" journalistic styles to differ, in this book I mean to trouble national categories, and here I want to explicitly push against the conclusion that there is a difference between "French" and "German" journalism at ARTE – especially not in any way that might enable speculation of nationally bifurcating sensibilities or temperament. Rather, when queried, journalists explained to me that they organized information in a particular way because they had been *trained* in a particular way – and explained to me that this training was quite specific and practice-based. Anja had been trained to think about news-making in terms of available materials and a set of embodied practices (writing down time codes, gathering and comparing quotations), while journalists who had been trained in France (as opposed to "French journalists") talked about having learned to think about news-making in terms of an intellectual tradition valuing narrative and a "line" of argument. They could recall particular courses, assignments, instructors who had instilled these practices. (One recalled, "I found it funny because my German colleagues here, we all studied journalism at the same schools and even had some of the same instructors.") These learned practices can therefore be attributed to particular (brick-and-mortar) schools of journalism; the cities and towns in which they are situated; and even generations of staff trained at these schools that, through their teaching, cultivate and reproduce these practices in their students. In other words, the ways in which ARTE journalists edited and organized news had to do with located and learned practices; being French or German did not somehow "mean" that that they thought about a news story one way or another, nor can we extrapolate that their practices imply something about French-ness or German-ness. (It was beyond the scope of my study, but one could further delineate similarities and differences in approaches to journalism at ARTE to journalistic training at particular schools of journalism – which would no doubt also reveal substantial intra-national differences, as well as trans-border similarities; cf. Boyer 2000, 2005.)

What's more, journalists who had worked at ARTE *Info* for many years or who had been trained there did not draw as clear distinctions between these stylings. One journalist who had gone to a European school of journalism in Brussels explained that his instructors had explicitly discussed several journalistic schools and traditions and encouraged students to craft a useful combination from among them.

Over days and weeks in ARTE's newsroom it became clear to me that journalists at ARTE, despite (or perhaps *because of*) conceptions of national journalistic difference, often strived to reframe their representations of current events in order to construe them as explicitly transnational or European. As the banking crisis continued to develop, in the daily *qui fait quoi* meetings, ARTE journalists pursued what they understood to be ARTE's French-German and European perspective on the story by raising the question of what Europe's role would be in mitigating the deepening financial woes of banks across the continent. A week after the first U.S. government bailout of flailing banks, the ARTE newsroom was abuzz with criticism of German chancellor Angela Merkel, who was seen as obstructing a European equivalent to the U.S. bailout measure. "*C'est la faute de Merkel! C'est la faute de Merkel!* [It's Merkel's fault! It's Merkel's fault!]" one of the editors in chief chanted, cheekily, as he entered the meeting room one morning, after the failure of the Royal Bank of Scotland and several other European banks. The crisis was understood as a test for the European Union and its ability to mobilize, collectively, a response that would ensure stability of markets not just in France or Germany, but in neighbouring countries whose economies were in many ways more fragile and susceptible to collapse, including the newer EU nations of Eastern Europe. In our daily meetings, there seemed to be a sense among journalists that "we're all in this together," as they chatted openly, switching between German and French, about the consequences of the crisis for a world in which national borders didn't seem, to them, in this context, especially relevant.

A German editor-in-chief asked at a *qui fait quoi* if the important question to ask wasn't, "Can't we have a French-German 'iron grip' [*bras de fer*] that could lead the European response?" His French colleague responded, "In any case, Sarkozy is the acting president of Europe, so if Paris acts, it's not only necessarily 'Paris.'" In these framings of what the appropriate questions were to ask of the situation, journalists were oriented towards the angles and language that they should employ in their reports, and the appropriate collective actors that should be

Figure 2.7 The set of ARTE's news program, ARTE *Info*. (Photo by author)

deployed as subjects, and objects, in their stories. Here, an editor-in-chief reframes French president Nicolas Sarkozy as the then-rotating president of the EU, and so "Paris" as metonym not for France but for Europe: We can therefore speak of Sarkozy's actions as *European* ones, the editor implies. In subtle symbolic shiftings (or overlays) like this one, in meetings in which journalists pool and negotiate ideas, angles of agreement and conceptions of common good are gathered and clicked together like Lego bricks. Journalists can then take these as a back to their desks as scaffolding and construct two-and-a-half minute reports around them.

Later that day, a journalist and editor put together a graphic that divided the screen into four parts, each quartile with an image of newspapers from a different European country, as the journalist evoked various disparate measures being taken in different EU countries (each securing deposits for differing millions of euros). Here was a cacophony of nations represented as a divided screen and seemingly random kinds of numbers which, it seemed to me, was intended to be disorienting. The image was used in three consecutive broadcasts, capturing and disseminating the news team's criticism of the lack of a common European financial response and policy.

Between and among editing styles, these reports came to take shape as trans/national and/or European in their comparative attention to the economic woes unfolding across the continent. Though journalists drew on national news sources as they constructed their stories, and their own disparate training about how such stories should be assembled and conveyed, there also emerged, between and among these, stories that journalists thought ARTE should tell for its French, German, and trans-European audiences. The approach isn't especially self-conscious or laboured; the French-German and European angles that develop in the *qui fait quoi*'s are a result of the daily conversations, interactions, and exchanges of information that happen as a result of the journalists pooling their ideas and news sources about what is happening in the world, and deciding on how particular events are relevant to everyone in the newsroom. As a result, news on ARTE constantly moves between the national, the trans/national, and global in motley ways that combine divergent editing styles and national news sources with a sense of common interests and goals.

4. ZOOM Europa

While ARTE *Info* crisscrosses national frames of reference, news sources, and "styles," there had been for many years another ARTE program that claimed to present a self-conscious, and in a sense, more direct "European" view of the world. Until 2005, the program was known as *Le Forum des Européens*. *Le Forum* was replaced by *ZOOM Europa* and, at the time of writing, *ZOOM* was replaced by a program called *Yourope*. These programs have had in common an editorial line (largely reproduced and passed along to subsequent shows) that has called for "an accessible engagement with Europe," profiling current events around Europe, in a way that has defined "Europe" in a broader geographical way rather than institutionally.

In some contrast to *Karambolage* and ARTE *Info*, *ZOOM*'s frame of reference explicitly gathered together multiple groups of European countries; each week it considered a theme that its journalists, producers, and staff considered to be relevant to some cross-section of European nations (which might as readily include Turkey and Russia as Italy). Weekly episodes have focused, for example, on animal rights across Europe, labour unions, corruption, aging populations, the dwindling reserves of fresh water across Europe, and approaches to the integration of newly arrived immigrants. Each episode would feature a series of in-depth stories, of about five minutes each, which examined the issue across three or four European countries. Teams of two or three *ZOOM* journalists would travel to places across Europe to film longer reports, or *ZOOM* would work with local journalists who could provide footage, usually for shorter stories. Much like at ARTE *Info*, themes emerged out of the daily meetings and conversations with staff, which included young journalists from France, Germany, and Italy. Themes and reports that would be featured for particular episodes were decided in meetings during which staff would debate the relevance of a topic and, above all, its seeming interest for audiences that were understood to include, but not be limited to, France and Germany.[16]

Journalists and staff were well-versed in trans-European current events and social issues partly because the news outlets that they turned to in their work were less nationally oriented than those at *Info*; at *ZOOM*, journalists more often turned to the "European" sections of national media, to the *European Observer*, *Le Monde Diplomatique*, and the European wire service *eurovision*. Yet during the two weeks I spent with the production staff and journalists of *ZOOM*, as two episodes of the show were filmed, edited, assembled, and translated, I found that the process of choosing "European themes," and then filling themed episodes with relevant reports, was marked by a self-conscious *politics* that wasn't as fully evident at *Info*. Indeed, the left-leaning ethos of the production staff's editor-in-chief and producer was clearly visible in the stickers and photocopied comic strips that were taped to their doors, most of which lampooned Sarkozy and his latest political initiatives. In meetings, discussions often turned to the political – even when we were talking about something else – as members of the *ZOOM* production team might bring up freedom of the press in Russia, Italian president Silvio Berlosconi's iron-fisted control over Italian media, or the seemingly imminent defeat of the Labour Party in the U.K.

I encountered a kind of political sensibility that seemed to inform much of *ZOOM*'s production work my first day at the program's offices. The head of *ZOOM* production, and its producer, invited me to sit in a swivel chair at a conference table as they inserted a tape into a player at the front of the room. Cécile and Eliza began to review reports that had been produced for a *ZOOM* episode about recent immigrants across Europe, sent from Germany. One of the reports was about about *clowns sans frontières* / *Clowns ohne Grenzen* – a group of clowns that travel from Germany to Eastern Europe (in this case, Romania) to perform for "underprivileged children and orphans," of whom many were recent immigrants from poorer Eastern European countries. In the report, the bus of clowns arrives, and we follow them as they describe what they do and as they interact with the children. Cécile and Eliza were critical of the somewhat awkward audiovisual relationship between the German adults and children. "Here's a story about clowns, and they don't even [hear from] the children," said Cécile. "We don't talk to the children at all, we only have the adults talking about the children. That's ridiculous." There were critiques of certain aspects of the composition – what was that bizarre guitar music in the background? how would they deal with the German lyrics in the French version? why *that* shot? why *that* cut *there*? But Cécile and Eliza became really exasperated when one of the German clowns explains, "The school is safe and clean – it smelled like *Putzmittel* [cleaning fluid] when we arrived." The producers took this to imply an assumption about the children's cleanliness, or lack thereof. Later in the report, one of the adults mentions that they leave their wallets in the bus (for fear of having them stolen). "*Mais c'est honteux, honteux,*" said Cécile [That is just shameful, shameful]. "Ça ne *va pas*, ça ne *va pas*" [That is *not* okay, that is *not* okay].

The incident, which snowballed into angry phone calls to the German production team and demands for them to re-edit the piece, indicated a kind of political sensibility that was at work at *ZOOM*, and which I noticed again and again as the weeks progressed, as I sat in on editing sessions and voiceover recording sessions. It became clear that for producers and staff at *ZOOM*, "Europe" often served as a kind of political orientation and ideology that was in a certain sense acutely antinational. During a brainstorming meeting for upcoming episodes and reports, one of the eight journalists proposed a story about national governments that hadn't paid their debts to the European Union. "France owes the Commission a monstrous amount of money," explained the journalist. Later in the meeting, another journalist asked about whether they might include something about the co-produced blockbuster film *Astérix*:

> It's being touted as the biggest French film in years, but it's actually pan-European – they've gone out of their way to include actors that are famous in various European countries, even if we wouldn't recognize them. One from Italy, I think … from Spain … so it's kind of the first European blockbuster.

A man who coordinates production for *ZOOM* at ARTE France, who attends the weekly meetings, frowned at this. "It's pure crap, that film.

Figure 2.8 A door at *ZOOM Europa*'s production offices covered in political cartoons. (Photo by author)

It's interesting that it's the first film of its kind to be marketed, in a way, as 'European' rather than French ..." "Euro-pudding," added the journalist. "But," replied the ARTE *France* producer, "it's 'European' purely because it can make more *money* that way." Several people nodded their heads. Someone made the joke, "Well, that's European, too!" Yet exactly what was at stake here was whether the film was "European" because it was an example of cultural interchange, or whether it was merely a commoditization of such interchanges, touting a trans-European cast in order to win easier distribution and to garner greater trans-continental ticket sales. *ZOOM*'s production team largely concluded the latter.

"Europe" at *ZOOM* seemed to discursively align with a politics of cosmopolitan open-mindedness and a sustained critique of capitalism that might be instrumentalized to cultivate trans-border social solidarities and multicultural inclusion. I watched one of *ZOOM*'s younger journalists, Nicolas, who grew up near Paris but who had received a master's degree in the U.K., edit a story about neighbourhood police, "bobbies," in the community of Lozells and East Handsworth, near Birmingham, England (for the same episode about newly arrived immigrants). The thesis of the approximately five-minute report, for which Nicolas had been in Birmingham with a camera crew to produce, was that police in the U.K. are improving their relationship with local immigrant communities by sending out bobbies to interact with the community in new, friendlier ways that are not limited to policing and arrests. The report began by explaining that Lozells and East Handsworth had seen three riots in the past several years tied to the ethnicity of immigrant groups. The community was Asian and Afro-Caribbean, and there were tensions between the two groups, but the story was mainly about the police themselves and how they were dealing with ethnic and community relations in the wake of the recent violence. The report was referred to as "nice police" – *police sympa* – on the various planning spreadsheets (*Mengengerüste!*) that we were using to organize production.

Yet, in reviewing the raw footage with an editor, Nicolas explained that it was difficult to find people who would agree that the neighbourhood felt safer since the police had begun their increased trips into the community. One woman who was interviewed said that things were a "mess." Another said that the community did feel more secure, but because it seemed like there were *fewer* police around rather than more. "Then how can it feel more secure?" replied Nicolas in the raw video footage, from off-screen, in French-accented English. As he edited the footage, he pieced together a report that included interviews with

Figure 2.9 In the editing studios of *ZOOM Europa*, a story is assembled about Birmingham "bobbies" interacting with the local community. (Photo by author)

two people who agreed that things were better since the bobbies were around. The edited piece takes us to the police headquarters, where we see how bobbies are trained to be culturally sensitive, and how to inter-act with the community in positive ways. The politics of the piece were clearly oriented towards a multiculturalism that sought to advocate for better engagement of police with immigrant communities in the U.K., proposing it as a model for other European nations: "Here, police have changed their tactics because they understand that they must be pres-ent in the community not only in bad times, but also in good, if they are to gain trust. Perhaps elsewhere in Europe, there is a lesson to learn," concluded the report.

In the pro-European politics at *ZOOM*, which tended to envision a particular social order rooted in politically leftist orientations and poli-cies that explicitly privilege trans-border comparisons and solidarities, "Europe" comes to stand in for governance and policy that might cor-rect the perceived deficits of national shortcomings in dealing with immigrants, poverty, or aging populations. Yet it is unclear if such a politics reveals something of the unifying fabric of European-ness, or if it is that these politics merely provide a convenient – because consistent – editorial perspective. (Indeed, while I was at ARTE, both France and the Netherlands voted in referenda to reject a European constitution. When I asked a member of staff at ARTE France why she had voted "no," she replied, "We didn't want *this* Europe. *This* Europe, today's Europe, is promoting globalization instead of protecting people from it – it's a free market Europe. I want an integrated Europe, just not this one." In other words, there is no clear correlation between leftist politics and being pro-Europe, and many would argue just the opposite.)

Given the holes and frays in the meaning(s) of a "European" politics, *ZOOM Europa* meetings, in contradistinction to those of ARTE *Info*, were often marked by discord and heated argument over the selection and execution of news stories. Though I was only at *ZOOM*'s studios two weeks, entire days passed in silence if an editorial meeting was particularly acrimonious. While some of this had to do with strong and conflicting personalities, I was also convinced that part of the problem with *ZOOM* was that, among ARTE's programming, it was one of the only series to require that staff work out, each week, a more or less explicit meaning for "Europe" (or, at any rate, a politics critical of the nation-state) as it was applied to various social contexts and problems. A left-leaning politics provided a means of siphoning off some of the ambiguity of how to narrate the relevance of Europe in many cases, but it also left room for ambiguities and arguments. One such argument, lasting almost an entire meeting, was about how much coverage (in terms of episodes) to provide an upcoming EU summit; it wasn't about the *institutions*, argued a senior staff member, it was about a social Europe. A senior producer disagreed: "It *has* to be about the institutions, first – otherwise, how do you put in place a social Europe?" Ultimately, while a certain emphasis on trans-border social justice informed *ZOOM*'s approach to "Europe," it was rarely without ambiguities that required and provoked additional discussion, and often, discord and dispute.

3

trans/national belonging

(inconsistent) sociality at ARTE

Sitting at lunch one day at ARTE GEIE in Strasbourg, as I finish my pizza, I look around the room. I've been trying to get a sense of who sits with whom in order to understand something about how people tend to group at ARTE. As I scan the space, I see that there are entire tables of staff, from France and/or Germany, who are chatting away in French or German. There is a table of staff – from France, Germany, and Austria – who all work in the same department, switching between French *and* German as they chat. Today I am sitting at a table of interns, all in their mid-twenties. At the table next to ours, five senior administrators sit together. At a table near the window, several programming staff from various departments eat with two members of the translation service. (I learn later that they are friends who all happen to live in the same neighbourhood of Strasbourg.) Near the room's entryway, six administrative assistants to the channel's highest administrators, and who work in adjacent offices, sit chatting. Near their table several technicians from ARTE's news department are finishing dessert. After lunch, everyone convenes at the coffee bar, just outside of the lunchroom, where these groups partly reshuffle.

Who eats with whom tells us much about the variety of social groups and associations that are relevant at this trans/national media organization. Workplace activities and organizational hierarchies organize social life and socialization at ARTE, as do linguistic competencies, nationality, age, and gender. Yet there were tables that both cross-cut these categories, or where the combination of ARTE staff eating together could not be categorized (at least by me) in any easy way. Indeed, I often found myself eating with members of both the documentary department and the audience studies department, or with administrators and administrative assistants. So the tables of ARTE's lunchroom tell us something, too, about the variety of categories that may be deployed in making sense of trans/national social worlds at ARTE, and about the ways in which various labelings may be only fleetingly, or inconsistently, relevant in understanding how people organize themselves in this trans-border context.[1]

In this chapter, I seek to understand something about how people think about belonging at ARTE, how these beliefs and practices intersect with ARTE's self-consciously trans-border French-German and European mission statement. I describe the sociality and trans-cultural negotiations that perhaps generally characterize trans/national or globalizing spaces, and attempt to shed light on a central contradiction that I found at this trans-border media organization. On the one hand, national culture, behaviour, and identity are everywhere at ARTE stereotyped and reified, reducing being French or German to formulae and cliché; on the other hand, ARTE staff found a sense of common belonging through a number of beliefs and practices that I discuss as "lines of flight" that seem to veer away from assumptions that "national identity" is fundamental, predominant, or explanatory.

This chapter does not engage directly with concepts or theories of "identity," but focuses on "belonging." Identity, like nationalism, is an overwrought concept across the social sciences, and rather than trying to connect ethnographic evidence at ARTE to a dozen divergent lines of argument about identity (and "identification" [Brubaker and Cooper 2000]), I focus instead on belonging. "Belonging" is not without its ambiguities, debates, and detractors (see Geschiere 2009), but my sense is that it offers a more particularly anthropological and open-ended gloss on the many ways in which humans think about, and articulate, who they are and where they belong in the world. In emphasizing belonging, I hope to leave behind what I understand to be the turgid quality of identity, especially in its implications – despite much critique and retheorization – of stability, solidity, and coherence.

I also circumnavigate identity because I want to draw attention to the ways in which sociological and analytical language is itself a kind of meta-problem with which scholars must continue to grapple. For if, as Richard Handler (1988) brilliantly remarked twenty-odd years ago, "cultural objectification is one contribution of social science to the modern Western world view" (15), pointing out that anthropologists, among others, had done much to "naturalize" and reify the "nation" as a bounded and uniform kind of "community," we still find ourselves struggling to disarticulate and to move beyond nation and identity. Andreas Wimmer and Nina Glick Schiller (2002) and Ulrich Beck (2006, 2007) have written about this tendency as "methodological nationalism," which Wimmer and Schiller (2002) define as "the assumption that the nation/state/society is the natural social and political form of the modern world" (301).

Recognizing the problem that Handler (1998), Wimmer and Schiller (2002) and many others, including Aksoy and Robins (2005), have articulated, I avoid discussing identity at ARTE in order to distinguish my own argument from the ways in which many ARTE staff *themselves* use the term. At ARTE, "identity" (*identité, Identität*) was almost always used alongside the assumption of circumscribed, bounded national communities. I therefore discuss how ARTE staff think about and talk about identity – how programmers and staff at a French-German and European television channel *themselves* deploy various abstract conceptions of (especially national) identity and culture, noting how and when they presume identity to be coherent, self-evident, and stable – but I myself avoid using the term analytically. In this way, this chapter means to excavate *discourses about* identity, nation, culture, and Europe, rather than in any way arguing that German-ness or European identity have content, or are always-already-meaningful, or consistently so.

Because this chapter means to challenge and trouble naturalistic and presumptive categories about nation, identity, and culture, I endeavour to employ an imperfect yet I think ultimately helpful set of nomenclatural strategies. I try to refer to ARTE staff by what language they were speaking (during a particular ethnographic moment) rather than what country they were "from." Many ARTE staff have complex biographies that track across several regions and countries, and in many cases it would simply not be accurate to oversimplify their trans-border trajectories by referring to them as either French or German. I sometimes do note when someone is "from France" or "from Germany" if I know that they have been hired in that capacity (ARTE has hiring quotas) and that they have primarily or only lived in that country. If they have

Figure 3.1 The lunchroom at ARTE's headquarters in Strasbourg. (Photo by author)

personally identified as French or German – that is, if they "claim" a nationally identifying label – I note that they "identify as French."

I do so not to be gimmicky or persnickety but because if one of my central arguments is about the subtle pervasiveness and tacit natural-izations of national ways of thinking, were I to merely and automati-cally assume that someone speaking French *identifies* as French (or merely "is" French, in all the foreclosure of "simply" equating *being* with *nationality*), I would reproduce the very line of logic I mean to throw into relief and to critique. Perhaps the person grew up in Swit-zerland and identifies as Swiss; or grew up primarily in Germany, but speaks fluent French after studying at the Sorbonne; or has a French parent and a German parent; or grew up in Spain but married a per-son in France, who speaks both French and Spanish. Beyond these contingencies – which some at ARTE immediately made clear, but others kept to themselves – a second reason for keeping national nominatives (what anthropologists might more broadly refer to as "ethnonyms") at arm's-length is because, as this chapter will show, such labels were loaded, like beasts of burden, with stereotypes, organizational politics, and assumptions of many flavours and varieties. To refer to someone as French or German at ARTE (and I would argue, in most contexts) is never neutral, but is often taken to indicate and imply a number of things about the person's background, appearance, and behaviour (and furthermore *authorizes* these assumptions) – and in some cases labellings of "French" and "German" may even imply a particular politics of acknowledging, or not acknowledging, Europe's growing sociocultural and intra-national diversity.

A majority of this chapter argues that discourses of identity and culture at ARTE, as evidenced by everyday discourse and talk, were almost always assumed to be synonymous with *national* belonging and behaviour in ways that understand being French or German as bounded, flat, and inflexible. I discuss the mechanisms of this "identity work" and the implications of this discourse for ARTE's mediational work. At the same time, alongside pervasive reifications of French-ness and German-ness, I found that certain forms of cross-national European solidarities and commonalities took shape *without* explicit or implicit reference to concepts of identity or to its usual connotations of stability and closure; alongside what is my own critique of national identity in this chapter, many staff at ARTE themselves outrightly rejected the capacity of this term to represent or mediate the manifold, dynamic sociality of this trans/national workplace.

national cultural stereotype at ARTE

During the first months of my fieldwork, one of the most interesting aspects of working at ARTE was trying to guess if people were from France or Germany. Finding myself in conversation with someone I hadn't met, at lunch, or posing a question after a screening, I would speak French (since I was better at it). Sometimes I could tell (I thought) from an accent that the person with whom I was speaking was probably, in fact, a native German speaker. But even if the person spoke with me in what I perceived to be near-flawless French, I soon learned that I couldn't assume that he/she was from France. For months I believed a woman in the docu-magazine department was French – her last name was Bucher (which I was pronouncing *boo-shay*), after all. Months later she told me that she had spent most of her life in Germany (although she had lived in France for fifteen years), and that her last name was in fact *Bücher*, which she pronounced (roughly) as *BOO-kuh*.

People at ARTE were often too bilingual to be linguistically "read" and categorized as French or German, especially since those from Alsace might speak French with what Parisians might hear as having a slightly Germanic twinge, and since dialects and accents across Germany could vary substantially – so much so, I was told, that some Germans had trouble understanding their German colleagues.[2] Like me, ARTE staff sometimes relied on linguistic competency and accents to determine who came from where – and people would tell me that a key characteristic of the French at ARTE was that often they wouldn't even bother trying to speak German.

But ARTE staff members in Strasbourg (and elsewhere) tended to have a mental list of French and German traits and visual cues that they could use to decide if a person was French or German. "I can tell by whether a person says hello," a German administrative assistant told me. "French people always say *bonjour* in the elevator, or if you pass them in the hallway. Germans don't do that as much." A member of the audience studies department commented:

> In the cafeteria, you can tell because the French tend to drink wine with lunch, Germans not as much. And French people eat dessert more than Germans. I [also] know from shoes. French people and German people wear different kind of shoes – Germans pay less attention to their shoes, they tend to be more informal ... French people seem to care more ... and French women wear heels more often.

"I can usually guess if people are French or German by the way they are speaking with one another," said a programming administrator. A French person can sort of talk about something for a while without saying anything, whereas we Germans are more direct, we get to the point. I find this difference very pronounced [*Ich finde, daß diese Unterschied sehr prononciert ist*]." A French administrator in the same department told me, "French people are more expressive with their hands when they speak ... they are more expressive with their bodies than Germans [*Ils s'expriment plus avec les mains ... avec le corps ...*]."

The ways in which people at ARTE read and categorized linguistic and bodily practices were immediate ways of discerning who in a room was likely to be French or German, not unlike those that anthropologists have observed in other socially dichotomized and borderland settings in Europe. William Kelleher (2003) has described, for example, the ways in which Protestants and Catholics "read" each other's bodies in Belfast, Northern Ireland, and Dominic Boyer (2000) has written about "corporeal expertise" when West German journalists assess East German journalists. ARTE staff, especially those who had worked at ARTE for a decade or more, had developed catalogues of behavioural differences between French and Germans that they used to make sense of how and why people worked well together (or didn't work well together) at ARTE.

"Let me tell you what happens at meetings," explained a German-identifying programmer on one of my first days at ARTE. We happened to be sitting in the president of ARTE's temporarily vacated, spacious office.

> You'll be in a meeting, and as you're explaining why you think something, the French interrupt you – they say, "No no, I think ..." The French are less goal-oriented in conversations – they digress, so a conversation or meeting can be a bit all over the place, and sometimes it's difficult to arrive at a set of objectives or a conclusion ... Though it's easier to arrive at an *agreement*, you see?

He paused to see that I was following.

> But the Germans are more direct. They let you finish your argument, then they say, "No, you're wrong, and here's why." It can take longer to reach agreement because it needs to be clear what is being agreed upon ... and everyone takes his or her turn.

Another German corroborated this description of French and German "argumentation styles," adding that the French will, after a long argument, say, "Okay, okay, we agree." But then, "a few days after the meeting ... suddenly you hear they're doing exactly the opposite of what you agreed to do!"

A personal assistant in the programming department explained: "Germans are obsessed with lists. In a meeting, you *have* to get to *every* point. And sometimes you're sitting there with your eyes rolled back into your head." The director of the programming department elaborated, "Germans are just more about following the protocol, the rules."

At a dinner party I attended, an argument erupted about whether it was appropriate to cross the road at a crosswalk if the pedestrian sign indicated Don't Walk. The German speakers in the room insisted that it was a very "German" thing to wait at the crosswalk, even if there wasn't a single car in the road. The French speakers didn't have so unified an opinion. Yet when I suggested that, during my summers in Berlin, I often saw people cross the street against the indication of Walk signs, German-identifying people in the Strasbourg apartment became indignant. "No, well it's *not* a German thing to do," one woman declared to me.

Much of the French-German talk was discussed as a means of knowing how to navigate daily life and work at ARTE. "It's learning to know what to expect," one younger staff person put it to me. If you're working with Germans, I was advised by the French, be sure to document *everything*, save emails – don't leave out *any* details. "Make sure if you meet with someone about something that you email the overseeing producer so that he or she knows about it." A number of German speakers told me about the French, on the other hand, that I should be sure to watch how much German I spoke, and with whom. "Many of the French are very sensitive about not speaking German very well, and I think they question your loyalty if they see you speaking too much German."

"German fastidiousness" and "French lackadaisicalness" were tropes and leitmotifs that tended to subsume French-German dichotomizations of practices and cultural sensibilities. Not only were the Germans understood to insist on lists and systematicity, they were also understood to be more interested in order and authority more generally. They were direct, less emotional, no-nonsense, logical, reasonable, predictable, while the French were, instead, indirect, emotional and prone to loquaciousness, spontaneity, and unpredictability. While on the one hand, there were specific narrative scripts that I heard circulating that "nailed down" differences in French and German behaviour – from email practices right down to French versus German editing styles[3] – there was also an encompassing hot-cold dichotomy in play (cf. Lévi-Strauss 1955). "Germany is the north [*L'Allemange, c'est le nord*]," one of my key informants told me one day, a minute or two after she noisily hung up her phone receiver, annoyed by I wasn't sure what. "We are *Latin* [*On est latin*]. We are probably closer to the Italians and the Spanish in our personalities … we love food, we love music …"[4]

Varieties of cultural stereotype therefore included bodily practices, social behaviours, and more amorphously, constellations of preferences and traits that were understood to fall at either side of hot or cold, northern or southern, emotion or reason. "That's so French!" or "That's so German!" could be, and constantly were, tacked onto any number of readily observed behaviours and ideas: a leather jacket; a person eating yogurt; sneezing without excusing oneself; a documentary proposal about the history of the colour spectrum.

National-cultural stereotype in the form of this nationalizing discourse and dichotomizations permeated everyday life and work at ARTE. Of course, because I was an outsider at the channel and neither French nor German, I am quite aware that I may have heard "that's how the Germans/French are" stories recounted more often than others. But stereotyping was part of the everyday look and feel of work and life at ARTE. Many office doors were covered in jokes or cartoons about French and German people. Meals and food especially provoked nationalizing commentary and joking because it was understood to offer clear evidence, literally, of differing national taste(s).

Presumed differences between French and Germans were also officially recognized and propagated at ARTE. For example, during a weeklong workshop aimed at improving cooperation and teamwork at ARTE, small groups were given blocks with which to build a structure. A member of ARTE's news department explained to me (and many others referenced this story, in what was a widely circulating narrative) that the German teams set down their materials, took inventory of them, and talked about what to do with them, discussing what kind of structure to build, while the French tended to begin building immediately, stopping to discuss what the structure should look like as they went along. "So this is what you find are the major differences between the French and Germans here in the news department?" I asked the journalist. "Basically. Yes."

ARTE even had an administrator, Béatrice Angrand at the time of my research, whose full-time job, divided among ARTE France, Germany, and Strasbourg, was to consider ways of facilitating coordination and mutual understanding of the French and Germans who work for ARTE – "to grease the machinery," as one administrator described it. Angrand coordinated meetings, workshops, and projects; one which circulated to inboxes while I was at ARTE had an ARTE France staff member spend a week at ARTE Germany and write up a report about her experience. Angrand (2009) had also co-written a short general-audience book called *Idées Reçues: L'Allemagne*, which was published alongside *Idées Reçues: Les Français*,[5] written by sociologist Nelly Mauchamp (2006). Each of these books is divided into brief discussions of "assumptions" and stereotypes about the French and Germans, such as *"Les Allemands* [sic] *sont un peuple guerrier"* (The Germans are a warring people), or *"Le français est arrogant, râleur, et indiscipliné"* (The French person is arrogant, grouchy, and undisciplined). I noticed one or both books sitting on several shelves in offices at ARTE France and at its headquarters in Strasbourg.

A

B

Figure 3.2 [A and B] Posted on office doors at ARTE; top, a photograph of
Nicolas Sarkozy and Angela Merkel seemingly embracing under an umbrella,
from a German newspaper; bottom, a photograph of two wall signs, the
first reading "Foundation for French-German Understanding," the other
"Psychoanalysis Clinic." (Photos by author)

on the "function" of national-cultural stereotype

One of the most common arguments invoked about national cultures and their stereotypes is that they provide a "rough but necessary social map" with which people must navigate complex social terrain. As Stacia Zabusky (1995), for example, explains in her ethnography of scientists working at the European Space Agency:

> Participants constantly talked about nationality. When people spoke about nationality, they were referring specifically to the "mentality" and "culture" that citizens of particular nation-states exhibited and practiced ... Such national stereotypes provided a means for instant ease of interaction when colleagues first began working together, because they organized the meaning of different nationalities in such a way as to tidy up expectations (and realizations) of clothing, cuisine, and customary behavior ... Such shared distinctions were useful ... because they helped people understand how to interact with others. (82–3)[6]

Such "mapping" explanations are still commonplace in discussions of national (and other scalings of) culture (or cultural generalization, to put it another way), perhaps especially in Europe (cf. MacDonald [1993] 1997; Darian-Smith 1999, 141–59). In positing that such generalization and stereotype provide a means of navigating multinational, multicultural, or transnational contexts, such analyses argue that processes of cultural stereotyping are "useful" because, though they may be roughly drawn or exaggerated, they gesture towards "real" nationally configured social differences (Ries 1997).

Others have argued that stereotype may serve additional, perhaps more complex functions. On the one hand, in an application of well-worn in/out-group theory (e.g., Barth 1969), reifications of national culture are understood to produce an "us" in contrast to the "them." Michael Herzfeld (1985, 1987, 2004, 2005), in his dynamic writings on "cultural intimacy," has demonstrated not only that national cultural stereotype is relational and fluid, but also that it often functions to articulate a common, informal, ordinary "we" counterpoised against official and state discourses. This production of community is not so askew from the "mapping" function of culture(s), but in this case the facticity of bounded generalizations is moot; it doesn't matter if the French really do drink more wine, only that *they* are not like *us*. I should note that several staff at ARTE argued exactly this – that their quips about wine, high heels, and so on were a way of upholding differences between the French and Germans, though the differences themselves might be inaccurate.

On the other hand, both anthropologists and *ARTEsans* argue for the irony and humour that inhere in cartoonish representations of (national) culture(s). Anthropologists have argued that cultural talk and stereotype tend to be enframed by irony and humour, and they have emphasized the polyvocal, ambivalent, and semantically excessive nature of European stereotype. Herzfeld (2001) argues, for example, that ironic self-conscious talk about Greek identity has dwelled in the "tensions between the cherished values of sociability and ... puritanical moralism" (70), which, when it takes aim at asymmetrical relationships of power, both "masks ... inequality and render[s] it viable and useful" (77). In a similar way, Neringa Klumbyte (2011) has argued that humour in late Soviet Lithuanian laughter "expressed and shaped national sensibilities" – through jokes about corrupt Soviets, for example – in ways that both "reaffirmed ... official ideologies" and which allowed for the "renegotiation" of socialist values: "Both codes of power coexisted ... and were neither clear examples of support, nor of opposition or resistance" (2011: 673). When deemed satirical, ironical, or parodic, the politics of culture talk is understood to be multidirectional, even as established social orders may also, at the same time, be acknowledged and reinscribed.

In some places and contexts, it may certainly be the case that cultural stereotype (and stereotypical culture) performs complex, ambivalent, and multidirectional kinds of social work, both opening and closing spaces of political possibility. But at ARTE and, I argue, in a number of contexts across contemporary Western Europe, these bindings-together of national culture may not be very ambivalent at all; theories of cultural stereotype must be able to both account for their sometime ironical or carnivalesque functions as well as, in other contexts, for their sometime inflexibilities and inaccuracies – indeed what Herzfeld has referred to as "falsifiability" (2001: 75). We are otherwise left with cultural-political equivocation (culture talk *both* confirms *and* resists power), without the capacity for characterizing some kinds of national cultural assertions (or stereotype), *tout court*, as reductivist and problematic.[7] Without recourse to such a conclusion, we are simply unable to clarify and emphasize the real political stakes and effects of some kinds of discourse.[8]

I would argue that this post-structural equivocation – a feature of *both* anthropological analyses and the educated common sense of ARTE folk themselves – may explain why the practice of cultural objectification and stereotyping remains so pervasive. Assertions that such talk is often tongue-in-cheek, or semantically manifold, empower ARTE staff to defend their use of cultural clichés as not "altogether" serious, and therefore as (more or less) inconsequential. ARTE staff were able to laugh off or shrug at this talk because, when they weren't asserting their sometime value for predicting or categorizing behaviour, they considered their quips about lazy Greeks or hot-blooded Spaniards to be at least partially ironic or tongue in cheek, and so in fact to be *refuting* the silliness or simplification of such talk and ways of thinking. Along these lines, I was often told that the traffic in stereotype at ARTE was, at base, "goodhearted," that people didn't really "mean" it, and that people didn't *really* believe that behaviour was so nationally organized or predictable. "*Détends-toi un peu!*" I was told at least once. "Lighten up!"

But my observations at ARTE suggest, jokes not aside, that instead of presuming that there is "some truth" to cultural talk and stereotype (how much truth we can never know, but *some*), or that it may somehow resist hegemonic power even as it seems to enable it (i.e., it undoes itself, though to what extent we cannot ascertain), we might rehabilitate attention to how some uses of culture misinterpret and misconstrue social facts and relations in the service of asserting and (re)producing particular social stabilities and homogeneities.

(re)producing the "French" and "German"

During programming commemorating the fortieth anniversary of the signing of the Elysée Treaty between France and Germany, ARTE's website featured a "quiz game," in both French and German, which asked users whether popular clichés about French people and Germans were in fact "true." Featured throughout the game, illustrating the clichés as they popped up on-screen, were cartoons of a highly stereotyped French woman and German man. France was represented as a woman in a slinky dress wearing the revolutionary French Phrygian cap of the *sans-culottes* revolutionaries, usually holding a cigarette or a dainty glass of wine, while Germany was a blond man dressed in a pro-recycling T-shirt and rugged jeans, holding a giant mug of beer and sometimes even a sausage.

The game consisted of four categories of questions from each of which the player must answer one correct question with only three allowable

Figure 3.3 ARTE's "cliché" quiz game, featured on its website. (Screenshot taken by author)

wrong answers. The categories included cross-cultural myths, art and culture, politics and history, and beer and wine. When a player selected a category, a statement popped onto the screen and the player selected if it was true or false. The quiz then informed the player if the answer was correct. If it was not, the quiz explained in a short paragraph why the answer was wrong, usually citing a statistic of some kind – how many litres of beer were consumed annually in Germany versus France, for example. The true/false statements and the answers the game provided included:

- The French do not like Germans [False]
- Paris is an expensive city [True]
- French people are unfaithful in relationships [True]
- The majority of Germans are blond [False]
- French people smoke more than Germans [True]
- Germans drink more beer than French people [True]
- French women are vain [True]
- Spoken French sounds better than spoken German [True]

Many people at ARTE enjoyed the quiz, though most people were seeing it for the first time when I brought it up on their computer monitors. Most laughed at the images and acknowledged the game's clichés. "That's so right!" they would say. Compellingly, however, even

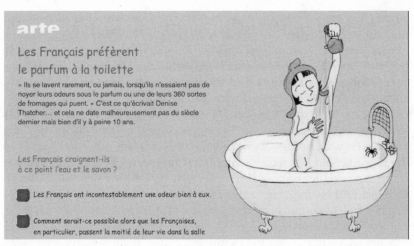

A

B

Figure 3.4 [A and B] From ARTE's cliché quiz game: the top question reads "The French prefer perfume to showering," and the bottom screen capture, which results when a player answers incorrectly, asserts "Germans [do] drink [a lot of] beer."

when they answered questions *incorrectly*, several staff who took the quiz almost immediately agreed with the game's correction: "I didn't expect that. But that makes sense ... French women *do* wear a lot of lipstick," or "That's true, actually. Most of the Germans I know here *aren't* blond." But here I would insist that most of the quiz's "factual" clichés – that French women buy more lipstick and so are "vainer" than German women, that German are *not* "humourless" because in fact a study in England shows that Germans laugh 35 times out of 100 at a joke but French people only 34 times – are, almost as much as the clichés the game sets out to refute – highly reductive, ad hoc, and ultimately serve to reproduce national cultural stereotype rather than to challenge its logics and mechanisms.

Indeed, I eventually came to notice the inconsistency of assignations of French-ness and German-ness to a variety of behaviours and practices. One of the clearest examples of this "flexible stereotype" was manifest in ARTE staff's perceptions of authority and hierarchy – in short, how they understood the functioning of *power* at the channel. Over coffee one afternoon, I mentioned to one of my regular informants in the documentary department that someone at ARTE France, in Paris, felt sorry for me having to live in Strasbourg – which they described as "*le province* [provincial]." She replied, "The French are like that. France is Paris only." Then she went on:

> You know, people say about the Germans that we are authoritarian, we are fascists, Nazis, all that ... but I think the French are much more authoritarian than Germans. They accept authority – whatever Paris says – and there is such a very strong hierarchy in France.

She explained that she saw this attitude towards authority reflected in her French colleagues at the channel:

> The French [in the department] just seem to accept when the administration changes something, without any challenge. It's the way it has always been in France, with the government. Whereas we Germans, we distrust the state ... authority for us doesn't mean the same thing.

This narrative about the French and their blind confidence in hierarchy and authority – sometimes explained in terms of the ubiquity of the French state and government – was often reproduced at ARTE, by German and French speakers alike. The French believed in hierarchy, and in the importance of power structures, to a fault; on the other hand, the

Germans had, as a result of the Second World War, learned their lesson about too eagerly submitting to authority.

And yet the Second World War and German history was *also* cited as evidence for the naturalness and continuity of a *German* fetishization of hierarchy and authority. "Germans have an affinity for authority and the State – which is of course how people explain the Second World War," I was told by a member of the cinema and fiction department. An administrative assistant explained to me one day, "You have to understand that, for Germans, everything depends on your rank, your position at the channel. For French people, it's where you went to school – that's how you are ranked, who has status. But for Germans, it's who you are in the hierarchy, your *title* that matters, and that's it." This story about schooling was one I heard several times.

> There are no elite universities [*grandes écoles*] in Germany the same way there are in France, even though that's changing. So for the Germans, you have power not because you went to a certain school but because you got a certain position, worked for that position. You have to believe in the system and how it works.

At the dinner party I attended, the trope of the German waiting for the Walk sign to change before crossing even an empty street was similarly linked to belief in the "system," in law, and in structures of authority.[9] "The French mistrust the State – that's their history," the Italian partner of an ARTE intern had commented. "It's true," said one of the Germans. "We respect authority, sometimes too much."

At the same time, I was told,

> At ARTE, if you are not an administrator, you are kept at arm's-length by the French. You are put in your place. With the Germans, each person has a role to play, and it's about fulfilling your role in the organization – because you have a kind of expertise no one else does – not about whether or not you went to *l'ENA* [École nationale d'administration – an elite graduate school].

A programmer in the documentary department put it another way: "Germans think that there is a structure of power, and you do your part in that structure. But it's not about who you *are*."

Over my months at ARTE, it eventually became impossible to decipher the various ways that ARTE staff were characterizing, qualifying, and ever-more complexly parsing differences between French and

German attitudes towards respect for power and hierarchy – who was more egalitarian or classist, which nation more blindly believed in the powers that be, whether or not "German culture" was prone to respecting the figure of the "father," and whether the court of Versailles explained much about how the French went about their daily business (cf. Elias 2000). Figure-pointing about power and authority was a nearly incessant feature of talk and discussion at ARTE, partly, of course, because so much of life and work at ARTE (as at most organizations) was defined by decisions passed down from higher authorities and by gossip about why such decisions were levied.

But talk about power and structure at ARTE also reveals much about the production of French-German and national difference at the channel: though ARTE staff regularly contradicted one another, and themselves, about how French and Germans produced and reacted to authority, I never heard acknowledgment of the fact that these claims about the "natures" of French and Germans were shifting and mutable. In fact, when I pointed out to a member of the documentary department, late in my stay at the channel, that I was finding the categories of what was supposedly typically "French" and typically "German" to be inconsistent (e.g., when I pointed out that more French speakers actually ate yogurt at lunch, not Germans), I was told by a documentary unit colleague, "Well, it all makes sense to *us*, when you've worked here for long enough."

Still, over my weeks and months at ARTE, I tended to notice that, in fact, when these national polarizations were not being discursively, self-consciously vocalized and produced, they were hardly obvious. I came to understand the production of national difference at the channel less as a means to an end – as a way of anticipating or predicting behaviour – than as a kind of end in itself: not only as a mechanism like mapping, or a task like listing, which seems to organize the world into limited, understandable, visualizable pieces of meaningful *sema*, but also as a kind of low-stakes agonism, or ludic pastime. What went under the headings of French and German – today yogurt is a "typical" French thing, tomorrow it's German – mattered less than the act of rendering differences to be evident, obvious, and (seemingly) capable of being organized. While surely some kinds of dichotomy and stereotype seemed to me more "accurate" than others – staff from France really did speak German less well than staff from Germany spoke French – many such assumptions were not systematically or consistently reproduced, at least to the extent to which I was able to discern. Furthermore, the most abstract or behavioural-humoural assumptions about national character – about who was hotheaded, impulsive, talkative, or better at decorating their houses – seemed to require the most iterative, elaborate kinds of narrative and narration. It was the *production* of a *making-sense-of* that seemed to matter more in all this talk about national difference, it seemed to me, rather than the real-ness of the "differences" themselves.

There is plenty of ethnographic evidence that lends itself to the argument that stereotype is, to a large extent, arbitrary. In her ethnography of identity, ethnicity, and stereotype in the Congo River Basin, for example, Stephanie Rupp (2011) challenges the long-standing distinctions of "pygmy/villagers" and "hunter-gatherer/farmers" through which anthropologists have bifurcated the people of this region because, as they argued, these were and are fundamental native distinctions deployed by these groups themselves. Rupp found that much of what she had learned about "culture" in the basin, and the way identity, ethnicity, and stereotype would function according to the villager/farmer binary, was simply wrong. Not only were these deployed distinctions relative and fluid (cf. Evans-Pritchard 1940) – one could pass from one to the other on the basis of seemingly unrelated issues related to one's social standing and reputation – the distinction itself was also problematic and something of a red herring:

> Far from conforming to the simplified, paired classifications of social identity based on presumed economic strategies and assumed political relationships, the diverse communities of southeastern Cameroon pursue various adaptable economic strategies, engage in many different kinds of social and political relationships, and identify themselves and shape relationships with others in dynamic ways. (Rupp 2011, 248–9)

A number of additional recent accounts of the politics of identity and belonging have similarly revisited and revised both anthropological and "folk" systems previously assumed to be predicated upon stable and utilitarian cultural wholes (e.g., Mandel 2008; Navaro-Yashin 2009; Ingram 2011; Niehaus 2013; Herzfeld 2015).

At ARTE, what was "French" and what was "German" was *made* and *remade* through a hundred daily comments and remarks such as *"Typisch französisch!"* (Typically French!) or *"C'est trop allemand, ça!"* (That's so German!). These in-the-moment assignations and designations (sometimes said for all to hear, sometimes for only "fellow nationals"), rarely functioned to "put name to" actual, stable differences, but were themselves the means by which national-cultural differences and expectations were constructed and upheld. They were a means, in other words, of calling French-ness and German-ness into existence as meaningful and explanatory categories. In this sense they are congruent with Althusser's (1971) theory of interpellation and Judith Butler's (1997) sense of performativity, which argue for the ways in which social roles are instantiated and performed when, a moment ago, such roles may not have seemed relevant or explanatory.

An emphasis on the performativity of nationalism and national identification (cf. Herzfeld 2005, 193–9) challenges our everyday assumptions that national origins and identity imply a series of stable ways of thinking and acting in the world, what was in an earlier moment of anthropology considered to be "national culture."[10] Nationalism offers a highly seductive (and today so taken-for-granted as to be hegemonic and nearly invisible) system of classification which obscures its historical contingency (there were, until fairly recent history, no French or Germans); never asserts that national sentiment is in fact regionally, locally, and individually highly variable; and which denies that what it means to be French or Chinese is simply never fully coherent, stable, or indeed knowable. It is not the case, I would assert, that stereotype is an extreme, particularly rigid, or merely wrongheaded "form" or version of national identity; rather, it more likely forms the everyday logical basis of how we think about, evaluate, experience, and ultimately oversimplify ways of being and belonging in the world. It is not the opposite of "more complicated" talk and discourse about the nation, but mirrors and buttresses such discourse.

three trans/national "lines of flight"

In what follows, I offer three glimpses of what I call trans/national lines of flight. The concept of a "line of flight" comes from Deleuze and Guattari's Anti-Oedipus: Capitalism and Schizophrenia (1972) project, but for readers uninterested in post-structuralist theory, I chose this particular Deleuzian metaphor (rather than "bodies without organs," for example) because one need not have read Deleuze and Guattari's *Mille Plateau*, volume 2 of *Capitalisme et schizophrénie* (1980) to grasp its meaning as, intuitively, a flying away from, a means of escape, but also (in its original French as *ligne de fuite*) as a kind of trickling away, of leaking. Rather than argue that what I evoke below are opposites or alternatives for nationalism and/or national ways of thinking and being (indeed, in much of what follows, nationalism remains a key language through which an alternative is nevertheless articulated), I argue that they are lines of flight that simply move away from, or perhaps merely leak away from, the solidities, flattenings, and circumscriptions of the nation-state. In this way, the following modes of identification and belonging that I describe remain trans/national; they are neither extra- nor post-national, nor fully tethered to the concept of nation in its usual connotations as coherent and enduring. Ultimately, these accounts reveal the ways in which national identity and even national belonging are, for some at ARTE, far too coherent and simplistic a vocabulary for the entangled, contradictory, and often ineffable ways that they think about and express who they are in the world.

1: neither here nor there

Paulette, an administrative assistant at ARTE, explained:

> I guess it bothers me because I *don't* really feel French around the French people here at ARTE. I sometimes get along better with the German women I work with – I think partly because I am Alsatian – I've realized that I'm *between* the two cultures, I grew up here on the border … and these German women – one of them grew up only ten miles from me, in Kehl, across the border – and so no, I don't think I'm French like Mr. Leluc [Paulette's boss] is French.

She continued, "I am not a German. I'm not completely French."

Nearly 30 per cent of ARTE staff grew up in Alsace or Lorraine, bor- der regions which have changed national hands (although in the case of Lorraine, only partially) several times over the course of the nine- teenth and twentieth centuries. Many staff at ARTE who considered themselves Alsatian understood themselves as neither fully French nor fully German, drawing on both to construct ideas about their sensibili- ties and attitudes, as Paulette described:

> I work well with Germans – we Alsatians work hard … And you can look around Strasbourg and see how organized it is, all squares, straight streets, very clean, very German. But am I *germain* [Germanic (but could also be translated as "to be related by blood")]? No … I have this, this [*snaps her fingers*] … French personality, I think, that makes me less rigid than the Germans … But I *understand* the Germans … I grew up with Germans, we went shopping every week across the border. The French and Germans

are very different ... The Germans come to a wall, they destroy it and keep going. The French, they throw up their hands and walk away. If you look at history, you see that this is pretty much true.

Not only does Paulette partly identify with German traits, partly with French, but she, like many other Alsatians I spoke with, had a tendency to objectify and position herself relative to both "cultures," but without fully claiming, or aligning herself, with either. "With the French and Germans, things are fine, now," said Paulette, speculating on the future of ARTE, "but who knows in five or ten years? The Second World War happened overnight."

"My mother's mother is German," a woman in the documentary unit explained in an interview when I asked her if being from Alsace was an asset at ARTE. "There are a bunch of [French] people here of my generation with a German parent or grandparent. There's always someone in the family who's from 'abroad' [*l'étranger*] – it's super far from here – 'abroad' – don't you know! I love when people say that. [*We laugh*]" Emma explained that she grew up speaking the Alsatian dialect with her immediate family. "I didn't speak French until I went to school ... My grandmother didn't speak French at all, only German and Alsatian." Growing up in Alsace, Emma watched both French and German television channels. "I wouldn't even notice when I would switch from a French channel to a German channel – it wouldn't even register." Like Paulette, Emma commented on the French and the Germans as if she were betwixt and between. "The French can't learn German," she told me at one point in the interview. "In France – I say 'in France' because there's France and there's Alsace ... they're just *blocked* [*bloqué*] when it comes to learning the language, I don't know what it is about them with that." She continued,

All the little differences – our dialect, the Alsatian social security system [which has a different statute than that of France] – it adds up and it means that we have a stronger regional identity than national identity ... It's not easy. It's not easy. [*Pauses*] We are culturally close to Germans, a way of thinking, little habits. It's an old cultural history [or, "story"] because this was Germany in 1870, and that has left its traces ... My grandmother went to a German school and so of course that still affects us younger generations ... there's still a background (*fond*).

... The border, it's open, people go to Germany to do their shopping because it's cheaper ... the latest thing that's become very *à la mode*, since about two years ago, is Alsatians who are buying houses in Germany – with the housing market the way it is in France, it's cheaper across the border in Kehl or Freiburg. They may still work in Strasbourg, but they're living in Germany ... In the end it's not farther than if you live south of Strasbourg. You can get a house for twice the size across the border than what you would get here. And if you speak German ... you can integrate very easily. People who live in this region have very few problems living across the border ... Someone from Paris might have some difficulty, but not people from the region.

Life courses of those who work for ARTE have often crisscrossed the French-German, and other, borders multiple times. Several young journalists on staff at one of ARTE's European news programs had spent recent years studying at universities in Germany; an Italian woman, living in France, told me she would soon go to study journalism in Brussels; a German-identifying woman had spent more than a decade living in France after graduating with a degree from a French university. At least three department heads in Strasbourg had one French or one German parent, as did a dozen other staff with whom I spoke; nearly all of the interns and younger staff had spent time, usually studying, abroad in the other country (and often elsewhere in Europe, too); and most everyone at ARTE's headquarters – and its national offices – had spent considerable time across the border.

Richard, a man who works as a translator in ARTE's news department explained that he was able to translate both French stories to German and German stories to French. I had thought he was a native French speaker, but Richard explained that he had spent the first decades of his life in Germany. He had been living in France for over thirty years, however, had settled in Strasbourg, and had a son with whom he spoke only French:

R: I've been at ARTE since we had offices in the other building in Strasbourg, the very beginning. I worked as a translator for many years, freelancing, and then worked temporarily for ARTE before I got my full-time job here ...

DS: So how did you end up in France?

R: I've have always had an affinity for France, since I was very young, a sort of love for French culture. I was always fascinated by France and would read books about France, then learned the language early on. I read French books by French authors, and then I became very interested in French philosophy. I fell in love with French literature, so that's what I studied at university in Paris. And so I never left.

DS: But do you go back to Germany? Do you miss it?

R: I do miss it sometimes, but I don't often think about it anymore. Of course I visit my family sometimes but I don't really think, "I am German" – not every day. Although sometimes my colleagues will remind me that I'm German, or something happens in the news and then I do remember, of course.

Karla, who works in the cinema and fiction department, explained in flawless French that she is German, but that her sense of self has transitioned over the years:

I first worked at ARTE Germany ... I had spent a year in France [after graduating from university], then was an activities coordinator and translator for a French-German exchange organization – that I had participated in myself when I was fourteen, thirteen years old ... France was a very close country for me [la France était un pays très proche pour moi] ... I'm from the south of Germany, so in any case it was very far.

In the beginning it was difficult, at ARTE Germany, because we didn't know how things should function, they were years of constructing the channel, how to distribute production, to develop a system of quotas ... There were always more and more questions. But for me, [this initial period] allowed me to understand how German channels operated, who was who, who did what ... and then with ARTE and the French audiovisual landscape, which was completely different. In 1996 I came to Strasbourg.

[DS: Maybe ... so it sounds like you may already have a sense of the French-German project, a French-German identity?]

... I could never be the kind of person that works a little way from home. I think that I would miss it, if I didn't work at a place like ARTE ... It's true that I don't notice when someone speaks ... for a long time now when someone speaks French to me, I reply in French, someone speaks German, I reply in German, I don't think about it ... We learn everyday [from each other], there are certain words I tend to say in French, some in German, we create a way of speaking.

But Karla explained that as she has gotten older, and as relations at the channel have seemed to her to grow more difficult, she has begun to feel, again, "more German":

I don't know what it is, I think it's age, but recently I do feel more German – I think that as you get older you kind of return to your origins. And so now I sometimes think to myself, "Well I'm German, and that's just what I think" … Maybe I don't have the patience anymore to sometimes explain myself.

Other ARTE staff confirmed that their sense of being French or German had changed over the years, had evolved during the time they had spent at ARTE, and that they would suddenly become "conscious" of one or the other identity as a result of something as simple as an annoying phone call, or in the wake of watching a compelling film. "Look, I can feel French when I eat with French people at lunch," one programmer told me. "I can even contribute to the humour and I feel completely included … But then after lunch, I go back to my office [which I share with a German colleague] and we speak German and that moment is over [*der Moment ist vorbei*]."

At ARTE people described feeling French, German, or something else, as a form of identity/*identité/Identität*, and "identity" for most people at ARTE, before gender or class, most readily invoked national belonging. It was also, however, a concept that some people readily dismissed or were sometimes careful, they told me, *not* to use. "I don't like the word 'identity,'" Cécile, a long-time programmer in the documentary-magazines department, told me during a conversation about differences between French and German people at ARTE:

The key word, the key word in this whole thing, it's *pragmatism* [*le pragmatisme*] but in the noble sense of the term, I'm not speaking of realism – this false realism in the name of which we lose spirit … You have to think about things in *practical* and not *theoretical* terms … Pragmatism is the many exchanges you have with your colleagues. Personally, I must say that I don't *live* the so-called French-German antagonism that people sometimes talk about. I have *exchanges* with colleagues who are human beings with their cultures and their sensibilities and in which I sense their approach, which comes from their education, just as I have mine, but which doesn't impede anything. I don't *live* it [*Je ne vis pas ça*].

Cécile recounted an incident in which she was travelling to Berlin for the filming of a program and forgot her passport:

I was so used to living … the excha – I wasn't even living any more in my head, the fact that, I'm not denying it, that countries exist with their national logics, but in a *common practice* [*dans une pratique commune*] there are moments when one just doesn't think about it.

If there is a place where the meaning of identity in its static quality loses its pertinence, it is exactly in a workplace like this one. The word "identity," if we can mean that it is "identity" in *movement* [*l'identité en mouvement*], then fine. But otherwise if we mean something static, that's not what I live, but I want to say that, this is a path that we began to clear before ... The first people who were recruited to ARTE, in the beginning, were French and German people who had lived in the country of the other, but who had lived in the other country *deeply* [*en profondeur*]. I had the experience of being a cultural attaché, during which I started to live and understand how Germans understood the French ...

For example, very amusing ... my German colleagues used to sometimes say to me when we'd have some kind of difficulty, "*Also, was denkt die 'Grand Nation'?*" [So, what does the 'Great Nation' think?] In France, I had *never* heard this expression, "*la grande nation.*" The expression just isn't used in France ... whereas in Germany it's become common ... and it expresses how Germany understands the way that France expresses a certain arrogance ... And I began to understand – I began to understand that French people would think of Berlin as "the capital," but that Germans didn't think of it that way, that they had a federal system and that cities didn't work that way, in Germany. And so it's in Germany, actually, that I began to distance myself from the notion of "an identity" [*une identité*].

And so that's what characterizes many of us at ARTE – this *relativization* [*rélativisation*] – of what we call national identity. I can't speak for my colleagues ... but that's how I've lived it.

Though ARTE staff are producers of trans/national media, they are also, as a part of this work, consumers of this trans/national media, and as either or both there is an interesting comparison to be made to viewers of trans/national and trans-border media in other contexts. I have in mind here an argument that Kevin Robins and Asu Aksoy made in the volume *Transnational Television*, in which they write of Turkish-speaking audiences in Germany:

> Turkish-speaking migrants cannot so easily relate to a singular and consensual knowledge space. The trains of thought that they ride travel across frontiers, and pass through different cultural and value spaces ... And, in so far as they are making comparisons they are, necessarily almost, aware of the constructedness, arbitrariness, and provisionality of those systems. They are more aware of the rhetorics, the ideologies and the biases that characterize different media systems. These transnational viewers do not

relate to knowledge, then, as they once might have ... (quoted in Chalaby 2005, 32; cf. Chalaby 2009)

While I disagree with Robins and Aksoy's assessment that transnational viewers and producers are "necessarily almost" aware of the constructedness of national communities – I argue in the first half of the chapter that national cultures are very often understood to be explanatory at ARTE – I would agree that among certain transnational viewers and producers there is a kind of "relativization" that Cécile evokes – what Robins and Aksoy describe as an "ironic stance to culture" (quoted in Chalaby 2005, 32). This relativization is perhaps understudied by anthropologists and others, but I would argue that in certain contexts such identity processes mark one important line of flight from taken-for-granted solidities and realities of national community.

2: ARTE / art

ARTE programmers' and staff's sense that they are television and media professionals working to advance a particular kind of vision of the world – an identification with their shared work and common purpose – provides an important glue that binds together ARTE staff across departments, perceived national identity, and even professional hierarchy. One of the most frequent ways in which this glue was regularly (re)applied was through talk about programs themselves. In the ARTE elevator I might overhear members of the documentary-magazine and performance departments chitchatting: "Did you see the film last night about Louise Bourgeois?" "Yes. Beautiful." Before a screening of an ARTE-co-produced documentary about New Orleans, I hear a programmer and a member of the translation department talking about how much they're enjoying the "Summer of the Seventies" programming. Covering the doors and walls of staff offices are postcards and posters from various ARTE productions that they are proud of, only some of which they have may have personally worked on. In ARTE's canteen hang several oversized film posters from the channel's most famous and successful projects: *Das Leben der Anderen / La Vie des Autres* (2006); *Lady Chatterley* (2006); *Sophie Scholl – Die letzten Tage / Les Derniers Jours* (2005); and *Gegen die Wand / Head-On* (2004), to name a few.

All ARTE staff regularly receive email invites to in-house screenings of soon-to-be-released ARTE films and programs (projected in one of several screening rooms, each one named after a famous European director). I found that these were generally well-attended not only by the producing department but also by a wide-range of ARTE staff, including personnel from the president's office and ARTE's news department, interns, and even tech staff and security personnel. For one especially prominent ARTE production – Ari Folman's *Waltz with Bashir* (2008), for example, a compelling animated documentary about an Israeli soldier's traumatic experience during the 1982 Lebanon war[11] – the screening room was completely filled with staff who came from throughout the building to the point that many had to sit on the floor and stairs. In the days and weeks that followed (as the film was released and began to collect critical acclaim), I regularly heard buzz and discussion about the film among staff who worked together and also among staff who barely knew one another.

Partly as a result, one finds at ARTE a kind of aesthetic sensibility, or aesthetic identification, which seemed to often provide ARTE staff with their sense of collective purpose and dynamic sense of sameness (although, to some extent, this was contingent on the success of ARTE's work). One administrative assistant I spoke with explained,

> ARTE is not like other channels. Sometimes I watch ARTE and I am proud that I work for a channel that produces these programs – really high quality programs. Last night I saw *Full Metal Jacket* [Stanley Kubrick, 1987], which I hadn't seen before and what a beautiful film, it really surprised me [*mais ça m'a étonné!*]...Where else can you see films like that on television? ... We provide an important service [*On rend un service important*] by putting films like that on television.

Conversations about "quality" television, creativity, the importance of making "good" television, the relevance of art for television – these formed professional commitments that contributed to people's sense-making of who they were and what they did in the world. As Dorinne Kondo (1990) wrote in her ethnography of Japanese artisans, "One must ... carefully attend to the meaningful, experiential aspects of work and to how those meanings are implicated in a larger system of power relations" (230). In recognizing that "the aesthetics of work cannot be separated from its politics," Kondo encourages attention to the ways in which work – and especially work that is understood to be productive or creative – enables (in a parallel process) particular kinds of collective self-narrative and self-construction.

People at ARTE surely had specialized professional roles to play in furthering the purpose of producing "good" television – for some it was editing, for others it was journalism, bureaucratic management of the production process, welcoming visitors at the front security desk, or finding just the right way to translate a word. Yet there was also a more generalized commitment to treating television and film as an art form, rooted in a commitment to aesthetics and the vitalness of creativity; a commitment to the belief that knowledge about the world sustains publics and democracies, and the notion, fundamentally, that they were together working to make the human experience less mundane. As these ideologies were voiced, circulated, and otherwise rendered apparent, they provided a cohesive, though hardly concise or stable, sense of belonging and purpose. Unlike the facile labels "French" and "German," these shifting assemblages of aesthetic values and beliefs about cultural production could not be gathered together into an ethnonym or tucked into a single word, and rarely did I hear this "sense" (idiom? vector?) of collective purpose acknowledged in any way that seemed congruous or contiguous with "an identity."

Staff cultivated these aesthetic sensibilities and commitments in small, everyday ways and personalized engagements. In nearly every ARTE office hung posters of ARTE films and programs that staff had helped to produce or had not helped to produce, as well as posters and photographs of what was often talked about as "beautiful things" (*schöne Dinge/belles choses*). Often these had very little to do with their particular role at ARTE: a print of a Gauguin painting, a *West Side Story* poster, a postcard-size *Water Lilies* reproduction, a black-and-white photograph of a worn-down pair of leathery boots, a tiny *Winged Victory of Samothrace*.

What's more, every six months or so, ARTE's headquarters in Strasbourg would literally be transformed into a gallery, as European artists were invited to create exhibitions of their work in the building's central atrium and along its hallways. Weeks might pass as artists assembled installations or hung their art, this always subject to much commentary on the part of staff. When completed, ARTE staff and friends of ARTE would be invited to a *vernissage*, a gallery opening that often included hors d'oeuvres and cocktails served by white-gloved wait staff. During the weeks that followed, installations were often participatory, asking staff to directly engage with the art in one way or another, either through talks given by the artist(s) or through activities designed to channel and display ARTE staff's creativity.

All this seemed to activate the staff's sense of aesthetic meaning and purpose by overlaying the channel's daily work with other kinds of engagements with art and beauty. Around ideas and ideals of quality media – which were actively connected to good production values,

A

Figure 3.5 [A and B] Above, seen from above, an art installation is assembled in ARTE's central atrium; below (next page), Jérôme Clément, vice-president of ARTE, offers a toast on the day of the exhibit's "opening" as staff, invitees, and members of the public gather around the completed piece. (Photos by author)

Figure 3.5 [A and B] (Continued)

groundbreaking film, and which further extended to good *art* – staff forged personal ties and loyalties to the channel's mission, their colleagues, and a sense of self that transcended (or perhaps altogether stood apart from) national distinctions and categories. Many at ARTE believed good art, like a good television series, to be not just French or German, but in some broader way, part of their European heritage, and beyond Europe, trans-human and universal.[12]

I came to be very aware of the many ways that "art," the Arts, and micro-material references to the formally aesthetic came to permeate the physical environment of ARTE – everywhere one looked there seemed to be claims to the importance or authority of art, seamlessly interpolated into evidence of ARTE's own audiovisual and cinematic production. Rituals like those of the art installation, at which ARTE staff gathered round to witness and demonstrate respect for the creation of art, seemed to be meant to parallel, and unify, their own creative practices. In this way, perhaps we might argue that Aristotelian and Kantian beliefs and ideals about the trans-border universality of beauty have come to provide an important idiom through which another line of flight transects this trans/national place.

3: movement

A number of ARTE staff travel to Cannes for the MIP (Marché international des contenus audiovisuels et numériques / International Market for Audiovisual and Digital Content), and to various television production conferences (often genre-specific) that are held in New York, London, and Madrid. In my months working at ARTE – even as a lowly intern – I participated in an ARTE-sponsored camping-canoeing trip, a play in the Lorraine, drove into Germany twice, and was invited to an ARTE-sponsored event in Brussels. During this time, I noted that members of the departments in which I was working travelled to various parts of France, to Germany (Mainz, Berlin, Hamburg), to New York, Chicago, Brussels, London, Cannes, Stockholm, Beijing, Seoul, and Geneva for ARTE-related work.

Many staff at ARTE consider themselves to be highly mobile travellers as a result of these and other kinds of border crossings. In Strasbourg, this partly has to do with the proximity of the border, but travelling to places across Europe and beyond seems to be one of the most popular leisure time pursuits of ARTE staff, who enjoy as much as six weeks of paid vacation time a year. ARTE's headquarters has an office that organizes discounted rates for group trips to various cities around Europe, and ARTE's intranet features dozens of listings for intrastaff vacation rentals and exchanges.

One of the administrative assistants with whom I had been sharing an office left for two-week vacation to Liguria, in northern Italy. Upon her return, she was effusive with details about the food, the wine, the architecture, the weather, the people she had found to be so relaxed and kind. As various staff would step into the office to welcome her back, she would launch into long descriptions of the wine – "delicious ... and so cheap, you wouldn't believe" – and the pasta – "honestly, some of the best food of my life." Stoppers-by would often trade information about where they had been in Italy or where they had most recently travelled; one staff member talked about her time in Spain, another about his visit to Tunisia. Even as her phone began to ring with projects and deadlines that had been awaiting her return, I would hear conversations ensue about Italy, travel, deals to be had, places to go, and food to be tried. Next to the intrigues and gossip of everyday politics at ARTE, talk of trips and travel were the normal stuff of chitchat and captured much of what ARTE staff understood themselves to have in common.

Travel, movement, and mobility are both real and meta/mediated at ARTE: Real because life and work in today's Europe, especially in media industries, have come to enable and compel trans-border movement. But meta/mediated, too, because the series, films, and webpages that staff produce, crafted among and between borders, itself reflects and encourages narratives about travel and transportation. The documentary-magazine department at ARTE alone has introduced a half-dozen pre-primetime programs that focus on recreational travel: *Les Nouveaux Paradis / Die neuen Paradiese* (The New Paradises), *Carnets de Voyages / Reiseskizzen aus...* (Travel Journal), *Tout le Monde à la Plage / Sommer, Sonne, Strand!* (Everyone to the Beach / Summer, Sun, Beach!), and *Prochaine Arrêt / Nächster Halt* (Next Stop) are just four recent examples of programming that deal directly with vacation travel. A broader array of documentary-magazine programs engage with mobility in other ways – one program taking us to taste the cuisine of various parts of Europe (*Cuisine des Terroirs / Zu Tisch* [Cuisine of the Land / At Table]), others bringing us to various parts of the world to examine local geographies and communities (*360° GEO, Horizons Lointains / LeseHorizonte* [Far Horizons]). In fact, an informal survey of ARTE's schedule reveals that as many as one in five programs broadcast by ARTE explicitly engages travel and/or transportation as a means of learning about other places and other people(s). Without parsing distinctions among these programs, it is worth noting in a general way that travel and mobility – from France and Germany to other parts of Europe, and from Europe to other destinations in the world – is one of the hallmarks of ARTE's programming. Because travel is a feature of life and talk at ARTE as much as it is of its production schedules and itineraries, there is clearly a permeability between real travel among ARTE staff – to broker audiovisual exchanges in Stockholm, to cross into Germany to purchase groceries, or to fill blocked-out weeks of vacation time in Italy – and the audiovisualized border crossings that form a centerpiece of ARTE's programming.

One woman at ARTE's *ZOOM Europa* program volunteered to me, after I described my project, that her sense of identity (*identité*) is rooted in her travel among cities and her love for urban life. She explained,

> I feel at home in most European cities – there is something familiar about them, whether I'm in London or in Spain or Moscow. There is a certain spatial organization that feels European to me, feels somehow comfortable. But in fact, I love most cities – I think I would define my identity as "urban" before I would say "European" – there is something about the feel, the energy, of cities that attracts me. I loved Beijing when I was there.

She did mention, however, that cities in the United States puzzled her:

> I was in Atlanta and a co-worker and I left the hotel to get some coffee and – can you imagine? – we wandered around for twenty minutes and ended up back at the hotel! Nowhere to sit and have a coffee! That was really strange to me, and made me feel very European.

Indeed, narratives about being and belonging at ARTE were as likely to refer to where one has been or where one would be going as they were about where one happened to currently reside. Cities were often mentioned as the kind of place where ARTE folk felt "at home" in the world, but so too were the very liminality and temporariness of travel and mobility themselves. Indeed, most staff at ARTE had moved to Strasbourg to work there from places in Alsace, France, and Germany, that made Strasbourg itself a sort of short-term, liminal place of residence. People at ARTE spoke of having moved to Strasbourg for ARTE and of knowing that they would one day be likely to move someplace else. One staff member in the documentary unit who had spent seventeen years at ARTE told me she had never thought of Strasbourg as home: "My life is here, but I do not *feel* like I am from here, and I am not attached to a place, really. I have moved a lot in my life." A staff member who had grown up near Strasbourg explained, "I am from Alsace, but I've lived in the south of France for ten years and who knows where I'll end up working next." Staff, especially those in

ARTE's higher echelons of administration, had known a life elsewhere before ARTE and would likely know a life elsewhere after their stint in Strasbourg – should they want to continue in television or film – in some other city in which the audiovisual industries were more concentrated.

One of ARTE's most popular programs, *Karambolage*, has sometimes featured a short one- or two-minute segment entitled "Ce qui me manque / Was mir fehlt [What I miss]." I first encountered the segment at the Maison de l'Europe (Europe House, the European Union's public relations office) in Paris during the city's Nuit Blanche all-night art festival, where a number of clips of the segment were being projected – in a kind of mosaic – onto a giant screen set up in the building's seventeenth-century courtyard. The segment features individuals who are living in a country of Europe that is not their country of origin; each person tells us about a food or object that he/she misses from his/her native country. A German woman explains that she cannot find a certain kind of buttermilk in France; a Portuguese woman living in Germany explains that she misses Portuguese lace; a German woman living in Rome stocks up on *Knödel* (potato dumplings) when she visits home.

The segment is, on the one hand, a longing for a national "home" and its familiar trappings – the people featured in the segment are, in a basic sense, homesick. But the segment is also a sort of desublimation of the seemingly overwhelming discomfort and foreignness of life abroad into the comfort that familiar objects can offer; the segments are not morose, but light-hearted, and the crowds of spectators that wandered in and out of the Paris courtyard would often smile and laugh at the individuals' selection of a particular kitchen tool or condiment.

Contradictorily (and thoroughly trans/nationally), "Ce qui me manque / Was mir fehlt" in some ways reproduces the container logic of the nation-state to which each person solitarily belongs (and which literally "holds" objects like lace, pickles, and dumplings) – and much of the critique I offer of *Karambolage* in chapter 2 also applies here; but the segments also perform a kind of ontology of liminality and displacement, displaying the everyday materiality of Europeans who live in places where they were not born, in unfamiliar contexts, for periods of time that may be indeterminate. It suggests that coping, and living in these other places, is both a matter of objects and an objective matter: We can identify what makes us long for another place, and in acquiring and, to some degree, fetishising tiny but symbolic material pieces of our (national) life elsewhere, we are ultimately able to adjust, displace, or re-place home.

Mobility, travel, and passage are themselves, then, sources of identification, social currency, and a means of self-understanding both at ARTE

Figure 3.6 People gather at the Maison de l'Europe to watch a video installation of "Ce qui me manque / Was mir fehlt." (Photo by author)

and in the programs which ARTE staff deem relevant for its French-German and European viewers. "Ce qui me manque / Was mir fehlt" provides a visual metaphor for the ways in which many ARTE staff understand who they are in ongoing relationship to movement, and to the multiplicity or contingency, of home(s). The assembly and dissemination of audiovisual texts, which frequently evoke journey and voyage, reflect and crystallize staff's own narratives about, and identifications with, them/selves in movement.

below and beyond imagined community

People at ARTE understand who they and others are in the world partly through trafficking in what are understood to be stable scripts and qualities subsumed into the categories and labels of national identity. French, German, and sometimes even European, ways of being and acting can be deployed so as to seem to comprise highly stable and predictable sets of traits and behaviours – at least at ARTE – and so are summoned forth as a means of explaining and stabilizing, in part, why people do what they do and act the way they act.

But if these labels work to simplify, or to make simpler-seeming, who people "are" at ARTE – freezing them into correlations and dichotomies – they do not tell the whole story. It is clear that ARTE staff, administrators and assistants alike, also draw on a number of other ways of thinking about the meaning of who they are and what they do at ARTE that eschew the boundedness and fixedness of national identity or identities, drawing upon a number of transcendent commitments and affective engagements predicated upon relativization, borderings, in-betweenness, humanistic creativity, and movement (cf. Friedman 2002).

How does an Andersonian notion of imagined community square with this evocation of belonging? There are surely aspects of sociality at ARTE that correspond to the main line of Anderson's argument. For one, national languages, spoken and written, do in some ways matter and function to distinguish people at ARTE (and the media they produce). And when Anderson (1991) writes that the idea of national community "[roots] human lives firmly in the very nature of things, giving certain meaning to the everyday fatalities of existence" (36), he gestures at the raw importance of meaning-making that nationalism encourages and enables, which I argue is partly the basis of pervasive national stereotyping at ARTE.

Yet there is also much happening at ARTE that I would argue lies above and below Anderson's notion of imagined community. The *banality* of national categorizations and distinctions at ARTE (Billig 1995) – shoes, wine drinking, yogurt – suggests that national community is often less ideological and abstract – less systematically or coherently "imagined" – than Anderson's thesis suggests, not least because, as I have argued, what it "means" to be French or German at ARTE is to a large degree variable, contingent, and context-specific. While some narratives of French-ness were perhaps derived from broadly shared linguistic and mediational communities (and variously adapted and redeployed at ARTE), others seemed *sui generis* and performative, taking shape only in the intimacy of face-to-face interaction. Ideas about national difference and behaviour are produced, I would argue, at a number of levels, but many (which may nonetheless appear to be well-known or widespread) come to be made meaningful, and to circulate, in local, interpersonal (and non-textual) interactions during which French-ness and German-ness are negotiated and reproduced (cf. Wogan 2001).

In a sense, we might say that this interaction occurs "below" Anderon's "imagined community."

In other ways, social life at ARTE lends itself to the conclusion that Anderson's conception of community is being partly transcended or displaced (and likely has always partly been so) by practices and modalities of belonging that are less self-conscious, less discursive, less recognized, and less recognizable. In their collective orientations to relativizations of identity, to the humanistic power of art, and to travel and movement, we glimpse kinds of belonging that are not predicated on closure or stability, and which therefore, I might suggest, avail themselves less to discursivity, discussion, objectification, and transaction. These orientations, sensorial entwinements, or lines of flight exist alongside or beyond the national imagination, but are less self-consciously acknowledged or narrated.

I have argued that we should understand belonging and lived commitments at ARTE as composed of both structure and people's active circumvention of structure, not in a both/and formulation, but as people variously shuffle between modes and models of belonging that are object-like and coherent, and non-object-like and in-coherent. The organization of social life at this trans/national institution necessarily teeters between notions of nationally bounded attributions of identity, and more dynamically expressed, and fluid, understandings of belonging. The Andersonian community does not quite capture the interplay of form and performance, nor the movement between objectifiable and non-objectifiable (but nevertheless potent) ways that staff at ARTE think about where they are and who they are in the world.

4

re-presenting history on and at ARTE

Through a variety of means and media, European integration and globalization have given rise to the production of new kinds of European histories. The European Union, as part of its 2007 "Citizenship" directive and budget, foregrounded "active European remembrance" as one of the program's four target missions and allocated funding to bring Europe "closer to its citizens" through a series of trans-European "memory aids" and "remembrance projects."[1] The Council of Europe, for its part, has funded and published a series of studies of national history textbooks and curricula (e.g., Pingel 2000; Ecker 2004), seeking to promote a comparative and trans-regional European historical perspective in schools (cf. Schissler and Soysal 2005; Nóvoa and Lawn 2002). Outside of European institutional frameworks, dozens of books have appeared over the past two decades proposing to delineate trans-continental histories of the meaning(s) of "Europe," many of which begin their bi-millennial narratives with chapters about Greek antiquity and early democracy (e.g., Pagden 2002, 3–4; Delanty 1995, 16–23; Den Boer et al. 1995; cf. Herzfeld 1987, 49–76).[2] Finally, a variety of European websites have emerged to offer a huge number of online textual and audiovisual resources for the teaching of the "history of Europe" and European integration: the non-governmental Centre Virtuel de la Connaissance sur l'Europe (Virtual Center for Knowledge of Europe) – just one example – offers over 9,000 historical multimedia documents, deeming itself "a genuine guardian of Europe's heritage."[3] These and other projects seek to re-present European history as a trans-continental and trans-border corpus of events and (hyper-)texts in which relationships between and among various collectivities –nation, Eastern Europe, Western Europe, Europe, and the world – are coming to be rearticulated and re-signified (cf. Rousso in Jarausch and Lindenberger 2007, 23–5).

Especially in the European context, the self-conscious formulation and writing of "History" and histories – what Henry Rousso refers to as the "regime of historicity" (in Jarausch and Lindenberger 2007, 31) – has been the privileged discursive mode through which national collective belonging has come to be established and mediated (cf. Herzfeld 2004, 3). If the nation-state has enjoyed a near-monopoly on the production of modern history and to the imagining and organizing of pasts (Berger and Lorenz 2008; Balibar in Suny and Eley 1996, 142; Hobsbawm 1992, esp. 92–100; cf. Calhoun 1997, 79), this chapter works towards better understanding why this largely remains the case, while identifying how French-German ARTE staff construe and cultivate parallel or alternative re-presentations of history.

This chapter outlines some of the ways in which ARTE producers and programmers engage with history. It does not posit a "Europeanization" of history in any simple way, except perhaps to understand this process as one that is deeply contradictory. ARTE producers employ a number of strategies and narratives in crafting historical programs that are meant to circulate beyond national borders. I begin by outlining how "history" was understood by ARTE producers and staff, and then move to consider a film that illustrates and exemplifies one kind of re-crafting of history at ARTE. With two further programming examples, I then seek to identify how national politics and State interests continue to intersect with, and to structure, "European" histories. A final section about the production of a particularly problematic documentary provokes us to consider why some historical scripts may avail themselves to revision more than others.

history on / at ARTE

At ARTE, history must be re-presented through the audiovisual means that lie at the channel's disposal. "History" at ARTE is talked about, foremost, as a category of programming and of documentary film that are among the channel's most frequently broadcast and among its most watched; historical documentary consistently garners ARTE's largest audiences and comprises as much as 30 per cent of the channel's total programming. During an average week, there may be more than twenty hours of historical films and documentaries on ARTE, and during my fieldwork the channel devoted two weekly theme (THEMA) nights to history. A majority of this programming, in turn, focuses on twentieth-century history and world wars – as much as 60 or 70 per cent of ARTE's overall historical programming.[4]

History "on" ARTE, however, can better be understood through history "at" ARTE – the ways in which producers understand what history is, what it is for, and how it should be (re)presented through the media of film and television. Staff at ARTE consult and negotiate their own historical knowledge and sensibilities as they work to obtain and produce history programming that must make sense across European borders; they often rely on their own sense of what they do or do not know about French, German, and European history as they evaluate what films might be of interest, and how these films' narratives might articulate with what an "average" German or French viewer might know about German, French, or Spanish history. It is through a constant tacking back-and-forth between what ARTE staff know or feel about history, and what they believe *audiences* should know or feel, that ARTE staff cobble together the channel's trans/national historical programming and perspective.

In some contrast to those who work for ARTE at its French and German offices, those at ARTE's Strasbourg headquarters see themselves as cultural brokers who must find historical-narrative middle grounds. A viewer's familiarity with the personages, dates, tropes, and symbols that are disseminated through national history books and schooling, and upon which the historical documentary genre substantially depends for its meaning and resonance, cannot be taken for granted at ARTE. Much of the work of the documentary department staff in Strasbourg consists of sifting through the narrative "poetics" of documentaries (Dornfeld 1998, 89–139) – the semiotic components and mechanics of documentary film – with something like national double vision: Do we need to explain here in voiceover what the *Bundesrat* is for French audiences? How can we translate *laïcité* here so that Germans won't be lost? Would a Finnish channel be interested in this story about the *Kindertransport*?

While reviewing a documentary about postwar Berlin, for example, departmental programmers discussed how much they needed to explain about Willy Brandt. The German-produced film, which ARTE had purchased, featured footage of the politician speaking at the Bund-estag (Germany's national parliament), but merely provided a subtitle with his name. ARTE's French-language version of the film would have to squeeze in an extra title or voiceover, agreed the department's pro-grammers, but how much? "I think we can leave it at German chancel-lor, and then the years [that he was in office] ..." "Yes but later [the film] refers to his *Ostpolitik* and I wonder if we need to introduce that here, or say something more about him, that he won the Nobel, or some-thing ..." Because the film had originally been produced in Germany for German audiences, it was taken for granted that audiences would know Brandt and have some sense of his role in improving relations with East Germany; this was reflected in the film's narrative structure, which then moved to Erich Honecker (leader of East Germany, 1971–89) welcoming Helmut Schmidt at the airport in East Berlin without indi-cating that Schmidt was Brandt's successor. "We'll need to put in a title to explain that," one of the programmers observed. "Otherwise French people will be lost [*sinon les français seront perdus*]."

The banal bureaucratic setting of such negotiations – an ARTE producer or two screening a film on a computer monitor and jotting notes – belies the many historical filterings and interventions that shape ARTE's production of trans/national historical documentaries. Though two staff may both be French, they are engaged in thinking about French historical sensibilities in a self-conscious, relativizing way; indeed, in the documentary department at ARTE's headquarters, the nationality of the editing programmer is understood to matter less than what he/she knows about a particular topic. I was often surprised by the knowledge a French programmer might express about what she thought German audiences knew about Versailles, or by a German pro-grammer's reflection about what French people knew about Soviet his-tory. When "general knowledge" about a historical referent could not be readily approximated by a programmer, a call would be made to a few colleagues down the hall to ask them, for example, if they thought Germans would recognize François Mitterand as France's president, or if he would need an identifying subtitle. In most cases, the solution was to include as much clarifying information as possible since ARTE staff were also aware that the channel's programming often circulated beyond France-Germany. But staff also wanted films to be as seamless as possible – and the more titles, or sped-up addendum voiceovers, the less easy, or pleasant, a film would be to watch. Depending on how "French" or "German" a documentary was, staff believed, the more dif-ficult the task would be of rendering balanced language versions in which the voiceover and textual identifications were roughly equal. One programmer told me that one particularly difficult documentary was about Hannah Arendt: "You can't imagine the difficulty we had – German words and concepts that just don't exist in French, all the postwar context and the fact that many educated Germans already know a good deal about Arendt, whereas the French ..." She smiled.

"History work" at ARTE is thus marked by highly self-conscious attention to differential historical knowledge. Staff negotiate differences in not only *what* histories are known – the historical figures, narratives, or dates which tend to have been publically inculcated – but also *how* history is understood: "history" as an idiom and category of knowledge is believed to hold different resonances or connotations for French and German viewers, and ARTE staff understand that certain historical periods especially require certain "nation-appropriate" tonalities and, sometimes, restraint. A veteran programmer explained, for example, that she works to mitigate what she sometimes perceives to be a French overemphasis, in certain documentaries, on the "state" and a vocabulary of "the state": "For the Germans, authority and the state ... there's a certain trauma [*un traumatisme*] for the Germans [*chez les allemands*], which doesn't exist for the French. So you sometimes avoid translating *l'état* as *der Staat* – you may use 'government' – *die Regierung* – or some other way of avoiding '*der Staat*.'"

At every turn, from the evaluation of proposals for documentary films, to the tweaking of a film's titles so that an image of the Académie française might be properly introduced to German audiences who may not recognize its building's cupola, staff attempt to objectify "History" and to consciously consider how much people know about it and how they are likely to respond to it. "History" thus comes to be doubly reified, as a body of knowledge that can be assessed and measured – the history that people may or may not have – and as an object to be shaped and manipulated through the concrete visual editings, and titlings that allow for this history to be pushed audiovisually across boundaries of language, schooling, and experience.

Constantly engaged in decisions about where to draw editorial lines between what they consider to be historically obvious and not-so obvious, ARTE documentary staff are essentially in the business of intuiting national historical knowledge sets. But encompassed by this exercise is the related task of deciding what audiences *should* know – providing a title for a French president or German playwright may not always be altogether necessary to understanding the larger narrative of a documentary, but staff at ARTE sometimes feel a title is editorially justified

when they believe audiences *should* be familiar with a particular historical character, location, or date.

One programmer in the magazine (short documentary) department
told me that she regularly "includes too much information" because
she believes "documentaries are to *broaden* what we know about history, to allow the French person to learn about German history, not to
just interpret it the way one would from a French perspective – that's
what's *different* about ARTE … what makes us different from France 5
or other national channels."

In deciding what films to program in the first place, and when to
include further explanations within films, programmers at ARTE
must reckon both with what historical knowledge may already exist
for German and French audiences, and how that knowledge should
be broadened or amended – that is, what should be added to the standard assemblages of French and German historical knowledge that programmers prefigure and imagine. Audiences tend to be presented with
historical documentary on ARTE that expect them to walk away knowing about as much about its relevant history – French or German – as
audiences would in the original country of the film's production.[5] In
other words, ARTE staff aim to assemble an amalgamation of historical
knowledge, through a painstaking editing process in which they pool
what they know, and what they think others know, in order to produce
as roughly equal French and German versions of a given documentary
as possible.[6] And yet, for some translation or editing decisions, there is
no clear way to avoid choosing a French or German perspective: "The
Germans didn't experience the end of the Second World War as *une
débarquement* [a military landing] but as *une invasion* [an invasion]," one
programmer told me, explaining the difficulties of producing programming about the fiftieth anniversary of D-Day. "So you have to think,
what word do I use for the film's German-language version? What
word are Germans *used* to hearing? What perspective do I take? Why?"

Because history is understood, by ARTE documentary staff, to be a
body of knowledge (or, rather, multiple bodies of knowledge) – which
are "out there," finite, and assessable – to which one can add or from
which one can, in a way, subtract (by omitting or revising information) – there emerges a certain degree of permeability between history
"at" ARTE and "on" ARTE. The channel's history programmers often
privilege historical documentaries which propose self-conscious and
reflexive approaches to history and historiography – programming, in
other words, which reflects their own history-production work. One
programmer in ARTE's documentary unit told me that "historically

critical films" (*les films historiques, mais aussi critiques*) are the best sort of documentary because "they make people think about ... what we take for granted ... [and] what we learn in school." At programming meetings, films were sometimes rejected on the basis of their being "too conventional," and not addressing fully enough the "question" or "problem" of history. ARTE's raison d'être – its mediating mission – is often broadly understood to imply not so much "education" as provocation: "*Laissez-vous déranger par* ARTE [Let yourself be unsettled / bothered by ARTE]," read one of the channel's early advertising slogans, which in France certainly alluded to, among other things, the channel's partly German perspective with which it would be confronting viewers in France.

Producers at ARTE are not interested in merely shuttling between histories, then, but also in talking *about* history (as History / historiography) and in cultivating through their work perspectives and approaches that convey histories themselves as (nationally) constructed epistemological frames. One of the clearest examples of ARTE's self-conscious, reflexive engagements with history as an object and a problem is captured in a documentary that the channel broadcasted in 2008, which I came across during my time at ARTE's headquarters. The way this documentary works to construct and exemplify particular kinds of historical subjectivities merits discussion at length because it illuminates some of the ARTE's key narrative strategies in relativizing, and editing, European "History" and, indeed, memory.

"Napoleon isn't really my thing"

The fifty-two-minute documentary *Chacun Son Histoire? / Zwei Nationen, eine Geschichte?* (2008), produced by ARTE in partnership with Alsace's regional France5 channel, asks if today it is possible to teach French and German high school students a shared history. The documentary follows a project launched in May 2004, in response to an initiative brought by the French-German Youth Parliament in 2003, to introduce jointly edited history textbooks to French and German high schools (Geiss, Henri, and Le Quintrec 2006). The central narrative of the film relates the story of a cross-national exchange program in which a French and a German girl each live with the other's family while attending high school. In their history courses, they use the new, shared textbook; meanwhile, the film discusses the editing and production of the

Figure 4.1 The joint European history textbook *Histoire / Geschichte: L'Europe et le monde depuis 1945 / Europa und die Welt seit 1945* (History: Europe and the World since 1945) (2006). (Photo by author)

textbook, bringing us into the editors' committee meetings, and exploring some of the national differences in the ways in which nineteenth- and twentieth-century history have been taught in French and German classrooms.

The film might be understood as an analogy for, or summary of, the historical project of ARTE, and in particular, the sensibilities of its documentary department, on several levels. For one, the film's title: the French translates as "To Each Its (or His) Own History?" and the German as "Two Nations, One History?" These different titles point to one of the central dilemmas facing ARTE staff: whether they are to bridge national histories through dialectical comparison or to construct anew some kind of trans-border and trans-European history through consolidation and standardization of these histories. The film self-consciously considers historical representation. And, as a film, it also offers a kind of meta-critique of textual histories from which it already stands apart as an example of a different medium, and means, for the re-representation of history. Indeed, during my fieldwork in Strasbourg, several ARTE staff conveyed to me that they believe that audiovisual-historical media can much better convey the lived experiences, and emotional resonance, of history better than texts or textbooks.[7] This audiovisual advantage was sometimes conveyed in terms of the "voices" (*voix / Stimmen*) that can (literally) be heard in historical documentary – those of former KGB members, political leaders, Holocaust survivors.

Much of the *Chacun Son Histoire? / Zwei Nationen, eine Geschichte?* consists of brief vignettes of high school students – inserted graphically into a background consisting of blown-up pages of the joint history textbook – who talk about what they know, and think about, various personages and periods of their respective national histories. The students' lack of knowledge is sometimes humorous, but the humour belies the film's revelation that German students often know more about French history than French students, and French students more about German history than the featured German students.

What's more, the students don't seem particularly attached to, or interested in, their own nation's histories. They seem to reject well-worn national narratives and subjectivities: a French girl states that Napoleon "isn't really her thing," explaining that Napoleon's rule wasn't "*très agréable pour les gens de l'époque*" (wasn't very nice for people at the time). A vignette of a German boy immediately follows in which he explains, *contra la patria*, that "*s'war ... relativ gut was [Napoleon] gemacht hat*" (it was ... pretty good what [Napoleon] did).

Figure 4.2 Screen capture from the documentary *Chacun Son Histoire?* / *Zwei Nationen, eine Geschichte?* The interviewed girl is inserted graphically into a blown-up page from the history textbook. She says, in French (subtitled here in the German version), "*Napoléon, c'est pas vraiment mon truc*" (Napoleon isn't really my thing). (Screenshot taken by author)

Near the end of the film a young woman explains, and seemingly summarizes the film's thesis, that she's not "really interested in history … or at least in memorizing dates." She continues, "It's different, though … when you hear about people's *suffering*." Then she adds, "Dates are dates, but suffering is something else" (*Daten sind Daten, das Leiden ist etwas anderes*).

This "something else" indexes a broader historical orientation, cultivated by producers at ARTE, which aspires to challenge not only national but also textual ways of knowing. As Hayden White (1973), Marshall Sahlins (1985), and especially Benedict Anderson (1991) have made clear, the nation-form is a world view and ontology that owes its origins, especially in Western Europe, to the rise of *print* technology

Figure 4.3 The boy says in German that *"s'war ... relativ gut was [Napoleon] gemacht hat"* (it was pretty good what [Napoleon] did). (Screenshot taken by author)

and books (though see Wogan 2001), which enabled its dissemination and promulgation. Anderson (1991) singles out the novel and the newspaper as having provided "the technical means for 're-presenting' the kind of imagined community that is the nation ... The idea of a sociological organism moving calendrically through homogeneous, empty time" (24–6). Books and other media printed in vernacular languages reflected and constituted nation-readerships and established differentiated "we's" moving alongside one another through history (Bhabha 1990), whose national protagonists and plot lines would be later formalized and disseminated through national educational systems (cf. Gellner 2006, 38–57; Balibar 2004).[8]

The ARTE documentary self-consciously calls attention to the roots of national communities in print, and printed histories, and moves to

critique textual knowledge as a limiting and problematic way of knowing. At one point in the film (see this chapter's opening image), the camera pans over piles of textbooks that have been used, says a voiceover,
as "weapons" like any other weapons, in the many conflicts that have
pitted France against Germany since the nineteenth century (cf. Nolan
2005). ARTE's historical documentaries tend to privilege non-textual
media (of which they are reflexively already examples) and, partly as
a result, historical narratives featuring protagonists who are everyday
people and whose experiences and stories complicate what one programmer described as "faceless masses." The high school students and
the film instead emphasize an individualist and affective engagement
with history through a language of experience and, often, suffering.
ARTE programmers explained that these particular and affective depictions stand in contrast to official, national, and textual representations,
which in this documentary are made to seem distant and contrived –
somehow apathetic to real-life (and audiovisual) stories of human mis-
ery and resilience. Perhaps counterintuitively, this "historiographical
cosmopolitanism" does not, then, "re-scale" history to trans/national or
global ecumenes ("we the Europeans," "we humans"), but is oriented
instead to persons and small groups who are able to voice their own stories about what has been lived: the immediate, the specific, the atypical.[9]

Later in the documentary we meet an elderly couple who were caught
on opposite sides of the border when Alsace was re-annexed by France
in 1914. "I was German, and then I was French," says the woman, in
German-accented French. She had been enrolled in German schooling
until Alsace was re-attached to France in 1918. "We used to have to learn
to count in German ... my brother and I had to dress up like Tyroleans
for a play," she recounts. As a boy, her husband, who was not living in
Alsace, explains that he was taught in school to despise Germans. The
film tells us that the couple has, despite this schooling and its ideological inculcation, been married for over sixty years. As the woman talks to
us about her upbringing and the difficulties of a trans-border romance,
we can see the couple's wedding portrait in the background.

Chris Rumford (2007) and others have suggested that Europe will
require a "memory culture that spans borders" (45; cf. Leggewie 2010) if
it is to displace the nation-state's entrenched twin regimes of historicity
and identity. I would argue, rather, that producers and programmers
at ARTE are working, in what might be a kind of interim strategy, to
partially *dis*-integrate national and collective histories through post-
textual, and post-collective, narratives of personal and individual experience. Viewers might be encouraged, like the young German student

Figure 4.4 The girl says in German, *"Daten sind Daten, das Leiden ist etwas anderes"* (Dates are dates, suffering is something else). (Screenshot taken by author)

featured in the vignette, to partly adopt the perspective of an alternative collectivity or, like the elderly woman, to oppose collective accounts through reference to personal experience and memory. History on and at ARTE in this way may be congruent with what Daniel Levy and Natan Sznaider (2010) have described, in their work on human rights and Holocaust history, as a shift towards "memory history" *(Errinerungsgeschichte)*. Memory history, they argue, "is a particular mnemonic mode which moves away from a state-supported (and state-supporting) national history. The previous (attempted) monopoly by the state to shape collective pasts, has given way to a fragmentation of memories ... Modes of collective memory are being cosmopolitanized and exist on supra- and subnational levels" (160–1).

While cultural producers in Europe and other trans-border contexts may, through various kinds of history work, seek to encourage and actuate the fragmentation or cosmopolitanization of national collective

Figure 4.5 The elderly woman recounts having to learn to speak German and learn German history in Alsace. (Screenshot taken by author)

pasts, we must also pay close attention to the ways in which these "new" histories come to be assembled, and recycled, out of national and nationalist remnants. Attention to the continuities and parallels among national and "European" narratives and ideologies of history complicates an account of transnational historical revisionism that might otherwise too simplistically gesture towards the novelties of *sui generis* trans-border processes. In what follows, I draw out some of the ways in which nationalist and statist politics – French, German, and others – continue to inform and intersect with the production of "European" histories.

À Göttingen / In Göttingen

The 22nd of January 2008 marked the forty-fifth anniversary of the Élysée Treaty, signed by Charles de Gaulle and Konrad Adenauer in 1963. Though mostly a symbolic recognition of reconciliation between France and Germany, the treaty established the Franco-German Office

for Youth (Office franco-allemand pour la jeunesse / Deutsch-Franzö-
sisches Jugendwerk), the very same student group which would propose the successful joint French-German history book on the treaty's
fortieth anniversary, in 2003. The treaty marks one of France-Germany's
newest and indeed only joint commemorations, a date freshly added
to recent historiographies and timelines foregrounding French-German
and European *rapprochement*.

The fortieth anniversary of the treaty was celebrated by ARTE
with a week of special programming, a number of special features
on its website, and even an online quiz game.[10] But on the forty-fifth
anniversary, I couldn't locate even a mention of the treaty on ARTE's
website nor was there any mention of it during the evening's scheduling. Though Truffaut's *Jules et Jim* (1962) – perhaps one of the most
significant films ever made about the complexities of French-German
friendship – had been screened that afternoon, I settled in for what I
thought would be an otherwise unremarkable evening of watching
ARTE in my apartment.

Around 7 p.m., however, a second or two of grey-white screen suddenly interrupted the evening's programming, accompanied by the
familiar voice of ARTE's soft-spoken announcer: "There's a song that
talks about reconciliation between France and Germany after the war,
and of brotherhood [*la fraternité*] in general. At ARTE [*chez* ARTE] the
French-German channel, we like this song a lot. Let's listen together."
A shot of birds in flight across an open sky appear on screen and then
we hear the first melancholy piped notes of the French singer Barbara's
Göttingen. Against black-and-white archival images of postwar rubble,
we hear the song's first stanzas. Though Barbara sings the original
French, her lyrics are translated into German on-screen; the lyrics are
highlighted in black as they are sung, suggesting that the viewer follow word by word, or even sing along (see Table 4.1). Then, mid-way
through the song, its key changes slightly and suddenly it is being sung
in German, with the French lyrics to the song appearing on the screen,
as the images proceed to document decades of French and German
history and reconciliation that followed the Second World War. More
images of postwar rubble and then of a little girl defacing the Berlin
Wall give way to Jacques Chirac and Gerhard Schröder holding hands,
and finally a waving European Union flag.

On the one hand, like *Chacun Son Histoire? / Zwei Nationen, eine
Geschichte?* the song offers a view of history that emphasizes personal narrative and experience, privileging sameness across borders over national
histories. Barbara sings that the children in Göttingen – "Herman, Peter,

Table 4.1 An excerpt of lyrics from Barbara's *Göttingen*, translated from original
French[12]

French	German	English
Bien sûr, ce n'est pas la Seine,	Na ja, dort gibt es keine Seine	Of course, it's not la Seine
Ce n'est pas le bois de Vincennes,	Und auch nicht den Wald von Vincennes,	It's not the woods of Vincennes,
Mais c'est bien joli tout de même,	Doch schöne Orte, die ich kenne	But it is pretty all the same,
A Göttingen, à Göttingen.	in Göttingen, in Göttingen.	In Göttingen, in Göttingen.
Pas de quais et pas de rengaines	Es gibt keine Kais oder Lieder,	No quays and no old tunes
Qui se lamentent et qui se traînent,	die klagen und kehren immer wieder	That lament and run on
Mais l'amour y fleurit quand même,	Und dennoch blüht auch dort die Liebe,	But love flowers here all the same,
A Göttingen, à Göttingen.	in Göttingen, in Göttingen.	In Göttingen, in Göttingen.
Ils savent mieux que nous, je pense,	Mir scheint, als ob sie besser wüssten,	They know better than us, I think,
L'histoire de nos rois de France,	die Geschichte Frankreichs großer Fürsten,	The history of the kings of France,
Herman, Peter, Helga et Hans,	Hermann, Peter, Helga, und Hans	Herman, Peter, Helga, and Hans,
A Göttingen.	in Göttingen.	In Göttingen.

Helga, and Hans" – are "the same" as in Paris. Paralleling part of what we learn in *Chacun Son Histoire?* / *Zwei Nationen, eine Geschichte?* the song suggests that the Germans may even know French history ("our French kings") better than the French themselves. The singer concludes that everything should be done to prevent war not for reasons political or economic but because, personally, affectively – conveyed with emotional vibrato – there are people she knows and loves in Göttingen, whose lives, experience has taught her, are in most ways just like her own.[11]

But the segment is a good example of the ways in which a European and seemingly supra-, post-, or anti-national narrative was often, at ARTE, entangled in other meanings and politics. In this case, one could argue that Europe serves as a kind of Trojan horse for what might ultimately be a story and message about the phoenix-like resurrection of France and Germany.

The segment depicts and advances a twentieth-century history in which France and Germany (and Europe) are for many years consumed by war, but which ends with French-German peace, cooperation, and (finally) European integration. The song's visual script shows France and Germany at war; overcoming deep mutual enmities; their leaders coming together to sign documents; and a Europe that finally emerges as a symbol and bastion of peace (cf. Shore 2000, 58). The sequence, employing an emotional repertoire of images and appeals (e.g., children emerging from rubble), ultimately seems to argue that France-Germany is the genesis and font of European integration, and they are joint guarantors of a Pax Europaea (of which ARTE, located in the symbolic borderlands of France and Germany, is of course the ordained cultural-mediational heritor).

Erased from this rather simplistic Franco-German story, however, are the complexities of the postwar period in Europe during which huge populations were displaced and uprooted (Judt 2006; Ballinger 2003) and borders were remade (both in Europe and among its colonies). Ignored or obscured by this narrative, too, is the collapse of socialist regimes across Eastern Europe with all of the attendant problems of sudden transition to capitalist regimes (Verdery 2000, 2003; Berdahl, Bunzl, and Lampland 2000). And some scholars have argued that it is precisely in France's and Germany's noisy (ongoing) celebration of a postwar, post-national cosmopolitanism that pressing questions about race and diversity have come to be drummed out (Mandel 2008, 109–40).

The lyrics and the story they tell of *Gottingen* are emotionally resonant, humanistic, universal. Yet they also provide an example of the ways in an audiovisual commemoration and celebration of Europe and post-national politics can ultimately enfold, and transpose, nationalist and self-interested historical rhetorics and politics. European and "post-national" histories are always in dialogue with a politics of the present, and they necessarily privilege some voices and versions of history over others. Nationalist narratives and world views often re-emerge, intact or in fragments, in "European" re-presentations of history, sometimes despite the intentions of producers who conceive of their work as transcending divisive national loyalties and as counteracting inculcated historical subjectivities.

Nach Fahrplan in den Tod

Because I am not a native speaker of French or German, my work with the documentary department mostly consisted of research and organizational work – I couldn't, for example, proofread scripts. One day, however, one of the programmers who works on history

programming at ARTE asked if my French were good enough for
me to transcribe an interview. I said that I thought it was and that
I could tackle the transcribing, and I soon found myself watching a
DVD that contained fifteen minutes of interview material, having
to watch it again and again in order to transcribe the words of a
French historian who spoke, haltingly, about the role of the French
railway company, the SNCF, in the Holocaust. Curious about what I
was transcribing, I asked a member of the department one day while
we were working on something else. "It's a disaster," she replied. "A
long story."

Apparently – and the details remain somewhat anecdotal despite
my efforts to confirm them – the programmer explained that in 2004
ARTE accepted for broadcast a three-part series called *Die Gestapo*,
originally produced for Germany's ARD television channel, which
would be rebroadcast in two parts on ARTE. One of the episodes of *Die
Gestapo* implied that the French national railway company, the SNCF,
cooperated with the Gestapo during their coordination of the deportation of Jews from occupied France. As the production process moved
forward and the French version of the film was being fashioned, word
trickled out that the film would implicate the French train company
in a collaboration which the company has never conceded, and which
in French courts it has vigorously denied.[13] As the documentary was
prepared for broadcast, the SNCF threatened to include ARTE in an
anti-defamation lawsuit. Heated discussion bounced between ARTE
France and its Strasbourg headquarters over whether or not to air the
episode; staff suggested to me that a personal friendship between
Louis Gallois, then the head of the SNCF, and then president of ARTE
France, Jérôme Clément (they had graduated together from France's
prestigious École nationale d'administration), had something to do
with ARTE France's special interest in quelling the dispute. A deal
was eventually struck whereby ARTE would be allowed to broadcast
the episode if it scrolled text across the bottom of the film, during
broadcast, that would essentially indicate that ARTE did not mean
to imply the culpability of the SNCF for the crimes of the Gestapo
in France. Much to the embarrassment and consternation of many
of those in the department and ARTE's headquarters, ARTE agreed
to scroll text that would "contextualize" (and undermine) the film's
principal argument.

Four years later, the filmmakers, it turned out, had made another film
for ARTE, *Nach Fahrplan in den Tod: Die Europäischen Bahnen und der Holocaust* (Destination Death: The European Railways and the Holocaust)

(2008), which was why I found myself transcribing the interview. The department realized that ARTE once again stood to anger the SNCF with a new round of filmic accusations.

The interview I was transcribing was an effort to avoid trouble. It had been organized by ARTE production staff in Strasbourg and Paris after a screening of a near-final version of the film. One of ARTE's German-identifying programming administrators asked a documentary unit staff member, also a German speaker, to explore the *Bewegungspielraum* (wiggle room) that might be introduced into the film that might soften the implication of the SNCF's culpability. With further discussion it was decided that a member of the unit should go to Paris with a production crew to film an additional interview, which might "add perspective." The interview, which would be inserted near the end of the film, was with prominent Holocaust historian Annette Wieviorka.[14] In response to the ARTE documentary staff's question, "Did the SNCF have an option?" Wieviorka carefully, and very tentatively, responded (and, in Strasbourg, I transcribed):[15]

01:05:48
AW: The wiggle room of the SNCF was extremely slim [*mince*], since its statute in some ways governed by the armistice convention which followed France's defeat, and which made sure that, in matters of transportation, the ... France would have to submit to the orders of the German occupier.

01:07:25
ARTE Docs: So it's just now an explanation since you have used the word "slim" [*mince*]. "Slim," that means, there is something, which is small, which is slim but there *is* something. And so [the director] wanted to know, "slim," what does that mean?

01:07:45
AW: I think that I used the term "slim" to avoid saying that there wasn't any margin because, I think there's always a little bit of, of, maneuver [*jeu*]. But, all in all [*globalement*], from the moment that France was defeated, where the country literally collapsed faced with the advance of the German army, and where the political choice was made to collaborate, there wasn't possibility for exception in the collaboration and in the deportation of the Jews for the SNCF.

01:08:51
AW: Maybe also, if I could add something, that, in saying "slim," I also meant that, we are talking about the SNCF as if it was one thing, but maybe it's necessary to break down what we call the "SNCF." The SNCF is a company, and in this company, there are like in all companies, different levels. So it is possible that in such and such place there was the possibility not of preventing the deportation but maybe, actually, of ... of acting in some way [but] I still don't see exactly how.

...

02:00:56
ARTE Docs: So do you see a kind of responsibility on the part of the SNCF concerning the transports?
AW: Um ... how to say ... um ... This question becomes difficult because ... there are complaints that have been brought against the SNCF. So "responsibility," what does that mean? Is it a penal responsibility, today, of the SNCF within a legal framework? In this case my answer is no. Is it that there is a responsibility of the SNCF in the deportation of Jews? Obviously, yes. In other words, we have, in sum, a certain number of administrations that have, or of companies, that made the deportation possible.

As I rewound again and again to try to discern a particular word or phrase, I found the scene on the monitor before me quite compelling. Here was an ARTE programmer, in heavily German-accented French, interviewing perhaps the most important French historian of the Holocaust, whose own grandparents had been arrested by the French militia and murdered at Auschwitz. The programmer was asking whether she thought the SNCF was legally responsible for the deportation of French Jews; she responded, in her careful and roundabout reply, that the French transport company *was* responsible, but perhaps not *legally*. He pressed her on the issue, later in the interview, asking if the French company could not at least have provided adequate water to those piled into the train cars. She replied that, in any case, how well people were treated on the train wasn't what mattered; what mattered was that the trains were headed to Auschwitz, where people were murdered: "I think that you always have to put the focus on that which makes all of this history unbearable, which is that you were deporting these people in order to kill them."[16]

In their production of this interview, to be inserted into the film to prevent legal turmoil, the producers, and the historian, were co-constructing a narrative that inflected (or perhaps deflected) the culpability of the French state during German occupation and for the deportation of French Jews. Wieviorka and the producers were carefully negotiating and crafting, through their interview dialogue, an argument that would both allow for recognition of the generalized "responsibility" of the SNCF for the deportation, while exculpating the rail company from actionable legal blame. This was a delicate audiovisual dance, in which the meaning of "responsibility" was very carefully managed (and would be further so during the editing of the interview) so that the film would balance delicately between *moral* and *legal* accusations. The meanings of a "slim" margin of maneuverability, "ordinary duty," and even the limits of the French state during collaboration were calibrated during the interview in order to set boundaries of the French state's "responsibility" that would be acceptable to both the producers and the historian.

If it is conventionally understood that the French and German state are hardly equal in their responsibility for trans-continental genocide during the Second World War, *Nach Fahrplan in den Tod* provides a window into the ways in which twentieth-century histories come to be partly renarrativized and renegotiated, as French-German transnational (and trans-state) cooperation spurs on reconsideration, and remediation, of this history. On the one hand, presumed national attitudes or dispositions towards the polemics of history do not, during these processes of re-presentation, emerge in ways that are simple or predictable; in this case, German, French, and Jewish identifications are in play, as well as professional and other personae, in ways that do not correspond to any "obvious" national configuration or opposition.

On the other hand, the film had to be re-edited in the first place because ARTE France met with resistance from the French state over what kinds of narratives about the French rail company were permissible and broadcastable. Indeed, one way of summarizing this social drama might be to say that, when German filmmakers attempted to retell a story about the French national rail company, the French state successfully reaffirmed its authority over national historiography. Though the formal intervention of the state comes to be complexly managed and, in certain ways, mitigated, the case of *Nach Fahrplan in den Tod* raises questions about what kinds of histories can be edited, and who is authorized to edit sometimes highly politicized (and potentially scandalizing) national histories.

A final example – this time involving ARTE France-affiliated producers seeking to produce a film about German history – sheds additional
light on why some kinds, and periods, of history, may be more easily
revisited and revised than other kinds of history.

L'Affaire Octogon / Schwarze Kassen

While working one day at ARTE in the documentary department, one
of the channel's most respected production managers, Tomas, walked
into my office and dropped a script on my desk. "I have a job for you,"
he said. "I've circled parts of this script that I think are wrong … They
say that these are facts, but can you check them? Do some research and
find out."

The film was *L'Affaire Octogon / Schwarze Kassen* (2008) produced by
Fabrizio Calvi and Frank Gerbely. The script referred to 150 cities in
(East) Germany that revolted in 1953 – was it really 150 cities, or more
like small towns and villages, asked Tomas. The script asserted that the
gouverneur of Liechtenstein had issued a certain money-smuggling Nazi
a Liechtensteiner passport in the final days of the war. Was it really the
gouverneur or some other kind of official, asked Tomas. Sifting through
dozens of websites, I cut and pasted answers to the questions as best I
could – there were few definitive answers that I could find.

But when Tomas returned to my office some hours later, he took
one look at the research I had printed out and said, definitively, "No.
There is no position called *gouverneur* in Liechtenstein." Liechtenstein,
he explained, is a kind of royal principality. (I wasn't sure this meant
the country couldn't have a governor of some kind, but Tomas seemed
quite sure.) He clearly already had answers to his questions. "Come
with me," he said. We found an empty office, pulled up two chairs, and
started watching a DVD of a fine cut of the film that had been submitted
to ARTE for a last round of comments before broadcast.

Shadowy, flickering sketchings accompany a narrator's smoky voice
and mystery-mood music plays in the background as we are taken,
through a series of black-and-white animations, back to the events of
the summer of 1944. The Second World War draws to a close as Germany weakens and Rome and Paris are liberated. In Strasbourg, the film
claims, a group of German officers meet to ensure that Nazi reserves of
gold will be hidden, and made available to a successor regime (Helmut
Kohl and the Christian Democrats), after the end of the war.

Tomas thinks the film is extremely flawed. We go through the script
together. When the narrator tells us that *"on a la liste"* – that *we have the*

list of those who attended this secret Nazi meeting – Tomas pauses the DVD and turns to me: "Why don't they show us the list?" We stare at a screen of disconcerting black-and-white sketches of Nazi officers but no list of names. This is the first of many pauses in which Tomas turns to me to ask me about the film's evidence: "Underline that in the script," he tells me, and I make a note. Tomas scrutinizes the film for visual evidence of archival records, or other "proof" of the documentary's assertions. At one point, after staring at the monitor for several minutes, he concludes the filmmakers may have forged a wartime passport that appears in the film.

Days later, Tomas asks me to write up a formal report of all we've scribbled across the film script. He can't let the film be broadcast – they'll have to re-edit, he says. He doesn't know how they'll fix the different kinds of problems with the film, which are as much about its "tone" as its historical accuracy.

Yet even as I was dutifully annotating the script with Tomas's ongoing criticisms, I wondered if tonality and historical accuracy were entirely distinct problems. Many of Tomas's comments I agreed with; as a documentary filmmaker myself, I could see that the film's visual evidence and too-emotionalized, direct appeals to the viewer were problematic.

Yet there was a kind of annoyance or anger in Tomas's over-and-over-again circlings and X's and scribbled question marks across the script. His constant corrections of transcribed German interview materials were often accompanied with comments about how "these people" didn't even speak German. And he mentioned several times that the film's producers were French and French Swiss.

Whatever the film's flaws, and those flaws were real, I sensed that part of Tomas's problem with the documentary was that its producers weren't "German." This wasn't their history, and the script was subject to such editorial scrutiny, in part, because the film couldn't claim to fully know postwar German history, couldn't claim therefore to revise this history, because its French-speaking production team wasn't authorized to do so, quite apart from whatever archival documents they claimed to have found uncovering a Nazi conspiracy.

Part of the issue was also that the documentary's conspiracy theory wasn't unfamiliar to Tomas and indeed to many Germans; Nazi gold and its laundering was an ongoing story that had been covered by the German press for years, and especially in the mid-1980s and early 1990s, when connections to the Christian Democrats had been suggested. The complicated and often contradictory evidence that was brought to light

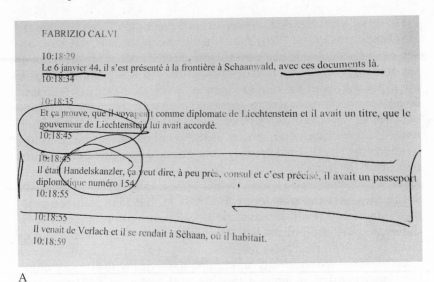

A

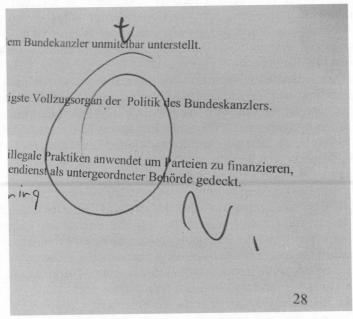

B

Figure 4.6 [A and B] Tomas's markings and edits from the script of *L'Affaire Octogon / Schwarze Kassen*. (Photo by author)

by German and Swiss press about trajectories of Nazi gold constituted a complex series of postwar events that were never conclusively connected to any contemporary politician. Tomas felt that the filmmakers didn't understand, and perhaps *couldn't* understand, the full political context of the controversy.[17]

Because the film had been submitted by ARTE's French production offices, the film came to be understood, in effect, as a source of French-German conflict, in which French producers argued for the sterling reputation of the filmmakers while Tomas and other German Strasbourg-based production staff held their ground that the film was inaccurate and far too emotional in its "poetic" style. The filmmakers were indignant. The highest levels of the channel's administration became involved. The film was discussed at ARTE delicately and in whispers. It wasn't so much the film's questionable "accuracy" that made ARTE staff uncomfortable talking about *Octogon*, I decided, but the film's ongoing threat to expose some of the staff's sharper-edged nationalist sensitivities.

While, in theory, French-speaking filmmakers can make a film about postwar German history as easily as German-identifying filmmakers, in reality "history" doesn't quite capture what is often at stake in these re-presentations: memory, and a "politics of memory," might be invoked to convey, in a sense, the deepness and ineffability of the ways in which experience (and self-conscious belonging in a linguistic [history textbook] community) is understood to authorize someone to edit "their" "history." In the case of *Octogon*, the French producers' affective signification of the Second World War – conveyed by their shadowy sketchings and eerie score – was rejected outright by Tomas. The Second World War, because it can still be invoked to attribute national culpabilities, remains highly sensitive historical ground, and while Germans at ARTE may work to open what have been highly intra-national conversations about the war to trans/national dialogue, both *Nach Fahrplan in den Tod* and *L'Affaire Octogon / Schwarze Kassen* suggest that there are limits to whom people understand to be authorized to participate in revision, and the extent to which "outsiders" can lay claim to certain kinds of historical expertise and authority.[18] Tomas's circling and highlighting constituted a *de facto* strategy of literally reinscribing historical knowledge in national identity and historical subjectivity. His fact checking and markings seemed to be not just an intellectual practice, but an emotive-affective one too.

re-scripting (some) histories

At ARTE, on ARTE, and for those who watch ARTE, historical scripts literally and figuratively mediate not only how people come to know how events have unfolded in time, but also how they are to position themselves as subjects within such narratives, and what kinds of affective engagements are appropriate.[19] The cases considered in this chapter demonstrate that some historical scripts may be more semiotically resilient than others, however. It may be that Napoleon is simply a less charged figure than Hitler, or that the contemporary resonances and politics of Napoleonic history are less recognized than those of postwar Germany: Historical anthropologist Michael Lambek has pointed out that the contemporary politics of memory surrounding the Second World War has everything to do with present-day politics of an ongoing "reimagination of Europe and its parts" (quoted in Cappelletto 2005, xi; cf. Lebow, Kansteiner, and Fogu 2006).

A transnationalization or "Europeanization" of history is hardly a foregone conclusion and this process (if we can posit linearity) may be slowing, stopped, or reversing. While *Chacun Son Histoire? / Zwei Nationen, eine Geschichte?* seeks to self-consciously *fragment* the textual scale of national histories without necessarily formulating a "pan-European" alternative, *Göttingen* illustrates the ways in which national political interests may be entwined with the elaboration of "European" historical narratives. *Nach Fahrplan in den Tod* makes plain the continued authority of the state in censuring certain editings of history, while *L'Affaire Octogon / Schwarze Kassen* reminds us that history is never "merely" about the facticity or accuracy of reporting events, but also about deeply held – and learned – affective responses, emotional(ized) memory, and the exclusion of "outsiders" from "insider" historical indignity and shame, in keeping with Michael Herzfeld's (2005) notion of "cultural intimacy." Closer attention to the particular tetherings and tanglings of narrated pasts with political presents may help us to understand why some historical scripts are being (are *able* to be) rewritten – while others remain more faithfully re-produced.

5

culture, "culture," Culture

At ARTE, "culture"[1] is constantly talked about. But even a casual visitor to the network's offices would soon discover that "culture" means no single thing, and is used in no single way. If ARTE proudly refers to itself as "the European culture channel," *la chaîne culturelle européenne,* and *der Europäische Kulturkanal,* the implications of "culture" in these linguistic renderings vary. In English, the ambiguity about whether ARTE is the European "culture channel," or the "European culture" channel, is perhaps especially instructive. It points us to the heart of the consequentiality of "culture" as the term is trafficked and employed at a media organization whose understandings of the term will partly determine what it produces and disseminates, and to what ends.

"Culture" is a key concept that pervades ARTE producers' work, a constant point of reference and sense of identity for the channel's administrators and staff, but it is also ambiguous, and an almost daily source of discussion and argument. Attention to the negotiations and conversations of media producers at ARTE about "culture" might help us to better understand, then, some of the central tensions that organize ARTE's constructions of national identity, French-German trans/national similitude, and European belonging.

At the fulcrum of this chapter are the complex vernacularizations and circulations of "culture" as this concept moves ever further from its prolific definition and theorization by anthropologists and academics, to pervade the everyday vocabularies of professionals in worlds of media, business, marketing, politics, and beyond. Raymond Williams captured part of the complexity of culture's contemporary status over thirty years ago. In his celebrated *Keywords*, Williams (1983) wrote,

> Culture is one of the two or three most complicated words in the English language. This is so partly because of its intricate historical development, in several European languages, but mainly because it has now come to be used for important concepts in several distinct intellectual disciplines and in several distinct and incompatible systems of thought. (87)

Although there are dozens of ways of delineating the meaning(s) of "culture" and how it has unfolded, in places and institutions in which it is self-consciously understood to be a useful, or necessary category or tool, its utility stems from the ways it is self-consciously delimited. Here I look to see which meanings of "culture" at ARTE are routinized and instrumentalized – but I necessarily hold its meanings and uses at ARTE in tension with those of anthropologists (who perhaps have grown to disprefer the term) and with my own sense of how human behaviour "holds together."

I hope to make clear that there is much to be learned by paying attention to the overlaps and disjunctions among and between an "informed" sense of *cultural analysis* as this is proclaimed by anthropologists, sociologists, media studies scholars, and other academics, and the sense in which "culture" is practically and more broadly applied by educated people – some who may even have degrees in social science – but for whom "culture" is a category that is less an analytical premise than a useful category for the work at hand, and a conceptual tool (either sharp or rough) for thinking about human sameness and difference.

In pages that follow I describe the self-conscious and patterned ways in which "culture" gets taken up by media professionals in a place where this term has manifold registers variously invoking the arts, social community, and national character. At ARTE, the ways in which "culture" is understood and deployed have consequences for the ways in which sameness and difference are conceived as national, European,[2] and human. I aim to illuminate some of the ways in which French and German notions of "culture" are understood to vary at ARTE,[3] and to suggest that partially shared meanings for "culture," and even "European culture," are also sometimes acknowledged. The reader might bear in mind that much of our social scientific thinking, especially about society and culture, finds deep roots in French (Montesquieu, Rousseau, Durkheim, Lévi-Strauss, Foucault) and German (Kant, Herder, Marx, Weber, Boas) conceptualizations of these terms. Indeed, it is in the fissures and gaps between "culture" as a presumably universal concept and analytical category – and as a particular, nationally constructed (and particularly Western European) idea – which I hope this chapter might somewhat uncomfortably rest.

the mysterious disappearance of the "culture" theme night

Until very recently ARTE broadcasted three evenings of themed programming, called THEMA. These blocks of air time, usually consisting of two films and some sort of introduction or debate, were organized around themes and were of three sorts: on Sundays, the cinema THEMA night, ARTE might broadcast, as they did one night, two equestrian-themed films, for example *The Black Stallion* (*L'Etalon Noir*) and *Bouzka-chi*, a docu-fiction about men and their dependence on horses in Central Asia. Other nights have been programmed around the work of Oliver Stone, the early career of Gerard Depardieu, or films about the *Belle Époque*. Tuesday night THEMA are about politics, society, and current events; recent themes have included Europe's aging population, Tibet, and young people's access to internet pornography. The Friday night THEMA was designated the "culture" THEMA, proposing a broad range of programming themes that have included everything from Catalonia to Checkpoint Charlie to Charlie Chaplin.

"The *problem*," Sylvie, a veteran programmer in ARTE's THEMA department, half-whispered to me as we chatted one afternoon in her sunlit office, "was that Friday night THEMA was never clearly defined, the editorial line was much too vague – it was the 'culture' THEMA, but what did 'culture' mean in this context?" She paused as though I, the anthropologist, might have an answer to propose. I smiled politely. She continued, "The French and Germans would sit around and ask themselves, in coming up with themes to propose, 'What themes seem "cultural" to us?' I have to tell you that, this, this touched off huge debate, was always a source of debate, which sometimes got really tense. [*A pause*] The Germans submitted to us a night of programming about *homeopathy*," she explained, changing her tone, as if levelling with me. "And this got the French bouncing off the walls, saying '*La culture! La culture!'* Culture is the *arts* ... it's *philosophy* ... it's certainly *not* home-opathy." But Sylvie explained that she could understand how home-opathy could be appropriately "cultural":

> Me, I proposed that ... medicine is also a sort of vision of the world, because the way we take care of ourselves is a vision of the world, it's ... medicine proceeds from modernity, it's ... well, cutting up the body by dividing it, okay well this is a kind of particular approach ... and what if we treated homeopathy from the perspective of whether it's reimbursed by the health care system, then it's also something current ...

I could see that Sylvie might conceive of a broader category of "culture" into which homeopathy might fit, and yet I sensed that she was less comfortable with this sense of the term, or editorial line, as it were. Though she eventually connected modern medicine to systems of ratio-nality, thus arriving at "culture" in some wider sense, she hemmed and hawed, and finally questioned whether this understanding of "culture" made for good television:

> You also have to understand, you must not underestimate all that is *impli-cated* by this approach. It implicates the filmmakers, the choice of *images* ... because the cultural approach to homeopathy, what would you have for images? Hmm? You can put an image of Paracelsus [a fifteenth-century advocate of homeopathy] but *le monsieur* wasn't filmed! ... You have maybe a few engravings but ... so what kind of film can you make? You're compelled to make a certain kind of film.

Indeed, I sensed that Sylvie was trying to convey to me that this "cul-tural" approach to homeopathy would result in something of a vague, and very boring, film.

Despite the fact that most programmers in the THEMA department, French-identifying and German-identifying, recognized the ambigui-ties of the Friday night "culture programming" – I heard at several points during my fieldwork that it had been a source of agitation – its subsequent cancelling led to an outcry from the THEMA department, whose members felt that the administration was trying to reduce the department's charge and influence. (The programming and audi-ence studies departments had recently been "providing" numbers to the department suggesting that ARTE's viewers were unwilling to sit through the three or more hours of the mono-thematic program-ming that comprise THEMA.) Department staff demanded meetings with administrators, angry emails were exchanged, and the "culture" THEMA was discussed and gossiped about in the cafeteria. Comments like, "Well, it obviously wasn't working – 'culture' is far too vague a category," were met with, "I don't see why we can't just accept that there are different ideas about what 'culture' means, that French and Germans might have different ways of approaching it."

In the end, the hallways of ARTE's THEMA unit were dotted with little stickers reading "I ♥ *thema*," marking defiant resistance to the administration's disappearing of Friday night "culture." The stickering of hallways and the generally strident tone of the debates leading up to, and in the wake of, the culture night's cancellation, mark it as an

Jérôme Clément
Président d'ARTE

Jean-Paul Cluzel
Président-directeur général
de Radio France

David Kessler
Directeur de France Culture

Seraient heureux
de vous accueillir à l'occasion du colloque

La culture
est-elle encore un enjeu politique ?

Proposé par **ARTE** et **France Culture** en partenariat avec **Le Monde**

Vendredi 1ᵉʳ décembre 2006
de 9h à 13h et de 14h30 à 18h

Figure 5.1 Insert from a mailing announcing an ARTE France co-sponsored colloquium entitled, "Culture: Is it still a political issue?" (Photo by author)

important social drama at ARTE that turned, in a fundamental way, on the ambiguous and contested meaning of "culture." This term was not only pulled between the French *culture* and the German *Kultur*, but was also left too vaguely defined – betwixt and between various renderings – to be serviceable. In the end, it was the THEMA department's renewed cohesion, pitted against programming department administrators that marked the end of the conflict over the meaning of "culture." But the definition of the term remains as highly contested at ARTE as it is crucial to the channel's ongoing operation, and its conceptions of what is appropriate programming for a hybrid French-German, trans/national, and global audience.

locations and locutions of "culture"

The Friday night THEMA controversy reveals the ways in which producers and programmers at ARTE are compelled to contemplate, negotiate, and explain "culture" in often highly self-conscious and discursive ways. Yet it became clear to me, especially during my months at ARTE France in Paris, that self-conscious references to "culture" as both a *problem* and *debate* seemed particularly resonant for French-identifying members of the staff.[4] German-identifying staff at ARTE's headquarters often wondered at how their French colleagues could speak about "culture" in such circumscribed ways, at its seemingly more specific referentiality, and about the series of fairly consistent debates the concept inspires about the arts, democracy, class, and the state. I spent several lunches listening to French-speaking colleagues talk animatedly about *la politique culturelle* without participating; sometimes German-identifying staff ate among them in silence. "You have to be careful," a German programmer warned me one day. "It's very political, and if you're not French, you can't really understand what this word means."

In this way the very extent to which "culture" was a debatable and debated category at all – a knowable, discursive, bounded category – was understood to vary greatly among French and German staff at ARTE. I wondered if this is why Sylvie implied that a *French* approach to "culture" was somehow more concrete – more filmable – than its German cognate: "Culture" could be contorted to somehow include homeopathy, she could agree, but then how do you *film* such a thing?

The idea that French *culture* is somehow more *filmable*, or *locatable*, than German *Kultur* is intriguing. On almost a daily basis I saw or heard some means of distinguishing French *culture* from German *Kultur*, almost always in reference to place – that is, where *culture* or *Kultur* could be found in the two countries. I would often hear ARTE staff agree, when they would fall into conversation about differences between France and Germany, that "culture" was less *centralized* in Germany than in France, where it was to be found in Paris, at the Louvre, in Jacques-Louis David's *The Death of Marat*. Germans would explain that they, on the other hand, organize government, education, media, and the arts through federal Länder, and sixteen regional cities – so that while key cultural references and symbols for the French were usually to be found in *la ville-lumière*, for Germans, *Kultur* in Germany seemed a bit more distributed or diffuse.

Some producers at ARTE employ a sort of opposition, or equating, of Paris and Berlin – indeed, one ARTE-produced talk/debate show is called *Paris-Berlin: Le Débat / Paris-Berlin: Die Debatte*. But German speakers would sometimes scratch their heads at the equation of Paris and Berlin as "twin cities." One veteran German-identifying programmer explained to me, "In France you have just one big city – Paris. We have several big cities, each one with its own museums, its own orchestra ... but the French are Paris-centric, they don't understand that Germany isn't like France." Another programmer pointed out, "The French are always trying to equate Paris and Berlin, but actually Berlin has only become an international city and tourist destination in the past few decades."[5] ARTE productions originating in Paris nevertheless often insist on the homology between the two cities, so that when stock footage is needed, for backgrounds or the opening segment of a show, alongside images of the Eiffel Tower and Arc de Triomphe, stills of the Brandenburg Gate and the Fernsehturm might be juxtaposed. German-produced programs (produced by ARD/ZDF) tended to employ a wider range of local and regional landmarks in order to audiovisually indicate the national context – from Berlin, yes, but also Frankfurt, Hamburg, Munich, or Leipzig. Indeed, in Germany, because the ARD public channels are distributed within each regional state, viewers might consider opening titles featuring images of Berlin a bit strange or out of place.

It became increasingly clear that, as the terms tend to be employed every day by staff at ARTE, "culture" didn't seem to be *located* in the same way for German speakers as it was for French speakers; and *culture* implied French-ness quite differently from the way *Kultur* might be connected to German-ness. Among French-identifying staff at ARTE, *culture* tended to evoke a distinct set of debates, most of which centred not on what it meant to be French or European, at least not directly, but which tended to call forth a much narrower range of polemic about the arts, *la création,* and *la politique de la culture.*

La culture was quite often used alongside or in the same strip of talk as *la création,* and the concepts are best discussed in tandem. *La création* (perhaps best translated not as "creation" or "creativity," but "cultural production") is a concept that French-speaking administrators and staff at ARTE often employ in describing what ARTE does differently from other channels. I would hear or read the word (always in French) on almost a daily basis at ARTE. Jérôme Clément, the first and longtime president of ARTE, now president of ARTE France, has frequently employed the term in his explications of what ARTE does and means. In a 2007 interview with the European Union-focused news website *EurActiv,* Clément explained, for example,

> Notre ligne éditoriale, elle, reste la même: culture, création, diversité, Europe ... nous ne sommes pas une chaîne d'information continue comme Euronews, France 24 ou la Deutsche Welle et, à la différence de France 5, avec qui nous coopérons, la création est au cœur de notre mission.
>
> [Our editorial line remains the same: culture, *création,* diversity, Europe ... we are not a news channel like EuroNews, France 24 or Deutsche Welle and, in contrast to France 5, with whom we cooperate, *la création* is at the heart of our mission.][6]

As suggested by Clément's asyndeton, at ARTE, French producers and programmers speak of the channel's identity, and *différence* from other channels, as having to do, almost interchangeably, with *la culture* and *la création,* as if these things referenced twin aspirations. I asked a French-speaking programmer and former cinematographer in ARTE's documentary department to help clarify this for me. He explained:

> *La création* ... it's a vast subject, but ... I would say that it's a certain intention to communicate a vision of the world, to create and *communicate culture* ... through the means of the audiovisual ... It's not to make money – that's an important distinction ... It's to communicate an artistic vision to the public.

This bridging of *culture* to *la création* might partly be attributed to the vocabulary and policies of André Malraux, who played a central role in French politics and society for the better part of three decades.[7] After Malraux convinced Charles de Gaulle to establish the first Ministry of

Culture in 1959 (then called La Ministère des Affaires culturelles), as the first minister of culture he endowed it with the mission to

> rendre accessibles au plus grand nombre les œuvres capitales de l'humanité, et d'abord de la France, au plus grand nombre possible de français, d'assurer la plus vaste audience à notre patrimoine culturel, et de favoriser *la création* des œuvres de l'art et de l'esprit qui l'enrichissent.
>
> [render accessible to as many as possible the capital works of humanity, and first of all those of France to as many French people as possible, to assure the largest audience for our cultural heritage, and to encourage the creation of works of art and the spirit that enriches it.][8]

Here, Malraux explicitly yokes the *patrimoine culturel* (cultural heritage) of France to *la création des oeuvres de l'art* (the creation of works of art).

French political scholar David L. Looseley (1997) argues that Malraux's conception of the state's support of art, as framed in the ministry's founding documents, centred on the ambitions of "promoting the national heritage at home and abroad[,] enriching it by encouraging contemporary creation[,] and, dominating and embracing these two, democratization" (37). Extending this argument, historian Marc Fumaroli (1991) notes that Malraux specifically hoped to buoy up national support of the *visual* arts because he understood the *image* to be particularly well-suited to the democratization and "uplift" of French society, especially as the country was undergoing a virtual communications revolution as a result of the huge popularity of cinema and introduction of television:

> Malraux had no intentions ... to make *books* a priority. It didn't seem to him that they could ever become a cult object and the object of mass culture. Instead images, more accessible to sensations and basic emotions, seemed better suited to the ... crowds ... Malraux saw himself as ... called to assemble the people ... in great communal audiovisual celebrations, the efficacy of which, at this date, had already been well attested to. (124–5)

The establishment of Malraux's Ministry of Culture laid bare the French state's claim to the administration and regulation of popular symbolic and artistic forms, especially as these began to accelerate in number and form as a result of their mechanical reproduction across the nation's screens both big and small: the CNC (Centre National du Cinéma), which had regulated the film industry in France since 1936, was summarily subsumed into the ministry upon its founding. The

French sense of "culture politics" (*la politique de la culture*, to be differentiated from our familiarity in English with "cultural politics") indexes what are today still highly effervescent debates about the "drastic increase of state interventionism after the Second World War, and, more precisely, of the increasingly predominant place occupied by the state in 'the management of national symbolism'" (Dubois quoted in Depétris 2008, 52).[9] *La création* can largely be interpreted as a political neologism emphasizing and legitimating the ongoing intervention of the state into evolving and emerging domains of public culture: "In ignoring *la création* of its own era as well as the new modes of expression and modes of thought," wrote Malraux in 1966, "a national arts policy sterilizes and ossifies instead of invigorating the culture of which it claims to be the guardian" (Malraux quoted in Depétris 2008, 56, author's translation).[10]

"What Malraux meant by culture was the highest and most lasting forms of artistic achievement," explains Looseley (1997). Malraux defined "culture," in his own words, as "those works that have escaped from death [*les oeuvres qui ont échappé à la mort*] (36). For Malraux and the state, writes Looseley, "culture was therefore to be understood as a humanist alternative to religion and a source of immortality in an absurd universe" (36). As Mark Ingram has noted in his excellent ethnography of French citizens' theatre, *Rites of the Republic* (2011), through the 1990s, *création* and culture were often used, in tandem, to push against the looming threat of "regressive populism" (and, I would argue, implicitly, perceived invasions of American-style "entertainment"):

> The inclusive goals of Jean Vilar [advocate of citizens' and popular theatre] were portrayed as promoting a theatre for the masses at the expense of singular individual inspiration and "minority" experiences ("minority," in this sense being opposed to "mass" and not intended to refer to an ethnic or religious identity). The rejection of a class-based conception of French society by theatre artists such as Planchon ... was consistent with the move away from a class-oriented portrayal of society by the French intelligentsia more generally in the 1980s. Theatre "creators" argued that, in attempting to address what "the people" wanted, "theatre for everyone" merely acted as a front for a market mentality and the transformation of artistic work into a market commodity. (14)

If *la création* plays an important role in ARTE's administrative vocabulary, it isn't accidental that its founding president, Jérôme Clément, spent several years at the Ministry of Culture, not long after Malraux's departure, before acting as director of the Centre National du Cinéma also housed within the ministry.[11] In his editorials and political writing, Clément (2002) seems to share Malraux's (and Planchon's) sense that *culture* implies something like a humanist (and anti-capitalist) political ideology: *"La culture* is not merchandise like other merchandise. It's a precious good, it's our soul," he has written (my translation). Elsewhere he writes,

> What is culture if not a different perspective on others, on the world? [It's] an openness, a curiosity, another way of accessing the real, whether it's expressed by the talents of artists (theatre, cinema, music), or directly understood by those who know themselves how to look, to see (*regarder*) ... Television is at the heart of a system of thought and social relations that can defend itself from the profitability of investment. The State must assume this responsibility, if only to accept the dominance of the market over men and spirits (*sur les hommes et les esprits*). (Clément 1992, n.p., my translation)[12]

It may not be altogether surprising, then, that Sylvie, and many of her French-speaking and French institutionally credentialed colleagues, seem to share a sense of what *culture* means, and are able to access a coherent repertoire of ideas and debates about turning *culture* into television (or vice versa). To what extent can *culture* be democratized through television? Are television (here the distinction from film is relevant) – as a popular and populist form – and *culture* – in the sense of artistic creativity – antithetical? "The French love to argue about ARTE and *culture* [this last word spoken in French]," an ARTE programmer told me at dinner one night, in German, when I raised this observation. "And Germans, we often just sit there and listen to them argue about this thing called *la culture*. It just isn't the same thing to us [*ist es nicht das Gleiche*]."

As understood by many at ARTE, *culture* was more circumscribed and political than the word's German cognate *Kultur;* it was hardly as all-encompassing or broad a category. For a majority of producers and programmers, the French concept referred to particular artistic and humanistic domains – a more-or-less closed set that includes the visual arts, music, theatre, and, more recently, film and television – which have been cultivated by the state as a means of not only democratization in its narrow political sense, but as a means of humanization, social integration, civilizational uplift, and closeness to the universal-eternal. *Culture* – in the ways it was often talked about by staff at ARTE – references objects and subjects that tend to be aesthetic, or closely related to the aesthetic, which can therefore be filmed, and re-presented, through the television and web pages, themselves audiovisual. Here we circle back to Sylvie's comment that somehow French *culture* is more filmable than its translation in English or German: ARTE is a "culture channel," for many of its staff, in this deep, but also narrow, sense.

Kultur *clash*

Sipping tea in the tiny cafeteria of ARTE Germany's headquarters in Baden-Baden, I ask Katrin about the differences between *Kultur* and *culture*, and if she thinks they matter at ARTE. I had met Katrin several times during her frequent visits to ARTE's Strasbourg headquarters, an hour or so away by train, so I knew she would have some perspective on the matter.

"Yes," said Katrin, without hesitation. "My colleagues have talked a lot about the difference between *Kultur* and *culture*." She paused, now considering her words. "For the French, *culture* [in French] seems to also mean *Zivilisation* [in German]. But in German, we don't have a word for *culture* [in French] the same way." I asked her if she had heard about the "disagreement" around the homeopathy / *homéopathie* / *Homöopathie thema* night, and whether she thought *Homöopathie* wasn't "cultural" enough. Katrin smiled and rolled her eyes in recognition of the story, explaining that she herself had worked on the proposal for the homeopathy programming. "For us, the *Kulturthemenabend* [culture theme night] could include lots of things, could include *Homöopathie*," she defended, "because the films that were submitted for that theme night were actually sort of *Kulturgeschichte*, really – *Geisteswissenschaft*, you see – which could be included in *Kultur*."

By *Kulturgeschichte*, Katrin meant "cultural history," which means more or less what it means in English. But *Geisteswissenschaft* isn't as easily translated – in English it might be rendered as "human sciences," or, with somewhat more severe linguistic contortion, as "the sciences and humanities," but either of these translations misses (and thus reveals) what is at issue here.

"For French, the categories are different," said Katrin. "If something is *science* [in French] then it's *science*, there's no argument. Let me give you an example. Are you familiar with a program that we had, called *Archimedes*?" "Sure," I replied, recalling that the program had run for many years. "Well this program, for the French, was *science* [in French], and that's it. But for Germans, this could also include *Geisteswissenschaft* – *sciences humaines* [in French] – and so this meant that we always had different ideas about what was appropriate for this show. The Germans would submit something like music, and the French would say, [in French] 'No, that's not science.'"

I asked a programmer in the cinema and fiction department at ARTE's headquarters, Angela, who has worked in the department for fifteen years, if a "cultural television channel" – I said this in French, then German: *une chaîne culturelle, ein Kulturkanal* – meant the same thing to her German colleagues as her French colleagues. Did *création* have an equivalent in German, was it as important? *"Hmm ... auf Deutsch? ... die Kreativität? ... Nein, es geht nicht"* (Hmm ... in German? ... *Kreativität*? [creativity] ... No, it doesn't quite work), she replied after sounding out the German cognate.

"In French, *la culture*, it's ... it's delicate ... almost taboo, it's almost ... *magic*," Angela finally reflected, in German. After a second or two of silence, we both burst out with laughter, but maybe for different reasons. I thought she was poking fun at anthropology, but she may have just been poking fun at *la culture*.

At stake in all this were the form and shape of categories of knowledge, categories which were at once linguistic and editorial, conceptual and practical: science, the humanities, culture, and the arts constituted different categories – and could be spliced together differently – in French and German linguistic renderings and connotations. Though editorial lines might blithely describe a program as "science," "art," or "culture," even colour-coding them in scheduling blocks this way, for many ARTE staff, the daily work of deciding what is appropriate for a certain category of programming – or for ARTE, period – is in reality often a process of careful negotiation of deeply held semantic organizations, logics, learned meanings, and competing senses of the appropriate.

"To understand *Kultur*," one programmer who had worked as a cultural attaché in Germany told me, "you have to understand the difference between *civilization* ... and *Bildung*. You can't understand Germany if you don't understand *Bildung*." Anthropologist Dominic Boyer (2005) writes that *Bildung* "still retains its semantic integrity against the sincere cosmopolitanism of its translators," and goes on to adumbrate a definition of it with a parenthetical litany of related English words: "(education, self-formation, self-cultivation, distinction, culture, civilization)" (52). But perhaps the most important sense of *Bildung*, for our more limited purposes here, is captured by its most simple and literal translation, as *formation*, or as its related verb *bilden*: to shape, to form, to build.

Kultur and *Bildung* are related through a trope of development, growth, and cultivation. Development and growth might most immediately refer to life course and education – this is the *modus operandi* of the *Bildungsroman*, in which we follow how our protagonist is literally developed – but *Bildung* shares this sense of cultivated knowledge and experience with *Kultur*. Both are redolent of the organic and botanical: "The German concept of *Kultur*," wrote sociologist Norbert Elias (2000), "refers to human products which are there like 'flowers in the field,'" (7). Elias himself used *Kultur* and *Bildung* sometimes interchangeably in his German texts.

Elias (2000) traced the close relation of these two terms to the early coalescing of German national culture among an educated middle class. Rather than in a centralized court or the state itself, much of German national identity came to emerge out of Germany's regions, the Länder, which were, in the early nineteenth century, Elias reminds us, still quite independent of one another. Whereas in France, talented middle-class artists and intellectuals, such as Voltaire and Diderot, were often absorbed into and legitimated by the highly centralized court society of Paris, in Germany "sons of the rising middle class who were distinguished by talent and intelligence were debarred ... from courtly-aristocratic life" (18). This "sharp social division between nobility and middle class" often manifested itself in expressions of hatred directed against princes, courts, and aristocrats; middle-class German authors, artists, and intellectuals increasingly expressed, both aesthetically and in daily conversation, "dreams of a new united Germany, of a 'natural' life – 'natural' as opposed to the 'unnatural' life of court society" (17). Klopstock, Herder, Lessing, and the poets of Sturm und Drang came to understand themselves as a vanguard of a new German social movement; these middle-class intellectuals were fundamental in constructing an opposition between what they understood to be French, "'ascriptive,' 'quality-based' values on the one hand" with more authentically German, "bourgeois values based on achievement on the other" (19).

While French-educated and -identifying staff at ARTE tended to conflate *culture* with the arts, German-educated staff tended to draw upon several registers of *Kultur*. In keeping with what Kara Kosnick (2007) has argued in her ethnography of German immigrant media, many German staff at ARTE would use *Hochkultur* when they meant to reference the arts in particular (81–7). This may reflect the (perhaps reciprocal) opposition that Elias (2000) identifies between *Culture*, in France, as having substantially emerged through and alongside courtly authority, while in Germany *Kultur* emerged through anti-courtly values of self-formation and education.

Furthermore, although culture, when linked to the arts, was often deployed to emphasize sameness and universality, Germans were more likely to add an "s" to the word in order to speak of distinct *Kulturen*, distinguished by their own histories and characters. "The concept of *Kultur* delimits," explains Elias (2000). "*Kultur* places special stress on national differences and the particular identity of groups" (18–19).[13]

a meta-cultural aside

Here (insert sound of needle scratching across a record) we might turn this last section's discussion partly on its head. Although one way of telling the story of *differences* in understanding "culture" at ARTE is to delineate oppositional historical-semantic sensibilities as I have done above, it is worth considering the ways in which this analysis remains beholden to the very notions of "culture" that it claims to disentangle, dissect, and set apart. In other words, we might think about how the preceding analysis of how "culture" comes to have meaning at ARTE – my ability to discern and categorize "ways of thinking" about "culture" – is *also* subject to assumptions about what "culture" is, and how it works.

Sylvie mentioned that a "cultural" analysis of Western medicine might argue that it is premised on the notion that you can "divide" and "cut up the body." Cultural anthropology performs a similar kind of surgical procedure. Its premise is that complex human societies and interactions can be broken down into discrete subgroups, each with their own beliefs, cultural practices, material traditions, and ways of life. In so doing, the anthropologist tends to emphasize difference, often working to disambiguate a group from those that surround it or which may otherwise seem to resemble the group under study. Although anthropology claims to examine both sameness and difference across human groups, and although similarity and variation are necessarily both in play as an anthropologist describes a community (e.g., indigenous North Americans are both similar to and different from settler and immigrant North Americans), in actual practice I would assert that ethnographic description leans more heavily on the inscription of difference between groups.[14] Few ethnographies make the argument that a particular group – Brazilian Yanomami, Londoners of Pakistani descent, Oaxacan peasants, or Somalis – are more or less *the same as* other groups around the world (except insofar as they may argue that all humans have something like families, rites of passage, systems of material exchange, etc., which is almost always a premise but rarely a central argument).

In preceding paragraphs, I have argued, in keeping with this pre-dilection to differentiate, that the French and Germans have distinct ideas about "culture," rather than emphasizing that their ideas of "culture" are largely the same, or that they have much in common, or that they substantially overlap, or, which I have indicated as my approach elsewhere in this book, that it is largely difficult or impossible to usefully differentiate "French" from "German" culture (or *ideas about* culture) without ignoring hundreds of years of trans-border movement, the uneven distribution of knowledge, education, and ideology across the two countries, not to mention conceptions of "culture" that have circulated to and from well beyond France, Germany, or Europe. It is not only the case that French or German conceptions of "culture" at ARTE may not be generally representative of broader sets of beliefs in those two countries – Ingram's (2011) *Rites of the Republic* details the complexities and discrepancies among beliefs about "culture" in southern France alone – but also the case that we have weak empirical grounds on which to stand and assert that conceptions of "culture" are best understood, in this case, as nationally dichotomous. It may be that it is an urban/rural division (to offer one alternative social grouping, and one which Ingram traces) which better explains the genesis and reproduction of these "French" and "German" discourses of culture; it may be the case that these understandings of "culture" have been co-constructed and so are mutually contingent and symbiotic; or that there is ultimately more *alike* between understandings of "culture" in France and Germany (relative to the rest of the world, say) than there is meaningful difference (I do not pursue this argument here). It may be true that the whole of my discussion – detailing this dichotomous difference – is an artefact, a byproduct, of this chapter's assumption that divergent *national* histories and divisions can explain the variety of ways in which people at ARTE talk and think about "culture" (with the erstwhile assumption that national populations and their ways of thinking can be parceled off and boiled down to pithy explanation).

Lest we become embroiled in deeper questions of epistemology, I mean only to once again suggest in this aside that national frames of analysis (re)produce national difference in ways that may in some ways be explanatory and useful, but which in many other ways surely obscure, or just get plain wrong, the non-dualistic complexities of ("culture" at) ARTE.

uses of Culture and culture at ARTE

In the actual complexity of daily life at ARTE, *culture* and *Kultur* did not always neatly oppose themselves according to categories of Frenchness and German-ness. Germans did not always imply *Kultur* in its more usually German-oriented sense of *Bildung*, and French-speaking staff could, by *culture* (when it is made plural), quite easily imply what is usually associated with *Kultur(en)*. More interesting than pinpointing the etymologies of *culture* and *Kultur*, perhaps, are the ways in which ARTE staff wielded ideas and ideologies about "culture" in order to strategically make use of its various registers of meaning. Regardless of whether and how these might converge or diverge nationally, ideas about "culture" at this "culture"/"cultural" channel were often self-consciously activated in ways that drew upon contrastive definitions of "culture" as, on the one hand, about beauty and humanist-universalist aesthetics and, on the other hand, conceptions of learned, patterned behaviour vertically transmitted through bordered social communities and polities.

When producers at ARTE invoked "culture," they tended to clarify whether they mean something closer to *création* and the Arts, or bordered group-ness; at least as often as staff referred to "culture" in Malraux's sense of universal humanist uplift, they were likely to enunciate "culture" as an idiom of social difference. The constant shuttling back and forth between these (and other) renderings of "culture" at ARTE was partly a result of the highly fluid composition of contexts in which the term gets used: meetings often consisted of motley assortments of primarily French or German speakers, staff who may have spent equal amounts of time in the two countries, or a colleague who was primarily educated in Spain. A diverse staff brought different sensibilities to the table as they evaluated program proposals, and so how "culture" was deployed in a given instance – as a category of programming, as a mission to be actualized, or an idiom of belonging – was very rarely self-evident. The word was used advisedly, and with deference to its capacity for controversy.

Indeed, staff at ARTE were highly aware of the politics of a term that is in France, Germany, and the rest of Europe, often politicized and polarizing. One outspoken critic of ARTE, Dominique Wolton (1992), wrote about "culture" and ARTE, for example:

> You find [in ARTE] the limits of cultural television. Not only does it not resolve the current problem – improving the quality of programs for the general public concerning culture – but it contributes to creating a culturally elitist ghetto ... The risk of discrimination is particularly clear with culture that reinforces inequalities ... and which nourishes snobbism and elitism. (n.p., my translation)[15]

Here Wolton critiques ARTE's pretensions to administer a sense of (high) Culture that claims to humanize and civilize through the dissemination of, approximately, the "Arts." Wolton interprets ARTE's status as a "culture channel" to be about privileging *la création* in an elitist or esoteric sense that leaves behind the general public.

Sensitive to these kinds of critiques, ARTE producers tended to worry about what sense of "culture" they seem to be transmitting through programming decisions. They hesitated to acknowledge too rigid a sense of "culture" at a channel where this is understood to be a potentially controversial word, though for different reasons, in French, German and a number of other European languages. On the one hand, to claim the French conception of *culture* as *la création*, ARTE restricts itself to quite a limited repertoire of programming rooted in the arts, philosophy, and other subjects that resonate with Malraux's noble sense of enduring human *civilization*, which sometimes opens the channel to criticism, like that of Wolton (1992). On the other hand, for ARTE to imply that its sense of "culture" is more akin to *Kultur*'s sense of sociocultural belonging – that it is the *"European culture* channel" instead of a "European *culture channel"* – exposes ARTE to what would no doubt be strident critiques and questions about how ARTE thinks it can go about defining what "European culture" is or means. As a result, claims about the meaning of "culture" at ARTE were always in motion *between* these.

Indeed, there was a certain strategy to the ways in which producers and programmers at ARTE drew upon and shuttled between various understandings of "culture." In claiming to be *culturelle* and/or about *Europäische Kultur*, ARTE could comfortably reside in ambivalence and ambiguity about its mission and intentions. Because it is a "culture" channel in both French and German senses of "culture," ARTE avoids the responsibilities of claiming to represent a social Europe by retreating to *culture* in some more limited, French sense of the word; on the other hand, in deflecting claims of elitism or limited relevance, ARTEsans could call upon a more encompassing sense of "culture" – and cultures (*Kulturen*) – refuting that the organization was only interested in *la création* and the arts, asserting its identity as a broadly European, general interest channel about life in Europe and European peoples: the *European culture* channel.[16]

European C/culture and aesthetic citizenship

ARTE producers often draw upon discourses of "culture" in ways that braid together, or overlay, *la culture* with *Kulturen*. And here the inventiveness of trans-border cooperation – and points of French-German discursive entanglement – become clearer.

A thirty-minute program about organ music begins with a number of still shots of the grounds of an old German church, in silence. Finally the camera enters the corridors of the building itself and we see a number of monks who, having finished with prayer, file out of wooden pews, turning off lights as they go; the shot is exquisitely framed, and the lights are extinguished in neat rows that bring darkness to the image in symmetrical pieces. The music starts, the deep booming noise of a centuries-old organ. Yet this is not Bach, but a contemporary, discordant piece, and the performer doesn't use his hands at all but only his feet on the instrument's pedals. The camera frames his feet in a perfectly square medium-shot, with the pedals just beyond the frame, so that the man's well-shined shoes seem to dance like puppets on strings. The frame skips to a shot from the rear of the church, so that the man seems tiny against a backdrop of pipes; it jumps back to a close shot, then we watch his feet hit the pedals from above – the performer's own perspective. The many camera angles against the discordant music, and almost disembodied legs of the performer, have the effect of something like a medieval avant-garde film.

"European culture" in perhaps its most banal historical sense – a centuries-old cathedral, organ music, Catholicism – is re-framed through highly contemporary filmmaking. The way the performance is shot and edited – with almost experimental filmmaking emphasizing the way the player's feet jump and glide across the organ's foot pedals; with marked emphasis of the formalism of the church's architecture and lines; and with the long shot of monks filing out of pews and switching off lamps that renders them almost machine-like – presents, alongside the organ music, the much newer art form of cinematography, insisting upon the ways in which a camera can craft and comment upon a performance or happening even as it merely re-presents it.

In this music program, *Die vier Jahreszeiten der Orgel / Les Saisons de l'Orgue*[17] (2008), a historical sense of European *Kultur* or *Zivilisation* overlays *création*. "European culture" in its sociocultural demarcation of group belonging meets up with *culture* in its French implications of universal human heritage and artistic expression (which, not by accident, as Fumaroli [1991] pointed out, was pseudo-religious in André Malraux's conception).

Indeed, it is often both through *culture* glossed as the "Arts" *and* as behavioural group-ness that European-ness, or a European sensibility, comes to be narrated and assembled. On ARTE's long-running *Cuisine des Terroirs / Zu Tisch*, viewers travel to various European regions to watch, in situ, how exquisite Bavarian desserts, Hungarian goulash, or Spanish tapas are made, often in beautiful rural villages. But at some point during these thirty-minute magazine programs, the camera leaves the kitchen and moves around the village, introducing us to villagers, where we might learn of impending depopulation, of the double-edged sword of tourism, or about how problems with the fishing industry are affecting the local economy. I asked the assistant program director of the documentary-magazines programming unit if there wasn't a strategy on the part of the unit to use these seemingly ordinary and visually appealing topics to introduce viewers to more complex trans-European social issues. She smiled. "Of course we always try to bring viewers new experiences, new knowledge, even in a cooking show," she told me. Yet there is, in ARTE's double identity as the *European culture* channel and as the European *Culture channel*, a kind of audiovisual Trojan horse: the arts come to stand in for European belonging and identity, and European cultural belonging is made to seem equivalent to European Culture.

It is in this superimposition of Culture and culture (to offer English words that are not without their own translational issues), of creative *création* and the boundary-makings of *Kultur*, that ARTE assembles and performs an *aesthetic* sense of European belonging. In its various reconciliations and superimpositions of French and German understandings of "culture," Culture, and cultures, ARTE programmers attempt to communicate to viewers, "This is what Europe *looks* [or sounds, or tastes] like." One of ARTE's former slogans in German, *Das hab'ich nie gesehen!* (I've never seen *that* before!) refers to the complex dualism of ARTE's programming, on the one hand about *seeing* and beauty – sensorial engagements with the Arts – but on the other about learning and becoming – *Bildung*, perhaps – the one often concealing, or appended to, the other. It is in ARTE's weaving together of *la création* – gourmet cuisine, the sublime drone of organ music – with subtle politics of sameness – the common problem of depopulated rural places, a shared history of Christianity – that we find the rudiments of what might be understood as ARTE's construction of something like an aesthetic citizenship.

"We are obligated here, at ARTE … to *create something new*," one of ARTE's senior administrators told me in my first days at the channel. "We have to create with the old, create from our national differences. *La création*, creativity, is essential [*La création, la créativité, c'est essentiel*]. That's how we can build European culture." Of course, perhaps the administrator meant, "That's how we can build European *Culture*." My guess is that he would not have much wanted to clarify.

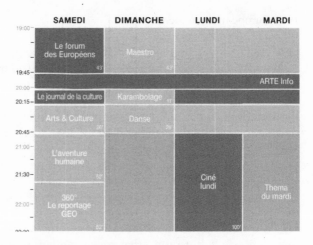

	SAMEDI	DIMANCHE	LUNDI	MARDI
19:00				
	Le forum des Européens	Maestro		
19:45	43'	43'		
20:00				ARTE Info
20:15	Le journal de la culture	Karambolage 11'		
	Arts & Culture 00'	Danse 26'		
20:45				
21:00				
	L'aventure humaine			
21:30	52'		Ciné lundi	Thema du mardi
	360° Le reportage GEO			
22:00				
22:30	52'		100'	

6

trans/national audiences

In a world presumed to be more globalized because it has become more mediatized, questions abound about audiences and to which audience(s) (or on whose behalf) these ever more widely circulating media claim to speak. If today there are a plethora of mass media, both broadcast and electronic, which claim to reach local, regional, international, cosmopolitan, transnational, or global audiences, little ethnographic research exists about how producers of these trans-border and multinational media contend with the problems of *who*, in fact, are the people engaging with these media: What tools and strategies do media producers deploy in order to discern who is watching? How do producers measure success in connecting audiences that have been historically, nationally, and locally constituted? What, in terms of content and narrative, seems to bring cross-border viewers together across presumably national habitudes and preferences? Finally, how do producers contend with fast-changing technology and the realities of twenty-first-century mediation in which audiences seem ever less coherent and able-to-be-cohered?

I will note here once more that this has not been a reception study – that is, a study of how audiences/viewers watch, engage with, and interpret programming. I chose to focus my efforts on understanding what was happening *at* ARTE rather than to also take on the question of how ARTE is watched and by whom (which would have, I concluded early on, spread my fieldwork too thin). I did, of course, regularly query a variety of people with whom I came into contact while in France and Germany about whether or not they watched ARTE and what they thought of it. And, I made a point of also asking a range of ARTE staff, on an almost daily basis, what they made of a program or film that had aired the evening before. But, in the main, I heeded the insight that Barry Dornfeld (1998) made in his pioneering *Producing Public Television, Producing Public Culture*, which argued for reconciling production and reception studies by recognizing that producers and consumers of media are not distinct, circumscribed groups (a model in which producers, as if sealed off in a secret room, send a "message" that audiences then "decode"), but rather that producers are *themselves* consumers of media and members of ARTE's audience. Like the PBS producers that Dornfeld worked with, ARTE staff often explicitly position themselves as viewers as they evaluate programming. Dornfeld (1998) reminds us,

> The very separation made between "audience members" and "producers" is an artefact of the history of mass communications scholarship tied to an industrial model of communications research. As such, it has become an ideological distinction that, when transcended, offers the richer conceptualization that production and consumption practices are intertwined. (14)[1]

Producers at ARTE contended primarily with two audience problems: On the one hand, media technologies – and how people use media platforms – are changing at a rapid rate. I was never fully able to decide, throughout my time at ARTE, whether producers and staff were able to ride and manage waves of technological change as these regularly swelled, or whether they were mostly being tossed and turned. Broadcast and internet technologies are changing (i.e., converging [Jenkins 2006]) in ways that keep producers and programmers guessing at how best to appeal to, and gather together, ever elusive audiences that today hardly resemble mid-century families gathered around a single household television, watching several consecutive hours, in real time. If the audience ever in fact cohered this way (Ang 1991), it certainly no longer does;[2] a massive proliferation of channels and on-demand programming over two decades have fragmented and dispersed viewers in ways that reorganize and interfere with the national (or transnational) imagined community (Marshall 2009; Turner 2009).

The question and problem of changing technology looms large in this chapter. But this chapter ultimately focuses on a second, related audience problem that I think is more interesting because it asks after the *stakes* of this changing technology. This related question has to do with the political economy of media – today largely understood at ARTE (and I would venture to guess nearly all media organizations) in terms of competitiveness. ARTE is a public media organization (with negligible advertising revenue) whose operation is funded, for the most part, by television taxes in France and Germany. But it also struggles, against the backdrop of a crowded world of media offerings, to regularly justify its existence, especially in a Europe with struggling economies and strained budgets. Although ARTE staff told me that they did not worry about (or even know) the size of its audiences in its initial years, over the last several years, administrators and government officials have increasingly scrutinized audience numbers as a gauge of the channel's reach and impact (and, implicitly, its legitimacy).

The upsurge in the importance of audience numbers aligns with Georgina Born's (2004) ethnographic evocations of neoliberalizing processes at the BBC:

> The BBC's infatuation with markets was ideologically and politically imposed. It generated a new value system in which entrepreneurialism was conflated with creativity ... [leading] to overcrowding in the centreground of programming and ever purer imitation of the BBC's rivals ... [This was] the inevitable result of the structural changes described, as well as of the BBC's continuing conviction that to retain legitimacy, the [BBC] must be popular, and that to be popular it had little choice in current circumstances but to ape commercial television. (178)

While I would not (yet) go so far as to argue that ARTE was aping commercial television, there was a pervasive sense that ARTE's days of producing television that they thought people *should* watch – without worrying whether anyone *wanted* to watch – were over.

Toby Miller (2007) summarizes debates about public versus commercial television by explaining that television has either been considered as a special kind of good requiring regulation – for example, the Federal Communications Commission (FCC) chair Newton Minow's famous appraisal, in 1961, that television programming constituted "a vast wasteland" requiring government (paralleling the founding ideology of the BBC and a number of other European public channels) – or that television was a widget to be bought and sold like any other – for example, Ronald Reagan's FCC head Mark Fowler's 1981 assertion that television was "just another appliance ... a toaster with pictures" (13–14).

Questions about viewers, audiences, and publics are necessarily related to long-standing questions about whether publics can and should be engaged, educated, or otherwise cultivated with television and other mass media, or if their purpose should be determined by demand and desires for distraction (Streeter 1996; McCarthy 2010; Ouellette 2002; cf. Debord [1967] 1994).

Even during my short time with ARTE, I witnessed the creep of competition and competitiveness (spurred on, in part, by the digitalization of television in France). During one of my first weeks at the organization, I arrived to find that several pages of audience number charts had been posted onto the walls of the building's elevators. People were outraged. "That's too much – they've gone too far now," were the first words of one of my colleagues as he arrived at the department. By later that morning, the charts and graphs indicating PDAs (*part d'audience*, ARTE's share of overall television audiences) from the previous evening's programming dominated conversation. At lunch, a senior programmer gestured to the elevators. "You see? This is what we're dealing with now – this idea that we're supposed to compete with TF1 or RTL – it's impossible." By the end of the day, however, it looked like the pages had been removed from the elevator – well, either removed or ripped down (remnants of paper and tape remained on the wall). That was the first and last day that PDAs were posted in elevators, at least during my time at ARTE.

What conceptions of (and debates about) audiences are in play at media organizations today, especially those that claim a trans/national or global scope? How and why do audience numbers matter? And, does a role remain for publicly funded media in light of the expansion, disintegration, and neoliberalization of media markets?

part I: the meaning of audiences at ARTE

How are audiences measured, and how do they come to be known and understood at ARTE? ARTE audience staff largely interpret audience numbers in ways that indicate still-national viewer preferences; measurement technologies and data, themselves nationally organized, seem to confirm (in what may be a self-fulfilling prophecy) nationally divergent viewing practices. At the same time, programming and audience staff have begun to develop innovative redefinitions of audiences and novel approaches in their efforts to reach, and to craft, trans/national publics.

national(ized) audiences

At ARTE's headquarters, I spent several weeks with the three members of its audience studies department. Their brightly lit office, equipped with five computer stations, and with big floor-to-ceiling windows overlooking the European Parliament and Council of Europe campus, was not a bustling place. Most of Sandrine, Marc, and Beatte's work consisted of culling spreadsheets of data for daily and weekly reports emailed to all ARTE staff's inboxes, or of silently streaming ready-for-broadcast programming on their monitors (with headphones) so as to reach an opinion about where something should be placed in ARTE's scheduling. After researching the past performance of various genres in various time slots, Marc would present the department's opinions and recommendations at a monthly programming meeting bringing together programming department heads and a number of the channel's administrators.

At the time of my research, ARTE subscribed to two national audience measuring companies, which release audience and ratings numbers several times a day; one targets audiences in France, Médiamétrie, the other those in Germany, GfK (Gesellschaft für Konsumforschung). The Médiamétrie software digitally connects to a huge audience database, with a variety of filters that one can select from, so that you can limit the data to visualize only ARTE's audiences, compare ARTE with another channel, or look at Thursday nights from 7 to 8 p.m. across all major channels, for example. Médiamétrie provides categories that can filter audience data according to gender (male or female), age (4+, 4–14, 15–34, 25–49, 50+), and two socio-economic groups, *CSP+* and *CSP-*. *CSP+* stands for a superior socio-professional category (*categorie socio-professionel supérieur*), including managers and executives (*cadres*) and professionals (*professions libéraux*). *CSP-* includes workers (*ouvriers*) and non-managerial staff (*employés non cadres*). There's also a category for *inactifs*, which somewhat ambiguously includes both students and the unemployed.

Every morning Sandrine would review with me freshly delivered audience numbers from the previous night's programming. "Well, see, this film didn't work because it is far too German." She was referring to the apparent lack of audiences for the film *Christine*, a 1958 coming-of-age story set in Vienna, which numbers seemed to indicate had only attracted an over-fifty-year-old, highly educated, mostly German demographic. Sandrine referred to these old movies as *patrimoniale* (patrimonial) – films that she said might include German *Heimatfilme*, for example, or a François Truffaut film. *Christine* was too German, but, by way of counter-example, she noted that Truffaut's film *Jules et Jim* (1962), which had also garnered a relatively small audience, was too French (although the narrative of *Jules et Jim* seems to, in fact, focus on the complexities of a French-German friendship).

When I asked Sandrine about what kinds of fiction films tend to best garner transnational audiences, she clicked through some audience data, refining her search to fifty recent fiction films that ARTE had broadcast during primetime to France and Germany. Next to each title was an audience share (*part d'audience*, or PDA) number representing the percentage of the total audience that a film had scored on a given evening. She moved down the list of films, sliding the eraser of her pencil down the matrix of behind-glass boxes on her screen: "See, okay, you would think this one would work – *Chocolat* (2000) – but it's been shown too many times." *Les Poupée Russes* (2005), a sequel to the popular *L'Auberge Espagnol* (2002), a film about European exchange students, had not "worked" well because, said Sandrine, it was not for a "general audience" (*grand public*). The high audience numbers, cross-nationally, for a 2004 film called *The Syrian Bride* (*La Fiancée Sirienne / Die syrische Braut*) confounded Sandrine, however – the German audiences were proportionally as strong as the French, even though, she said, "normally Germans could give a damn about anything having to do with the Middle East and the Maghreb." In reading up about this film later that day, I noticed that the film had been co-produced by French, German, and Israeli production companies. When I mentioned this to Sandrine the next day, she was surprised. "Really? Well, then that's probably why it worked well in Germany, too." When we later looked up *Christine*, the film that Sandrine had said failed with transnational ARTE audiences because it was a German *Heimatfilm* – far too German for French audiences – we discovered that, though the film is set in Austria, it was co-produced by French and Italian film companies, was originally in French, and had a French director. Sandrine was, again, surprised, but argued that the film still has quite a German "air" about it (*"mais ça a l'air d'être allemand"*).

Sandrine, Marc, and Beatte were prone to narrating and explaining audience numbers in almost exclusively national terms. As Sandrine cut and pasted together Médiamétrie and GfK data into tables and charts that she would send out to ARTE inboxes, the side-by-side national data seemed to consistently confirm that ARTE's transnational and European audience(s) was/were split by French and German national programming preferences; in fact, for audience studies staff, it seemed there was hardly a Franco-German or European audience or public to speak of, since the numbers seemed to indicate on a daily basis that a given program would disproportionately attract French or Germans, but rarely both in any kind of equal, proportionate way.

And yet there is much room for interpretation in these data. If media scholar Ien Ang (1991, 1996) has written extensively about the problems and assumptions of national audience measurement technologies, cross-national comparison of audience data is especially tricky because audience numbers are counted differently in France and Germany. Whereas France's Médiamétrie breaks down viewer categories into 15–34 year olds, 25–49 year olds, and 35–49 year olds, Germany's GfK has a single age category for viewers aged between 14 and 49 years old. What's more, the criteria that determine when a viewer has technically watched a program and counts as an audience member differ in the two countries; in France, one must watch for only thirty seconds, but in Germany it must be for a minute or more. The data were variously aggregated and compared in ways that surely could not take account of differences in survey techniques and demographics (level of education in German audience data versus in French data, to give one more example). Finally, as Sandrine pointed out, ARTE's ratings were often skewed by national coverage of sporting events, national political news coverage, or other kinds of intra-national happenings; the audience studies department simply could not always acknowledge or account for the ways certain programs might seem to have "failed" in Germany, but had actually, for example, languished as a result of an intra-national football match televised at the same time on a different German channel.

National bias and origins of the data were rarely acknowledged by staff. Though the data could be interpreted to show that French and Germans had very different ideas of what made for "good TV," the data were rarely recognized as already-nationally bifurcated and oriented, or in need of further contextualization or some kind of alternative measurement or agglomeration. As a result of how audience data were narrated and made meaningful, and of how the data were already nationally structured, audience numbers tended to avail themselves to the conclusion that a given film or program was either too "French" or too "German" in ways that were readily attributable to national preferences for a given genre or topic. Sometimes it was just the "air" of a program...

Politically themed nights of programming that ARTE broadcast on Tuesdays were understood to most clearly reveal audiences' national proclivities. A roundtable of experts talking about the Congo? This was a "disaster" for German audiences, explained Sandrine, because Germans don't care as much about West Africa (as a result of differences in French and German history). A discussion about the Russian natural gas giant Gazprom? The French didn't watch because they tend to be less interested in Eastern Europe and Russia than Germans. And yet Sandrine had no way of explaining the correlating proposition that German audiences are more interested, according to this same data, in theme nights of programming about hair, China, and diamonds, whereas French audiences seem to prefer programming about camels, prisons, and viruses. In these cases, national interests clearly make little sense as explanations. Yet, for almost any other germane genre, topical theme, or geographical area, audience studies staff could readily narrate and explain the numbers in terms of national difference and interests. "Our major 'handicap' is our bi-national audiences," Sandrine told me the very first day I spent with the audience studies department. "It's why ARTE will never have the audience numbers of other channels."

At the same time, even national audiences seemed, according to Sandrine, Beatte, and Marc, to be disintegrating and dissipating as a result of changing technologies. French television went digital during my fieldwork at ARTE, switching from its longtime Hertzian technology, thereby adding five or so channels to those that most every French household receives, suddenly reducing ARTE's – and every other major network's – national share.

"There is no loyalty anymore. People don't watch TV like they used to," Marc explained to me. "People aren't watching the same thing from one week to the next anymore." Beatte, whose job included monitoring ARTE's website traffic, went so far as to tell me that she could tell very little from the "hits" (visits) that www.arte.tv/guide/fr or /de registered, that they were only starting to collect and parse data about who was streaming ARTE programming, and what was happening to ARTE's audience as a result. ARTE had only recently become capable of monitoring how long people were watching online videos, and it was already clear that most hits correlated to less than thirty seconds of play time. Beatte's initial assessment was that users of ARTE's website were diverse and multinational in ways that seemed quite different from what the broadcast data seemed to indicate – ARTE's web audiences seemed, predictably, to be younger, but they also seemed to be more interested in trans-European topics and materials that could be accessed on ARTE's website in English. "But we just don't know," concluded Beatte. "We only just began presenting internet data at the programming meetings." As the measurement technologies were shifting, so too was the audience studies department's sense of who the channel's audiences were, and whether and how they cohered.

Talk about audiences at ARTE, then, tended to cast its transnational and European publics as alternately bifurcated, dispersing, or simply untrackable: ARTE's European audiences were understood to disassemble into national preferences; national preferences were understood to be fragmenting as ever more media filled the space once ubiquitously occupied by only a few national channels; and *all* the data – national and otherwise – were understood to be ever less reliable as audience viewing practices changed and diversified. Indeed, audiences were much less discussed as coherent audiences or publics, or as *the* audience or *the* public, but almost always referred to as *les téléspectateurs* and *die Zuschauer* – implying a disconnected assembly of viewers.

re-gatherings: ARTE as on-screen/off-screen

Partly because ARTE understands its multinational audiences to be divergent and dispersing – or in spite of this reality – the channel has begun to reconsider its audience(s) in ways that work towards reanswering the question, What is television? – a question that television scholars Graeme Turner and Jinna Tay (2009) argue has become once again central for today's broadcast industries (5).

Understood to be dispersing across channels and platforms, a singular ARTE audience was also, against the fray of nationally divergent spreadsheets and ever less reliable measurement data, partly being self-consciously reassembled. Several administrators with whom I spoke told me that the channel more and more thinks of its viewers as "reaching ARTE" not only through multiple media platforms, but also through the channel's physical presence at various festivals, concerts, debates, and events. The president of ARTE France, in a 2008 Radio France interview with sociologist Frédéric Martel (2006) at which I was present, cited ARTE's recent participation in the Festival de Verbier as one of its greatest recent successes – not only in terms of television audience numbers for the broadcast event, but as a result of having sold thousands of tickets to the event and having brought together "ARTE viewers in a different way ... around live music."

ARTE has found in recent years that one of the most successful means of increasing its visibility and interaction with viewers – even as these seem to elude the channel in measurement spreadsheets – has been its in-person presence at various film and art festivals, which it sponsors and in which it participates.[3] In late 2007, I attended the first of several of ARTE's sponsored public cultural events, located about forty-five minutes outside of Paris at a cinema and stage theatre complex called La Ferme de Buisson. I had seen the event mentioned on ARTE's website, but also in ads papered along walkways in the Paris subway. The title and theme of the event, TEMPS D'IMAGES (Time of Images), intended, as described in the festival program brochure and advertisements, to question the era in which we are living, which has become saturated with and defined by the ubiquity of images. (See this book's introduction for additional discussion of the TEMPS D'IMAGES festival.) Most of the events – which included ARTE films, original plays, student films, and performance art – focused on a kind of reflexivity towards the medium in which they engaged, and others: there were films about film, performances about film, films about performance, a play about television, and so on. One play I watched, for example, featured a stage endowed with several television screens on which we sometimes were able to watch characters' internal monologues. The theme of the festival seemed to signal and underscore ARTE's own reflexive role as a meta-medium, a kind of frame in which to present other kinds of emplaced (re-placed?) media – including screen and broadcast media like ARTE's own films and television programming, but always alongside or within more immediately present, personal, live, and interactive performances.

In early 2008, during the Nuit Blanche of Paris – an all-night city-wide event including everything from open museums to guided tours of government buildings to film and live performances – the staff of the production studio of ARTE's *Karambolage* program set up a large screen in the courtyard of the Maison de l'Europe (the Europe House), a beautiful seventeenth-century mansion which serves as the principal point of information about the European Union in Paris. The video installation, called "Ce qui me manque / Was mir fehlt" (What I Miss), consisted of a giant projection screen divided into sixteen squares, in each square a video clip play and pause. Every minute or so a different clip would play, in which a person living in a European country other than that of his/her birth would describe a particular food or object that he/she missed from his/her home country. The event drew crowds throughout the evening, some of whom I heard make remarks reflecting their familiarity with *Karambolage* and other ARTE programming, and others who seemed less aware of the channel or its particularities. (See chapter 3 for a fuller discussion of "Ce qui me manque / Was mir fehlt".)

ARTE participates in and sponsors (either in whole or in part) dozens of such events and festivals each year in France, Germany, and other

European countries, including several that travel across Europe. Three ARTE-sponsored events of particular note are the EuroGlobe Festival, the European Film Festival, and most recently, the *Europes* Festival – a diverse collection of events that travel to cities in thirty countries. ARTE's recognizable logo, orange and askew, appears across various ads for these festivals, as well as on banners and posters at the festivals themselves, "enframing" these various events, in Erving Goffman's (1974) sense of that term as *also* ARTE; in other words, we are to understand the performance of a play at an ARTE-sponsored arts festival to be intertextually linked to the various plays that ARTE regularly broadcasts. ARTE staff and administrators recognize the ways in which ARTE might extend its presence in its viewers' lives – not only increasing the brand's visibility, but also forging bridges between forms of ARTE media: an ARTE-sponsored concert broadcast on ARTE during which segments of ARTE television played on giant screens; an ARTE-hosted roundtable debate about the 1960s in Europe after which an ARTE documentary was screened – an event which, in turn, was filmed and featured on ARTE's website.[4]

ARTE is therefore increasingly "on-screen/off-screen," broadening the range of what it can claim as its programming, to include screenings, performances, debates, concerts, and readings that can directly engage with, and confront, audiences that are, in these contexts, less usefully translated into data (ticket sales, in comparison to television audience numbers, are negligible) but more easily understood by ARTE staff who are able to personally observe and meet with viewers in various transcontinental spaces. In these contexts, ARTE's audience is more often referred to in the singular because, at events, viewers become in-place and differently cohesive and coherent; when speaking about an event (in contrast to when they spoke about television and web audiences), I found that ARTE staff tended to refer to *the* audience in the singular, as "the public" (*le public / das Publikum*) rather than as an assemblage of abstract viewers.[5]

Considered to be one of ARTE's most successful programs of 2009 was a live performance of Verdi's opera *La Traviata* in Zurich's main train station, complete with a full orchestra, even as passengers went about their business buying tickets, boarding trains, and drinking coffee. ARTE received much positive publicity for the event as commentators reflected on the ways in which the channel was trying to refashion not just opera, but also television, by reimagining and innovating production models.[6] *La Traviata*, as well as each of the other various live events that ARTE sponsors and televises, demonstrates how ARTE is

shifting its approach from a focus on audiences as inconstant or dissipating, to live persons that might be gathered around opera, a political
discussion, or theatre.

ARTE's off-screen programming is a way of recollecting audiences
that are engaging less regularly, or less predictably, with its on-screen
programming, nevertheless bringing its viewers together around the
same kinds of themes and politics that orient its on-screen trans/
national sensibility: a Verdi opera, a debate about the political legacy of
the 1960s in Western Europe, a series of contemporary plays originating
in a number of European countries. These events are intended to foster
the same kinds of solidarities and sensibilities that ARTE's programming is meant to cultivate. Yet events like an opera staged in a train
station offer the added possibility and benefits of real-time collectivity and interaction among attendees, a kind of collective effervescence
ever more difficult to inspire through the shifting technologies and (in)
coherencies of traditional broadcast media.

The emergence of Anderson's (1991) national "imagined communities" relied, in part, on an imagined *simultaneity* of experience that readers thought they shared with others as they read novels or the news.
Such simultaneity – both imagined and real – has dwindled as media
have multiplied across screen technologies. Off-screen engagements re-
establish such simultaneity of experience, albeit in a differently mediated way; mediation in this case operates merely as a frame for, and
secondarily to, something much closer to face-to-face (i.e., unmediated)
social interaction.

Of course, such gatherings are in some ways limited by the physical size of their settings, and often, too, by language (which arguably
explains why a majority of ARTE-sponsored off-screen "happenings"
are musical). But these events are also able to amalgamate the immediately local and the trans-local in interesting ways; a Verdi opera set in
Zurich's main train station takes advantage of the immersive trope of
travel both real and imagined, and by relocating the opera in Switzerland it might argue for the relevance of its narrative to contemporary
Swiss society (and its provenance as more broadly European).

ARTE audience staff and administrators talk about audiences in no
singular or absolute way – but I would argue that they understand the
challenge of constructing a trans/national public at once as an intrac-
table problem of divergent audience data – national, inconsistent, and
ever less knowable as a result of ongoing technological shift – and at
the same time as a collectivity or demographic that might be otherwise forged and recollected through events and media happenings

Figure 6.1 Photograph from the filming/performance of *La Traviata* (2009) in the main train station of Zurich, Switzerland. In focus are the two leads of the production; visible in the background is a crowd of onlookers, spectators, and passersby. (Photo by Martin Stollenwerk, used with permission)

meant to *also* constitute ARTE television. In this way, television producers at ARTE are working to reach and reconstruct audiences not only as charts of discrepant data, but as people-in-place who might be interpellated as sharing common interests and identifications.

part II: the stakes of public media

Since ARTE began broadcasting from Strasbourg in the early 1990s, public television channels across Europe have faced growing challenges that threaten to permanently weaken or altogether eliminate publicly funded media from European airwaves. During my fieldwork at ARTE, French president Nicolas Sarkozy, citing a "new era" of mass media, proposed a law that would prohibit public television channels from commercial sponsorship, streamline and reorganize public television into a smaller number of divisions, and have the president of

France Télévisions appointed by the French head of state (i.e., Sarkozy) rather than by a separate, independent commission. Since public channels have increasingly relied on commercial sponsorships to remain competitive, Sarkozy's reorganization of media funding has resulted in a huge loss of funding for public television in France.[7] Italy's RAI public channel has likewise been subjected to several budget cuts and continues to be threatened with privatization by media mogul and prime minister Silvio Berlusconi.[8] As Georgina Born (2004) has pointed out about even the once-stalwart BBC:

> For all the high-level statements of public service vision issued by senior management over the course of the nineties, their preoccupations and the policies they unleashed worked in a contrary direction ... new guiding values were given low priority and displaced by other dominant concerns: efficiency, markets, value for money, audit and accountability. (252)

Alongside diminished budgets, digital televisual technologies have replaced antennae, providing viewers with access to a greater number of channels. On a typical night of programming during my research at ARTE, an audience report revealed that 5 per cent of all television viewers in France had tuned into the film *Rambo* (broadcast by a new digital channel), while only about 0.5 per cent of French audiences watched ARTE. American television series such as *Grey's Anatomy, CSI, CSI Special Victims Unit*, and several other police investigation spin-offs already garner, on a nightly basis in both France and Germany, upwards of 15 per cent of counted viewers. The fact that *Rambo* registered a million viewers suggests the effect of changing television technologies on public television: at least in France and Germany, there has been a net migration away from public television towards private channels whose programming focuses mostly on popular music, reality-based programming, and American-produced series and films.

On the one hand, the numbers seem to indicate that people would rather watch *Rambo* than a documentary; on the other, public media have been systematically undermined by governments who have favoured neoliberal policies of privatizing audiovisual industries over the past twenty years. These two issues – the one related to demand, the other to supply – were often understood by ARTE staff to exist in some kind of reciprocal or feedback relationship: audiences complain that most of what is on (advertising revenue-driven) television is terrible, but they still watch it; governments then argue that people seem to want to watch bad television and so can't justify the expense of funding media that people aren't watching ... This was understood to be a central neoliberalizing conundrum and feedback loop from which ARTE could not seem to escape.

For ARTE staff, the macroscopic policy-oriented problems and political economies of media were a source of localized, daily consternation. I cannot recall a meeting in the documentary department in which there wasn't reference to ratings and an argument about whether or not their logic of popularity should be heeded. Ratings and concessions to ratings were among those aspects of "the reality of ARTE" that people were most concerned I understood and would convey: "Audience numbers are the only thing that matters these days," people would tell me. "That's the sad fact." People would lower their voices when they talked about rumours that, should ARTE's market share in Germany fall below 1 per cent, the German government would cancel its partnership with ARTE France. No one could quite verify if this was true, but everyone had heard that it was – and ARTE's numbers in Germany never far exceeded this mythologized percentage.

Fretting over numbers had become central to everyday life and work at ARTE. ARTE's anxieties over its audiences, public image, and popularity may help us to understand how the problem of relevance is being negotiated by television producers today. These tensions and anxieties also reveal the mounting pressures under which public media especially, and increasingly, find themselves.

ARTE's audience aporia

A special episode of the popular German late-night talk show *Die Harald Schmidt Show* (now broadcast on ARD Das Erste) poked fun at ARTE with an opening segment that, in French (with German subtitles), announced that the night's show would have a special focus on the *plus ardent télé du monde* (the most passionate television in the world) – ARTE – with its *soirées 'Thema' prometteuses* (its promising "theme" nights). The talk show's exceptionally "French" opening segment featured a voiceover mocking the calm timbre of ARTE's ubiquitous female announcer. In the standup comedy which followed, host Harald Schmidt joked that ARTE was a good channel on which to watch films and theme nights about sex, and that it might as well call itself the "boobies channel." In a later segment, Schmidt came up with new slogans for German television channels, revising ARTE's German slogan (at the time): *Sehen sie selbst* (ARTE: See yourself) to *ARTE: Wir haben die ganze Intellekto-Scheiße* (ARTE: We have all the intellectual shit). The segment was shown to me

by an ARTE documentary department programmer because the programmer felt Schmidt had exactly, hilariously put his finger on ARTE's
popular image in France and Germany as a high-brow, elitist channel
with esoteric and difficult-to-understand films, documentary, and current events shows.

Schmidt also put his finger on one of ARTE's latest strategies for coun-
tering this image and for increasing its audiences: programming about
sex and sexuality, often featuring nudity. Theme nights and debates
about sex, the clitoris, internet porn, and orgasms garnered some of
the highest of ARTE's audiences in 2007 through 2009. Programmers at
the channel were somewhat ashamed of the strategy; of ARTE's online
on-demand videos, the documentary film made for the clitoris theme
night far exceeded any other ARTE film in number of downloads. "It's
so embarrassing," a woman in charge of ARTE's on-demand content
told me. "People are starting to think that that's what ARTE does now –
sexy television (télé sexy)."

The strategy reflects a long battle that ARTE has waged against its
popular intellectual image as the channel that people readily acknowledge as worthwhile and "high quality," but which they do not watch.
A widely circulated anecdote at ARTE is that, according to a recent
street survey that asked people in France what television they regularly
watch, almost half of those polled mentioned ARTE, despite audience
numbers which show that only about 4–5 per cent of French people
regularly watch ARTE; indeed, several people at ARTE told me that
when they tell people they work for ARTE, people often tell them that
they love ARTE, and then refer to a program that hasn't aired in five or
more years. In an interesting twist to Bourdieu's (1984) studies of the
stratification of culture, most everyone could refer to ARTE *as if* they
watched it – knew that they were *supposed* to find it interesting – while,
in reality, they rarely if ever did.

Worried that it will lose its legitimacy and so its funding, ARTE has
in recent years sought to increase its ratings by producing more "accessible" programming; the word is always "accessible," and partly refers
to programming about travel, popular science, animals, and foreign
cultures that tends to be more heavily expository and narrated than
ARTE's programming has traditionally been. But it has also included
various programming nights that are more sensationalistic and, well,
sexy – themes like "Teenage Sex Addicts," "[Islamic] Women Who
Refuse the Veil," and more celebrity-oriented American films like *The
Game* (starring Michael Douglas, 1997) and *A River Runs Through It* (starring Brad Pitt, 1992). This on a television channel that once prided itself

on broadcasting avant-garde and experimental work by little-known filmmakers and documentarians.

The audience studies and programming departments, with data indicating that ARTE's audiences are dwindling and aging, have steadily applied pressure to ARTE's production units to solicit and recommend programming that might appeal to a broader, younger demographic in order to compete with new digital channels and a proliferation of web-based video media. In the documentary department (and, as far as I could tell, in most every department) this was interpreted as a retreat from ARTE's editorial lines providing alternative, intelligent television – in other words, as a dumbing down and capitulation to the low production standards and spectacle of mainstream media. A longtime member of the documentary department explained to me in an interview that ARTE will "never have the audiences":

> We'll never have the audiences. Never! (*Mais jamais!*) We'll probably only ever have 3 or 4 per cent of the audiences in France … less in Germany … but if we broadcast these banal films, only documentaries that are "accessible" – the stuff you see on France 5, or M6 – we might get 6 or 7 per cent, yes, but where does that leave the "difference" of ARTE? We'll be another France 5, and then what's the point?

A senior member of the documentary department put it this way:

> The problem is, look … people watch television to relax. They come home from work and they want to watch a Hollywood film or a police show. They don't want to think. ARTE documentaries – look I watch ARTE from time to time but I watched a Kubrick film on ARTE last night and I had to really *think*, you know? [*We laugh.*] I mean, it's a beautiful film, I'm glad I saw it, but some nights I come home and I'm tired and I don't *want* to watch ARTE, to do the work of watching – I flip on TF1 and I watch whatever for an hour, and I eat, and I go to sleep … People don't want to use television to challenge themselves, it's pure escapism. And the audiences we want – people interested in long-form documentary or political debates – unfortunately for us, those people tend to not watch TV! They read books or go to see films at the cinema.

The ARTE staff and administrator describe varieties of a fundamental aporia in which the channel is mired: To gain audiences – and retain its legitimacy – the channel believes it must relinquish the perceived elitism and difficulty that audiences are said to perceive in its transnational culture-oriented programming. Yet, if it does so, while it may retain or gain audiences, it may lose its sense of purpose, difference, and raison d'être.

It isn't easy to step back from the transitioning of television, or to offer straightforward analysis or criticism of these trends, most obviously if the situation is understood as "do or die" (i.e., that an ARTE with too-dwindled audiences is likely to be defunded). Yet one way of thinking through such questions of demand, supply, and the purpose of public television is to resituate the technology and uses of television in terms that are not beholden to notions of audience reduced to size and revenue.

a (mild) polemic

Anthropology reminds us that television is a human technology – not unlike paint or a hammer – without, *a posteriori*, a privileged ideological end or use value.[9] Indeed, video and television have been used in otherwise low-technology settings as a tool for the reproduction of social knowledge to younger generations (Michaels 1984, 1994), or as a practical means of recording and displaying social collaboration and kinship during ritual performances (Turner 2002). It does not inherently or necessarily lend itself to social uplift, control, capitalism, or advertising and selling products, but is a technology merely enabling a certain kind of widespread dissemination of image-text-sound. To remember this – the multiplicity and fluidity of the social uses of media technologies – may seem pedantic or banal, but it is an increasingly important exercise given the encroaching assumption, or resignation, that television has been lost to entertainment and consumerist desire – or that, more or less inherently, watching television is an escapist practice (cf. Ginsburg 1994, 9–10).

Historically, public and governmental interventions into television have arisen out of myriad politics with highly variegated – and mostly incalculable – ideological effects. In the U.S. context, Anna McCarthy (2010) has written about the ways in which television was understood as a tool for disseminating conceptions of successful capitalistic living and citizenship to a postwar American public (14). Under John Reith, the BBC has provided perhaps the clearest example, bar none, of the self-conscious instrumentalization of television as a means of fostering particular national and civic solidarities (Born 2004, 23–96; Burns 1977; Briggs 1995). Anthropologists and other scholars have described a number of additional contexts across the world in which the small screen has been pressed into the service of teaching and crafting modern citizens and political subjects (Postill 2006; Abu-Lughod 2002; Mankekar 1999; Dornfeld 1998). Yet when and where citizenship has been yoked to television, it has nearly always been directed at a *national* population and nationally governed subjects who might, through audiovisual intervention, be interpellated as citizens, and inculcated into civic participation and a national civility, allowing for the transcendence of intra-national differences (especially those of class and race) (McCarthy 2010, esp. 83–116; cf. Mankekar 1999, 165–223). In other words, television has long been the handmaiden of politics, but these have overwhelmingly been national governmental politics, largely because television infrastructures – like those of electricity and the telephone – have more or less been state-constructed and state-regulated, corresponding to and residing within national boundaries.

In some important ways, ARTE differs from earlier televisual projects of governmentality. As one of the last founded major public television channels in the world, the media ecology in which ARTE today finds itself is radically different from public television that thrived in the mid- or even late-twentieth-century. The channel therefore provides an opportunity for reconsidering the role that public, non-private, or semi-public[10] media might continue to play given the contemporary context of now mostly privatized mass media industries. In a world in which television – palm-sized, downloaded, embedded, VR, or 3-D – is now widely considered to be more or less analogous (at least in terms of pricing models) to a toaster, I argue that ARTE remains, and should remain, a model for a "space apart" from an overwhelmingly neoliberal media marketplace.

As a governmental project, ARTE necessarily bridges the French and German states to the production of widely circulating audiovisual texts; it cannot, therefore, be said to stand outside or apart from national politics and interests, nor can state and public interests be fully disconnected from those of corporations, the market, and profit (McCarthy 2010, 3–4). Nonetheless, as I hope to have demonstrated in this book, state or corporate interests align in no simple way with the diverse and multiple sensibilities of those who work at or for ARTE, and production processes at the channel always draw in multiple authorships in ways that provide for a variety of kinds of programming and programs, which are themselves assemblages of semantic intentionality and compromise.

· No longer predicated on the consolidation of the nation, but not quite European, and hardly global, ARTE produces media that shuttle between, and variously conciliate, logics, scales, and narratives of belonging. Its programming therefore represents (and sometimes gives voice to) a variety of cultural perspectives and communities, which articulate a variety of political claims and social priorities. Situated within and among borders and boundaries, this is a highly self-conscious project that must continually ask after what ARTE is and means, requiring answers that may be as contradictory as they are tentative. This, ultimately, may be both the channel's greatest strength and its greatest weakness: audiences – or audience data, in any case – can only shed quite a dim light on the impact and meaning of a media organization that (for the most part) continues to push against defining its purpose in terms of commerce, popularity, or entertainment.

While it may be true that ARTE is – Harald Schmidt was not entirely wrong – the place to find "all the intellectual shit," there are very few places left in the landscape of global television for debates about the political legacy of the 1960s in Europe or for a series about philosophy. Although such programs seem hardly to be in demand – and even if we could ascertain that they are objectively not wanted by audiences – there are good reasons, in explicit opposition to the logic that audience numbers should adjudicate or legitimate the circulation of some kinds of media and not others, to insist upon the importance of preserving public media like ARTE. In what follows I hope to demonstrate why this is especially true in today's Europe.

producing public (multi-)culture

In early 2011, ARTE's long-running *Metropolis* program broadcast the recent composition *Nya (Trusting in Life)*, choreographed by Abou Lagraa for the Contemporary Unit of the National Algerian Ballet. *Nya* was produced by the Mediterranean Cultural Bridge, a project financially supported by French and Algerian governments which, according to the *Nya* website, provides "a chance to create, to imagine and, above all, to give a more accurate picture of … young Algerian people." The description continues:

> These young people get their strength from their eagerness to learn, their rich cultural heritage and their virtuosity in hip-hop dance. The purpose of this training is to set classical ballet basics and to teach the fundamentals in contemporary dance, while respecting the unique identity and history of each dancer.
>
> *Nya*, an Arabic word meaning "to trust in life," was an obvious title for this creation. In fact, in Algeria, ever since our earliest childhood, we have learned this word from our parents, a word related to God and which is

part of everyday vocabulary. The one who possesses this *Nya* will be able to turn all the suffering into strength, and will help to blossom, to open up to the world. This creation is a diptych, two pieces on two different musics illustrating both French and Algerian collective memories: *Boléro* by Maurice Ravel [and] *Songs* by Houria Aïchi.[11]

Metropolis broadcast a three-minute excerpt from the *Songs* half of the performance, with dancers combining movements like breakdance spins with more fluid gestures drawn from modern contemporary dance. Thin sprays of mist at the front of the stage impart a kind of smoke-like fog that hovers just above the floor, and as the performance continues the dancers are able to take advantage of the stage's increasingly slick surface; their spins accelerate and their dancing at times resembles controlled slipping in a way that is mesmerizing and beautiful. The thirty-minute current events and arts magazine *Metropolis*, which each week compiles excerpts from festivals, exhibits, arts, and events happening in cities throughout Europe, is one of a very small number of means by which such a performance can be conveyed to an audience larger than those able to buy tickets to the Paris theatre where the dance was performed. The dance, and the Mediterranean Cultural Bridge project, challenges audiences to think about culture and cultural difference in ways that fit no easy box. *Nya* is about a crossroads and assemblage of identities and identifications – not just about French, Algerian, Muslim, and European identities, but also about being at once religious and secular, both French-Algerian and Algerian, masculine and feminine, and a number of other seemingly incongruent or irreconcilable ideologies and embodiments. In *Nya*, these are braided into a performance seamlessly combining hip-hop, modern dance, classical ballet, and breakdance.

Public media that are able to at least partially ignore how many and what kinds of audiences are tuning in can provide visibility of cultural practices, exchange, debate, and, ultimately, representations that may not always be popularly validated or compatible with audience demand (cf. Ginsburg 2005). Such representations matter, even if they are only passingly acknowledged by French, Germans, and other Europeans as *also* "legitimate culture" alongside ARTE's programming about paintings at the Louvre or eighteenth-century continental philosophy. We should also remember that if ARTE garners only a 1 per cent audience share in France-Germany, this very roughly translates into something like 500,000 viewers – which does not include the wider distribution of ARTE's programming to six other major European television channels, and widespread access to its programming through web-based video and media. As a programmer in ARTE's performances department explained: "When a tiny per cent of audiences watch an opera on ARTE, this might be a hundred thousand people, compared to the few thousand that can see it at the theatre."

Furthermore, in her study of postwar American television, McCarthy (2010) reminds us of the importance of high-level public debate *surrounding* the production and programming of television – quite apart from the issue of reception and audience numbers – as potentially facilitating politically influential conversations among governing elites:

> From its inception, television assembled and connected members of distinct sectors of the governing classes who were seduced by, or at least curious about, its potential as an instrument for inculcating the values of liberal capitalist democracy. The existence of TV's mass audience provided these powerful people with opportunities to talk about and give form to the amorphous collectivity of the nation ... TV stood for certain ideals of access, legitimacy, and popular identification, and it therefore occupied a privileged place within ambitions of rule. (8)

Figure 6.2 Performing *Nya*; visible at the front of the stage are thin streams of mist. (Photo by Aït-Benalla)

In this sense, *Nya* seems an important displacement of, and inter-vention into, certain kinds of representations of French-ness and German-ness usually encountered on more "popular" (read, revenue-producing) French and German television.[12] Performances like *Nya*, dotted across ARTE's programming, hold potential for displacing – especially among government officials and elites who are likely to pay at least passing attention to what ARTE is airing – outmoded, overly simplistic, and problematic representations of French-ness, German-ness, and European-ness. This is because ARTE is a project that dwells, at its best, in cultural innovation, trans-cultural discourse, transactions of difference, and creativity.

The caveat here is, of course, that ARTE must recognize and accept the responsibility conferred by its exceptionalism. If we can commend the dynamism and complexity that ARTE – and other public media – can impart to representations of demographic constituencies and "culture," the channel must continue to cultivate thoughtful (and thoughtfully entertaining) programming. As Georgina Born (2004) has eloquently written about the BBC: "The BBC's role can no longer be primarily to represent a unified nation … It is to provide a unifying space in which plurality can be performed … It is a space in which plurality not only of information and opinion, but of expression, of aesthetic and imagina-tive invention, must have full rein" (517).

conclusions and provocations

media

When I began studying ARTE as a college senior, I thought I would be studying how mass media are "forging new kinds of transnational and global identities." I thought ARTE would reveal how national identities were being amended and amalgamated, remade by image/sound/text into trans-border sensibilities and commitments.

Fifteen years later, I realize that what I have been studying is, in fact, the emergence and application of a particular constellation of *beliefs* about media and about mass media's unmitigated power to cultivate and modify large-scale identities (which, at the outset of this project, I shared). In my introduction, I discussed this media ideology as trans-cultural mediationism. By this I mean a set of assumptions about a causal (and reciprocal) relationship between "global media" and "global identities" (or, "transnational media" and "transnational identities") – the idea that the more media expand and move across borders, the more they engender a world of shared sensibilities and mutual intelligibilities. This belief sustains ARTE as an institution and motivates many who work within its walls. The more people around the world who listen to pop music, who identify as fans of Harry Potter, or

who watch ARTE, the more "connected" the world is in some fundamental cultural way, giving rise to -isms like transnationalism, cosmopolitanism, globalism, and post-nationalism.

But if I learned anything from fieldwork at ARTE, it is this: Between
"trans-border media" and the "trans-border identities" which they are
thought to engender, there rest myriad interferences and contingencies.
From my perspective, after eighteen months or so of research, it was
more or less clear to me that ARTE does not produce anything like a
widely held or coherent French-German or European "imagination,"
although this was one of the founding goals (and a remaining impetus)
of the media organization.

In part, this was because ARTE has always had audiences limited in
scale as a result of other available channels and media outlets (of which
the number hasn't ceased to grow). In France, during the first ten or
so years of the channel's existence, only five or so national channels
were freely available (through terrestrial technology), so ARTE stood
to garner a considerable percentage of audiences; but in Germany, ever
since its inception, ARTE has existed alongside a dozen or more available channels.

And yet, although the past several years of digitalization have meant
a diminishing number of viewers who either stumble onto, or are loyal
followers of, ARTE's broadcast programming, an increasing number of
people visit ARTE's website to stream one or more of its programs.[1]
ARTE is recognized as being on the cutting edge, perhaps even the
frontrunner, of European television channels in its digitalization, rendering its website sleek and its programs easy to find and download
across several platforms (there's also an ARTE iPhone app, of course).
Few at the channel believe this à la carte model of viewership offers the
same possibilities for the cultivation of a collective sensibility, however.
These limitations (which apply arguably to all mass media today) raise
questions about whether and how mass media – (in what sense are they
"mass"?) – are able to give rise to "imagined communities" in today's
world.[2]

Although scholars like Milly Buonanno (2008) have argued that an
age of "narrowcasting" has replaced broadcasting (in which television markets are ever more thinly sliced according to interests, demographics, or geography), television studies scholar Graeme Turner
(2009) cautions against a reciprocal "digital orthodoxy" in which the
national institution of television is characterized as "paternalistic, old-
fashioned, and anti-democratic," while user-generated content and

digital technologies are celebrated as "liberat[ing] the consumer from political and regulatory containment" (57). He continues,

> It is important to recognize that what we are witnessing in this era of plenty is a diversification of the media diet, not the simple substitution of one form of consumption by another ... If we take a global view, there is limited evidence to suggest audiences have decided, categorically, that they no longer require the core public function of the national (public or commercial) broadcaster ... While this capacity may not necessarily be uppermost in the audience's mind as they make their choices, it is important to recognize that ... broadcast television retains the capacity to construct a sense of unity and belonging ..." (62)[3]

The question for this brave new world of "post-broadcast" television is not, I think, best framed as an "either/or" – either (national) television still contributes to a (national) sense of belonging or we are being atomized into particulate viewer-users with no sense of collective belonging. Rather, the question must be *dragged down* from imagined community – or else relocated *away from* imagination – to fundamental, researchable questions that will help us to revise *how* and *where* meaning is ultimately produced in this multiplatform ecology. This isn't a return to "media effects" research, but a thick description that might capture the particular dynamics of fragmentation (and/or diversification) of shared understandings of the world, and the particular practices through which everyday people engage with media technologies to make sense of the world around them. It is no longer analytically sound, in a post-broadcast world of memes, Al-Jazeera, ringtones, YouTube, and Snapchat, to presume that Chilean television crafts "a Chilean view of the world" or that its narratives are necessarily "dramas of the nation." Such relationships must be recast as *questions* rather than as readymade equations of mediation and identification, and all the more so, I think, for those media that claim to be international, global, or transnational in scope (Stankiewicz 2011).

Although ARTE cannot be said to ever have held the power of a Reithian BBC, neither is it as publicly marginal as an arcane YouTube series. The space between these is problematic for theorists because it is "too small" for Anderson's (1991) imagined community but "too big" to dismiss as cult, peripheral, or fleeting. Perhaps we might draw upon something like Stuart Cunningham's (2004) conception of "public sphericules" – a bit like Habermas (2009), but effervescent (bubbly!) – that might offer one means of reorganizing or perforating the too vast, too coherent "imagination":

> The spatial metaphor of fragmentation, of dissolution, of the centre not holding, assumes that there is a singular nation-state to anchor it. Thinking of public sphericules as constituted beyond the singular nation-state, as global narrowcasting of polity and culture, assists in restoring them to a place – not necessarily counter-hegemonic but certainly culturally plural and dynamically contending with western forms for recognition – of undeniable importance for contemporary, culturally plural societies ...
> (Cunningham 2004, 152)

It will not do, however, to simply replace "imagination" with "public sphericule" (or some other concept-metaphor) if the latter retains the problematic equation (rarely argued or proven in any careful way) that mediation automatically "gives rise" to social collectivity/ities. Rather, the breaking-down (carbonation?) of Anderson's imagined communities must establish the actual mechanisms that operate between mediation and collectivity – in other words, we might ask not only how and when sphericules form, but about how stable they are: How and when do they collide, expand, fizzle, or pop?

What's more, if we imbue these sphericules (or an alternative concept-metaphor) with affect and emotion – Cunningham (2004) argues that sphericules might better convey the "'*affective*' as much as '*effective*' dimension of public communication" (152, my emphasis) – perhaps these gas-filled, frothy bubbles and bubblings might better evoke the ways we are left with what Susan Sontag (1977, 9) might have discussed as "traces" of our encounters with pluri-media (what Michael Curtin [2009] calls "matrix media) – impressions, twangs, resonances, inklings, recollections, and, of course, images (but in the soft focus of memory, or coloured by nostalgia) – that percolate and "float up" in us rather than inculcate or inhabit us as media were (and to some extent still are) presumed to do in more rationalist, stable, linear, and spherically intact models.

I have tried to evoke, in my ethnography of ARTE, the ways that programmers' and producers' motivations and goals, along these lines, do not form into, or draw upon, any kind of stable European sensibility or imagination. The programs they produce take shape as they are assembled, bit by bit, as producers and programmers navigate their own impressions, hunches, and rememberings – shaped though they may be by training and education – in meetings, editing suites, and film studios. They do not pluck ideas from some broader collective "thing" (or narrative, or set of narratives, if you'd prefer) that can be called (i.e., consolidated into) an imagination or imaginary (at least I don't think this kind of formulation would help to explain very much). Rather, ARTE staff make a series of up-close, particular, concrete decisions that accumulate and gain momentum as a program sputters through the organization's concatenated, multilocal production processes. Programs (and ARTE's overall programming) are constituted through an accumulation of intended meanings –what Amahl Bishara (2012) has generatively called "accumulated authorship" (57) – but also, as I have shown, through *un*intended meanings (*banlieu* as melancholy), affective short-circuits (e.g., anger at a script), and gaps, conflations, and silences (e.g., mistranslations, approximate translations, the untranslatable). As we have also seen, what are understood by ARTE staff to be broadly humanistic, transnational, or cosmopolitan ideals and narratives often come to be embedded in, and entangled with, local, national, and narrower interests, assumptions, and claims to knowledge (if indeed we can even fully pull these apart).

Mediation at ARTE has to do with concrete knowledge, decisions, and interpretive moves – manifold and complex – that cannot be reduced to, derived from, nor extrapolated into "imaginaries" or an "imagination" in any broadly explanatory way. *Whose* imagination, after all? With reference to what stage or context of the production process? Should I conclude that iterated newsroom decisions to include Turkey in ARTE's maps of Europe amount to an "imagination" of an enlarged or more broadly inclusive Europe at ARTE? I would argue that I should not. Is my argument that national culture looms large at ARTE an argument about a Europe *imagined* as national, or as similar to a nation? I would argue that I'd prefer to avoid implying that national culturalism is "in people's heads" since it was at least as much a byproduct of not entirely mental production practices – and because, as I have pointed out, such an assertion is subject to a number of exceptions and caveats – conditionalities that the concept of imagined community would compel me to ignore. But, but … aren't there a number of imaginations in play, however intersected and contingent, worth recognizing nonetheless for how they are made, at moments, shared or stable? I would ask why we seek to preserve a concept that does not readily avail itself to the kinds of layered, dynamic, intersectional, particulate, and ultimately *different* kinds of descriptions and evocations that media pluralisms and ecologies today demand.

Although there is much more to say about mediation, my argument has been that mass media (often by way of imagination-imaginaries) are too often made to *stand in for* the social, to represent the social, and as evidence that some kind of cohesive social world exists. I hope that my description has hovered much closer to what people actually said and did, eschewing the assumption that a coherent "European imagination," or "imaginations," must have been in evidence at ARTE.

culture

Discourses of "culture" at ARTE diverge as a result of differential French and German understandings of this term as it emerged over the eighteenth and nineteenth centuries. But what I also learned about "culture" at ARTE is that, even when it is suspended in quotation marks, statements like the latter nevertheless invoke one of the central logics (and powers) of "culture," which is to differentiate and to *produce* coherent, delimited human groups. I hope to have drawn attention to this "cultural practice" because it was one very much in play among many ARTE staff themselves (who were, for one, concerned with devising and applying meanings of French-ness and German-ness, in terms of "culture" and otherwise) – a practice I meant to describe and think about, but without merely imposing, alongside or instead of these, my own (somehow superior) scholarly assessments of group-ness. To this end, I have tried to espy culture through something like a mirror that is at once opaque and translucent, both reflective and two-way. From the safety of my two-way mirror I have observed, described, and analysed the social world of ARTE, and much of my commentary has been critical of deployments of "culture," especially as national "culture." Sometimes, however, I have tried to draw attention to my own image (the image of an anthropologist) staring back at me, this person who assumes and puts to use the implications of "culture" (even when I did not use the word) to offer potentially circumscribed differences that split off the French from Germans at ARTE. For the most part, I have tried to push against such analysis and group production-differentiation; but in some ways, I am unable to fully escape its implication, for example, that these pages capture what (most?) people at ARTE are like – even with all my caveats, exceptions, and qualifications.

I hope, nevertheless, to have paid attention to "culture" and the ways the word is implicated in, and enables (and even encourages) straight-forward reference to "the French" and the "Germans" (and the "Euro-peans," the "Americans," etc.), as if these labels can faithfully convey likely cognitive and behavioural patterns and predilections. At ARTE, more than many other places perhaps, these labels are inadequate and often misleading; but I am not sure they hold any more explanatory power in a café in the Latin Quarter, or in a beer garden in Munich. Do these group terms map onto language use? To a substantial degree. But do they help to predict a person's ability to work in a group? Likely attitudes towards centralized authority? Do they explain why someone eats a daily yogurt? In asking collective labellings to gather together such predilections – especially when we are able to demonstrate how various claims simply do not align with (rarely verified) "realities" (yogurt!) – "culture(s)," quite simply, begin(s) to fall apart – perhaps especially national ones, but, again, see Stephanie Rupp's *Forests of Belonging* (2011) for a discussion of the fallings-apart of ethnonym and stereotype in the Congo River Basin.

All this is intended to suggest that we (anthropologists and non-anthropologists) pay closer attention to the ways that "culture" gets deployed – both when it is explicitly invoked, and when it is analytically implied, among anthropologists and the people in communities with which we work. As anthropologists have long asserted of their own uses of "culture," but sometimes also of others' uses of "culture" (see Comaroff and Comaroff 2009), the ascription of belonging – especially the circumscribed, bordered belonging of "culture" – is never without political implications and real-world consequences. I have tried in these pages to describe these politics in plain terms, showing how a sequence about how the French eat cheese, a photograph of the "wasteland" Parisian suburbs, a ballad about French-German reconciliation, and interpreta-tions of audience numbers, each in their own way reveals assumptions about who is authorized to give name and meaning to social worlds while, simultaneously, other kinds of (uneven) realities about belonging (and *important*, often *dynamic*, aspects of supposedly uniform belong-ing) are silenced or flattened. These kinds of descriptive practices are, in other words, *claims* to illustrate and define belonging, claims which work to ensure the stability of particular kinds of social order while others (other possibilities for social dis/order) are left unrecognized or unacknowledged.

In today's Europe, it especially matters when one reduces represen-tations of German "culture" or Germans to beer drinking or ancient monasteries, not only because these reduce the complexity of the history of the German nation-state, but because they also ignore the presence of immigrants and the ways immigrants have shaped and continue to shape Germany. This isn't only or necessarily about cultural citizenship (Rosaldo 1994, 2003) or multiculturalism, with all of its attendant politics (Shohat and Stam 2014; Rodríguez-García 2010; Vervotec 2010), but more straightforwardly about acknowledging (by rendering present) the demographic change and complexity of today's France, Germany, Europe, and world – closer, perhaps, to what William Connolly (2005) has discussed as pluralism. The "absent present" (Derrida 1967), throughout this book, has been and is the manifest reality that the population of Europe is changing quickly – and with it, much of what Europe (and European "culture") means and has meant.

If we seek to allow for difference and change in Europe so that different kinds of people can feel welcome there, anthropologists and non-anthropologists must (continue to) write against and speak back to mainstream (and not-so-mainstream) definitions and deployments of culture-qua-closure. Perhaps especially, *national* culture enacts and reproduces a retrograde misapprehension of a social planet that is today defined by unevenness, movement and migration, intersectionality, and confluence (if not necessarily convergence) – requiring what Alexis Shotwell (2016) calls a "distributed ethics."

But the answer is not, I have also argued, in any simple way the transcendence or melting-together of national "cultures" or belonging. The problem, once more, may lie with the kinds of conceptions of difference and similarity that the "culture" concept enfolds. If we think about national cultures as islands, monolithic spheres, or bounded communities, transnational and global processes are, correspondingly, understood through tropes of slow collision, hybridization, or amalgamation. In ARTE's media, these self-conscious processes were often represented by juxtapositions of French and German flags, switchings back-and-forth between French and German, or of conjoined silhouettes of the Eiffel Tower and the Brandenburg Gate. But such depictions, which imagine a joining together or bridging of cultures, tend to evacuate power and ultimately reaffirm holistic culture(s) as building blocks of cooperation and progress.

The complexity of contemporary global processes escapes any single metaphor (Tsing 2000). As human populations grow, disperse, communicate, and differentiate, there are violent collisions at the same time as there is growth of underground, rhizomic-like circuitries while, at the same time, some collectivities and solidarities swallow others whole, like the cartoon of a shark whose jaws yawn down upon a fish. Understandings of the world that portray "cultures" as clashing, merging, homogenizing, resisting homogenization, or arranging according to some other pattern or concept metaphor – even my sometime use of "assemblage" in this volume can be simplistic – may capture some particular event or dynamic, but necessarily miss something of the always-shifting tectonics of semi-global comings-together and comings-apart. Culture, I think, misleads us towards thinking through singularities that seem to be, then, naturally interconnected, pluralized, networked – when I would argue that it would be somewhat closer to the mark if we *began* with pluralities, interstices, intersections – multicommunities, pluri-subgroups, crisscrossed networks, braidings / frayings, and

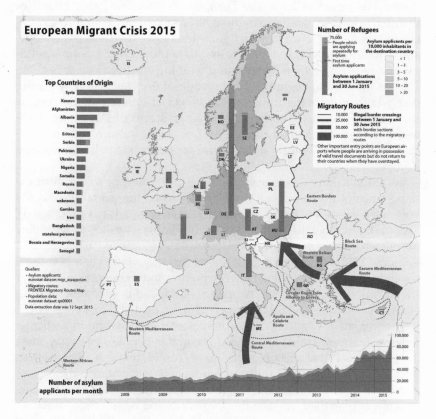

Figure 7.1 Asylum applications in Europe between 1 January and 30 June 2015. (Image from Wikipedia commons based on data from Eurostat)

haphazardly glued-together assemblages – as always already-comprising (and compromising) national-global dynamics. Thinking through "culture(s)" continues to obviate a rethinking and retheorizing of the World as neither a singular community, nor comprised of singular communities.

Europe

As I write this, Europe continues to emerge from an economic crisis. Refugees arrive in waves over land and by boat from the war in Syria and from armed conflict and poverty in other parts of the Global South. Britain has voted to leave the European Union, and other countries threaten to follow. Jihadist extremists have carried out a mounting number of attacks in France in which hundreds have died. Across Europe, and across the world, xenophobic and hate-mongering far-right political groups are gaining adherents and winning elections.

I was inclined to begin this final section of my conclusion by stating that, whether or not the arguments and theories I present in this conclusion seem plausible or convincing, the real stakes of this project have less to do with "imagined community" or "trans-cultural nationalism" than with people living, and those who are struggling to live, in today's Europe.

But I don't think this is true. To argue this would be to diminish the importance of debates about the fabric of social life (social theory). As Foucault has put it (which a great many social scientists have re-quoted), "People know what they do; frequently they know why they do what they do; but what they don't know is what they do *does*" (quoted in Dreyfus and Rabinow 1982, 187, my emphasis). I refer to this quotation here because it reminds us of the crucial link between politics and the seemingly small or trivial "micro-decisions" that happen at ARTE and myriad other institutions, public or private. Social theory reminds us that decisions at ARTE – however small – "add up" to express power in the world in particular ways as real power that affects and constrains people's everyday lives. This power isn't just a result of the image/sound/text that emerges from ARTE, but one that ARTE staff and producers convey among themselves and to others (including other elites) through their cobbled-together conceptions of who they are, who Europeans are, and who "others" are.

I have tried to show how ARTE's deployments, explicit or implicit, of "culture" variously circumscribe inside(r)s and outside(r)s. But here I would underscore that, despite myriad critiques of the culture concept and radical ethnographic experimentation, anthropologists and social scientists, too, are still quite beholden to the notion that "Japanese society," or Alsace, or Latin America, imply social sameness at some level (to some unknown degree), taking for granted "imagined" social scalings (national, regional, continental) across which difference can be presumed and described.

In a Europe in which "Europe" hardly signifies what it once did – various demographics indicate that European societies are diverse in complex ways (not just because of immigration, but intra-European migration, etc.) – what does, and what can, "Europe" mean? Does it too eagerly imply coherence and commensurability or comparability with other continental locatives (North America, Asia, Africa)? I would maintain that the way we teach and train undergraduate and graduate students continues to take regionality, and its implication of some degree of broad cultural similitude, at more or less face value. How might we rethink "Europe" in a way that undoes assumptions built into the very word (and sense of the World into which Europe, like a puzzle piece, neatly fits), presuming concentric semblance and contained difference, to instead emphasize social imbrications, intersectionality, non-linearity, unmoorings, fuzziness, bubblings, and/or anti-geographical practices, solidarities, and lines of flight?

In some ways this is the Gordian knot of a project about Europe, which seeks to complicate "Europe," while being beholden to European ways of thinking, speaking, and writing. As Talal Asad (2007) has written:

> The very identity of a people as European ... depends on the definition of a selective civilizational heritage of which most of the people to whom it is attributed are in fact almost completely ignorant – a heritage with which even individual members of the elite (the civilization's guardians) are only incompletely familiar. This legitimizes the internal inequality of those embraced by the civilization as well as their difference from other peoples. In other words, it is not simply that a heritage is invariably selective; it is that the people are defined by the civilization that is supposed to be their heritage. And yet, sociologically, the people who are said to belong to that civilization are highly differentiated by class and region and gender. (10)

In his many writings on the problem of European discourses of self and other, Asad (1973, 1997, 2000, 2003) reminds us that the "myth of Europe" is predicated upon a kind of insistence on sameness, of solidarity, in the face of apparent intra-national (and transnational) difference.

As he argues above, the power of this claim has for centuries been expressed through a notion of civilization that people in Europe have long adhered to and into which they have been too happily enfolded.

What are the resiliencies of (European) civilization, of its power to include and exclude, and in what ways is our social theory beholden to (a product of) its implications of inclusions, of insides and outsides, of roundedness, purity, and sophistication? Questions of belonging at ARTE, of representations of belonging by ARTE, and of my own representation of ARTE all, I think, return us to the limitations of social solidities, imagined communities, and of assignations of sameness and difference to which we still seem anchored. The complexities and politics of a twenty-first-century Europe (and world) demand another kind of language, other modes of analysis (and synthesis), and new (simultaneous, multiple) metaphors – ways of saying / thinking / writing through which the warp and woof of un-bordered, cross-bordered, or trans-bordered, belongings can be more fully recognized, evoked, and dignified.

notes

introduction

1 Although Appadurai (1990) did, of course, discuss "disjunction" and was centrally concerned with the ways in which American media might take on quite different lives in the non-West (and vice versa), I would contend that the article has overwhelmingly been cited to argue for the permeability of borders and the global "flows" (which Appadurai discusses as "scapes").

2 This is, of course, more or less Jean Baudrillard's (1995) argument about the "simulacrum" in which the representation or copy replaces, or becomes indistinguishable from, the original and (implicitly) authentic.

3 Note that this argument is different in scale, if not also in kind, from an argument about media effects. The latter has mostly been framed as a question of behaviour and whether and how particular behaviours are framed and/or learned during engagement with media like violent video games, whereas I am interested in the understandings and uses of media at the level of the states and societies – at the level of "culture," to put it another way – and *beliefs about* whether and how media can be used to coalesce, shape, or remake these.

4 To offer one measure (subject to various caveats), the number of paper panels with "media" in the title at the 2008, 2010, 2012, and 2014 American Anthropological Association meetings were, respectively: 10, 34, 81, and 110.

5 There are several important exceptions to anthropology's mediational lacunae – Hortense Powdermaker published the ethnographic account, *Hollywood: The Dream Factory* in 1950, and we should note that a long tradition of anthropological filmmaking preceded the emergence of an anthropology of media (although many of these films tended to echo written accounts in their inattention, ironically, to the role of media technologies in the sociality of the communities that they documented). Margaret Mead (along with her partner Gregory Bateson) was an early and important advocate of visual anthropology as a methodological innovation and of attention to the relationship of culture and media more generally, as was the groundbreaking ethnographer and filmmaker Jean Rouch, whose films (even in the 1960s and 1970s) often referred to or explored the local meanings and impacts of radio, television, and film.

6 As Ginsburg, Abu-Lughod, and Larkin note in *Media Worlds* (2002), part of anthropology's interests in media may also be owed to a turn towards ethnographic methods in British cultural studies (4–5).

7 Among these are Dornfeld (1998), Mankekar (1999), Born (2004), Dávila (2001), Kosnick (2007), Wilson and Stewart (2008), Griffiths (2002), and Larkin (2008), among dozens of more journal articles.

8 See the "European Commission // 40 Years / Eurobarometer" report at http://ec.europa.eu/public_opinion/topics/eb40years_en.pdf, accessed 20 July 2015.

9 Note that just because much of the world is familiar with Madonna, Batman, Shakespeare, and Hello Kitty – and that their fandoms span borders – does not mean that a person in the United States and a person in Thailand share any kind of substantive understanding of Madonna that would amount to an "imagination," and I would argue that even the "global soup" of pop culture and Hollywood imagery does not amount to much of a coherent "imagination" or narrative (and not a concomitant "identity") except through additional recourse and reference to other kinds of social contexts in which these are received and made sense of.

10 In certain ways, Anderson's (1991) argument about "Creole Pioneers" comes closest to what I will argue constitutes, at ARTE, a transnational or post-national sensibility; that is, it was more clearly the act of working together, travelling together, and so on, that seemed to foster non-national ways of understanding self and other (see chapter 5).

11 "French" and "German" labels missed much when it came to ARTE staff's biographies and senses of self, which were often complexly transnational; many were from the Alsatian region, for example, and considered themselves to be neither fully French nor German. For this reason, in this chapter and elsewhere, I refer to ARTE staff as "French-speaking"

or "German-speaking," depending on language use at a particular ethnographic moment. In some cases, staff could speak both languages comfortably and readily identified as inhabiting a cultural borderland between (or beyond) France and Germany; referring to staff as French- or German-speaking offers one way of undoing the naturalness of "French" and "German" as monolith-like identitarian categories by emphasizing the temporal contingencies of language use and switching at ARTE (which coincided with many staff's abilities to deploy and enact different kinds of selves in different professional and social contexts at ARTE).

1. *bienvenue à ARTE / wilkommen bei ARTE*

1 In fact, production at ZOOM was divided 40 per cent between French and German poles, with the remaining 20 per cent produced by ARTE's headquarters in Strasbourg.
2 Furthermore, while a large part of ARTE's budget is provided by French and German governments (which accrue revenue for public media through an annual tax), much of ARTE's production work is subsidized (sometimes up to 50 per cent of costs) by European institutions through the MEDIA and EURIMAGES film subsidy programs (to support film production/industries in Europe and to encourage bi- or multi-national co-produced films).
3 Several books have been written that trace the long history of ideas about European unity. See the concise first chapter of Marie-Thérèse Bitsch's *Histoire de la construction européenne de 1945 à nos jours* (2004).
4 The Maastricht Treaty, Title 1, Article A.
5 Cris Shore's *Building Europe* (2000) provides a careful anthropological analysis of European bureaucrats' attempts to engineer certain kinds of social cohesion through policy and deployment of ideas about shared "culture."
6 *Rapprochement* has the additional overtone of reconciliation, and so holds particular resonance for the French-German context.
7 See chapter 4 for further discussion of the use and cultural logic of the Paris/Berlin homology.
8 For more on this conundrum, central to understanding ARTE and its evolution as an organization, see chapter 6 on audiences.

2. producing trans/national media

1 In fact, with few exceptions, ARTE is always a *co*-producer of its programming, never producing without the participation of another channel or source of production funds.

2 See chapter 5, on audiences, for further discussion of editorial lines and their centrality to ARTE's articulations of its identity and meaning in broader landscapes and global economies of media.

3 Lila Abu-Lughod (2004) writes, to this point, "Most radio and television around the world has been state controlled or in the hands of culture industry professionals who, as Stuart Hall (1980) has argued, tend to share the 'dominant codes' of the nation state. Whether to create loyalty, shape political understandings, foster national development, modernize, promote family planning, teach privatization and the capitalist ethos, make good socialists, or innocuously entertain, mass media have been viewed as powerful tools for social engineering" (12–13).

4 See chapter 5 for a fuller theoretical engagement with conceptions of "public" and the "public sphere."

5 One could argue, of course, as I will come close to doing in this section, that what the "classic" problems of philosophy are themselves to some extent vary nationally, and to a much greater extent trans-globally.

6 On the issue of the social lives of theory, see Dominic Boyer's (2001) thought-provoking article, "Foucault in the Bush: The Social Life of Post-Structuralist Theory in East Berlin's Prenzlauer Berg."

7 Audience data collected during fieldwork research, Weeks 30 and 31, Summer 2008.

8 *Karambolage* episode from 28 September 2008.

9 In the French-language version of the segment this is rendered: "En France, vous le savez, l'un des principes fondamentaux de la Constitution réside dans sa 'laïcité' et c'est la raison pour laquelle vous ne trouverez que très rarement une Bible dans la chambre d'hôtel. Ou alors, il faudrait, pour respecter l'égalité des croyances, mettre également à disposition des clients le Coran, la Torah etc, etc. En Allemagne, l'immixtion du religieux dans la société est beaucoup mieux admise. Par ailleurs, le protestantisme, religion – comme on le sait – très implantée en Allemagne, fait une grande place à l'Écriture Sainte." The German-language version of the segment renders this: "In Frankreich ist eines der Grundprinzipien der Verfassung der 'Laizismus', also die Trennung von Religion und Staat. Deshalb werden Sie dort nur ganz selten eine Bibel in einem Hotelzimmer finden. Oder man müsste, um alle Religionen gleich zu behandeln, den Hotelgästen auch den Koran zur Verfügung stellen, und die Torah, usw, usw.In Deutschland wird die Einmischung der Religion in die Gesellschaft besser toleriert. Und der Protestantismus, der wie man weiß in Deutschland sehr verbreitet ist, räumt der Heiligen Schrift großen Raum ein."

10 In the German translation this is rendered, interestingly, "This man, whom you all know well, is of course [*natürlich*] French …"

11 In French: "Monsieur que vous reconnaissez est bien sûr un monsieur français, figurez-vous que ce monsieur-ci, mais oui, que vous connaissez bien lui aussi est également un monsieur français ... Tous deux sont dans leurs cuisines françaises et tous deux ont une petite faim. Ils s'apprêtent à déguster un délicieux en-cas: voici donc une baguette bien croustillante, un bon camembert normand et, bien sûr, un petit ballon de vin rouge." In German: "Dieser Herr, den Sie alle gut kennen, ist natürlich Franzose. Und dieser Herr hier, den sie natürlich auch sehr gut kennen, ist auch Franzose ... Beide Herren sind in ihrer französischen Küche und beide haben ein wenig Hunger. Sie werden gleich einen köstlichen Snack zu sich nehmen: wunderbar knuspriges Baguette, leckeren Camembert aus der Normandie und natürlich ein Glas Rotwein."

12 "Religion in Germany," *Wikipedia*, https://en.wikipedia.org/wiki/Religion_in_Germany, accessed 21 March 2017.

13 It isn't just social class that structures, and is structured by, *habitus*, "taste," and lifestyle, though class most concerned Bourdieu (1984). *Distinction*'s treatment of taste explicitly focuses on the specific circumstances of "French" sociality and class structures, thus the book's relevance must be both relativized and broadened in light of the increasingly complexity of what it means to be "French" in the first place; in other words, *habitus* itself as a nationally relevant framework might be re-examined to take into consideration more contemporary, and fragmentary, dispositions towards French-ness.

14 This is a lyric from the national anthem of East Germany (the German Democratic Republic, DDR), written in 1949, *Auferstanden aus Ruinen* (Risen from Ruins), by Johannes R. Becher, music by Hanns Eisler. The lyric has been long recognized by East Germans for the irony of its "one Germany" when the song in fact signalled Germany's partition.

15 ARTE's "desk" stories, Pascale Guimier emphasized, are about a minute longer than those of France 2, which are one minute and forty seconds. "This allows us to be more complete," he explained.

16 More reports were shot in France and Germany than elsewhere, however, given the availability of production staff in these countries and the reduced costs of filming in Paris or Berlin, where ARTE producers were readily available.

3. trans/national belonging

1 Among the 250 or so staff that work at ARTE headquarters in Strasbourg, about half identify as French, half German, with a handful of self-identifying Austrian, Belgian, Swiss, and Luxembourgeois, and Italians

who are also sometimes counted among its staff (as official assignations of national origin). There used to be a designated coordinator of co-production activities with Spain's TVE channel, and with Poland's TVP, though these posts no longer exist at present. Almost 70 per cent of ARTE's staff are women; according to ARTE's human relations department, during my fieldwork the average age of staff at ARTE GEIE headquarters was forty-four. At any one time, there are about thirty university-aged interns distributed among ARTE's various departments and offices.

2 A heavily Swabian accent could be particularly challenging for northern Germans, for example.

3 Aesthetic practices were understood to differ between French and Germans on a number of levels. Colour was something the French understood better than the Germans, according to the French. "Everything the Germans send us is a little bit greenish," a French executive producer told me. A German editing style – like a German speaking style – was often understood to be less roundabout and more to the point. French and Germans alike agreed that the "mood" and ambiance of a film or program was more important to the French than the Germans. (See chapter 2's discussion of news production for more on these differences.)

4 And yet, she added, there wasn't "a whole lot" between the French and Spanish – she couldn't imagine a French-Spanish ARTE ever coming to fruition.

5 Interestingly, one book title is *L'Allemagne*, referring to the nation-state Germany, while the other is *Les Français*, the title referring to the French people themselves.

6 Whether Zabusky (1995) was merely reporting a "native" explanation for the use of stereotype or would posit an explanation that is coterminous with the scientists' is partly what is at stake in anthropological engagements with European stereotypes.

7 What's more, national cultural stereotype at ARTE was only sometimes "funny," or, as best I could tell, intended to be "funny." As often as they were followed by a smile or laughter, references to French parochialism or German unfriendliness were invoked to justify programming, hiring, and budget decisions. ARTE's culture of stereotype was not always, or even often, ironic, especially for those who were, through its logics, denied a broadcast or a job.

8 We might also set in conversation the politics of stereotype in Europe with studies of racial stereotyping in the United States. What might the politics of the stereotypical "Frenchman" have to do with "mock Spanish," for example (Hill 1993), or, perhaps more consonantly, with the emerging field of whiteness studies (e.g., Hartigan 2005)?

9 See Dominic Boyer's Spirit and System: Media, Intellectuals, and the Dialectic in Modern German Culture (2005) for an ethnographic and thickly historical-theoretical account of notions of "system" and structure among cultural producers in Germany.

10 The Culture and Personality School, largely formulated by Ruth Benedict, Margaret Mead, Gregory Bateson, and Geoffrey Gore, was perhaps the most concentrated and influential moment of anthropological theorization of national "cultures," with entire national cultures characterized in analogy with personality and psychological types (in which some cultures were, essentially, hot-blooded, others cold).

11 The film was nominated for the 2009 Academy Award for Best Foreign Language Film and won the 2009 Golden Globe for Best Foreign Language Film. ARTE France co-produced the film with Bridgit Folman Film Gang, Les Films d'Ici, Razor Film Produktion GmbH, and Noga Communication.

12 But see chapter 5 on differing political orientations of the French and German state towards support of the "arts" and its conflation with "culture."

4. re-presenting history on and at ARTE

1 According to the EU's website, these aim to "[foster] action, debate and reflection related to European citizenship and democracy, shared values, common history and culture" in order to "[bring] Europe closer to its citizens by promoting Europe's values and achievements, while preserving the memory of its past." See http://eacea.ec.europa.eu/citizenship/programme/action4_en.php, accessed 22 March 2017.

2 While some of these works are more "critical" of an attempt to construct a coherent European history or cultural history of the idea of "Europe," they evidence, nonetheless, efforts to make sense of the emergence of "Europe" as a central historical problematic, and introduce inquiry about Europe during historical periods in which, until very recently, the continent was understood to be more or less irrelevant. Pagden (2002), for example, acknowledges the extremely thin basis on which Europe can be said to have meaning in the ancient Greek world (3) – and yet in attempting to gather together what evidence he can, works to establish the relevance and the continuity of its meaning across great stretches of history and into the present.

3 The EU's "European Schoolnet" (http://www.eun.org/web/guest/home, accessed 23 February 2010) and "Learning Resource Exchange for Schools" (http://lreforschools.eun.org/LRE-Portal/Index.iface, accessed 24 February 2010) also offer thousands of texts and illustrations for teaching European history.

4 Historical programming data based on ARTE's twenty-four-hour programming schedule, November 2008.

5 This may be partly because many staff at ARTE's headquarters have studied in both France and Germany, have grown up on the French-German border, have spent part of their childhoods in the other country, or have bi-national parents – see chapter 3 on identities and identifications for more on the producers' own sensibilities.

6 Though it must be acknowledged that the extent to which films avail themselves to historical-cultural translation substantially varies, as does a particular programmer's own knowledge of French or German history.

7 Indeed, in the last pages of the textbook featured in the film, ARTE itself appears as an example of a new chapter in French-German history, literally suggesting that ARTE comes near the end of text-based histories of France-Germany (Geiss, Henri, and Le Quintrec 2006, xx).

8 As Stefan Berger (2007) notes, European histories differ in the extent to which there was agreement among historians about how to write national histories; whereas France had something of a "well-established ... national story line," and in newer nation-states like Italy and Germany historians often competed with state representations of history (55–6); nonetheless, by the early twentieth century inscriptions of national story lines tended to be "remarkably similar in makeup and structure" (61).

9 Perhaps ironically, anthropologists have tended to characterize "non-Western" and indigenous peoples as imagining the passing of time this way, less as events assembled in causal-linear succession – inscribed, printed, and disseminated – than as oral, personal, and moralistic narrativizations of human vulnerability to the workings of time. E. Valentine Daniel (1996) discusses this dichotomy, for example, in the Sri Lankan context, as one between presumably "objectivist" Western "history" and "transcendentalist," non-Western notions of "heritage" (27, 13–42; cf. Fabian [1983] 2002).

10 See chapter 5 for a discussion of the use of stereotype in this online quiz game.

11 The song's lyrics are all the more compelling because in 1940 Barbara (née Monique Andrée Serf) was forced into hiding with her family under Nazi occupation. Then only ten years old, the traumatic experience would come to influence much of her artistic work. See Sophie Delassein, *Barbara, une vie* (1998).

12 German lyric translations are from ARTE broadcast; English translations are my own and take some liberty in an attempt to retain some of the song's original alliteration and rhyme.

13 The case against the SNCF and the French state was brought by Georges Lipietz and his brother; exhaustive documentation about the case, and

links to various legal decision texts, can be found on Lipietz's website,
http://lipietz.net/spip.php?rubrique75

14 Wieviorka is the author of *Déportation et génocide: Entre la mémoire et
l'oubli* (Deportation and Genocide: Between Memory and Forgetting)
(Paris: Hachette, 2000) and *L'ère du témoin* (The Age of the Witness) (Paris:
Lavoisier, [1998] 2002), among many other books and articles.

15 Translated excerpts from original French transcription:

01:05:48

AW: La marge de manouvre de la SNCF a été extrêmement mince, puisque
son statut est en quelque sorte régie par la convention d'armistice qui suit
la défaite de la France, et qui prévoit qu'en matière de transport, les ... la
France doit soumettre aux ordres de l'occupant allemand ...

01:07:25

ARTE Docs: Donc c'est justement maintenant une explication comme vous
avez utilisé ce mot 'mince.' 'Mince,' ça veut dire, il y a quelque chose, qui
est petite, qui est mince mais il y a quelque chose. Et donc [le réalisateur]
voulait savoir, 'mince,' ça veut dire quoi ?

01:07:45

AW: Je crois que j'ai utilisé le terme de 'mince' pour ne pas dire qu'il n'y
avait pas de marge parce que, je pense qu'il y a toujours un petit peut de,
de 'jeu.' Mais, globalement, à partir du moment que la France a été vain-
cue, où elle s'est littéralement enfondrée devant l'avance de l'armée alle-
mande, et où le choix politique qui a été fait a été celui de collaborer, il n'y
a pas de possibilité d'exception dans la collaboration et dans la déportation
des juifs pour la SNCF.

01:08:51

AW: Peut-être aussi, si je pourrais ajouter quelquechose, que, en disant
'mince,' je voulais aussi dire que, on parle de la SNCF come d'une entité,
mais que il faut peut-être décliner ce qu'on appelle la 'SNCF.' La SNCF
est une entreprise, et dans cette entreprise, il y a comme dans toutes
les entreprises, différents échelons. Donc il est possible que à tel ou tel
endroit il y a eu la possibilité non pas d'empêcher la déportation mais
peut-être, effectivement, de ... d'agir encore que je ne vois pas exacte-
ment comment.

...

02:00:56

ARTE Docs: Donc est-ce que vous voyez une sorte de responsabilité de la
SNCF concernant les transports.

02:01:07

AW: Euh … comment dire … euh … Cette question devient difficile parce que … il y a des plaintes qui sont portés contre la SNCF. Donc la responsabilité, qu'est-ce que ça veut dire ? Est-ce c'est une responsabilité pénale, aujourd'hui, de la SNCF dans le cadre des procédures ? Dans ce cas-là ma réponse est non. Est-ce qu'il y a une responsabilité de la SNCF dans la déportation des juifs ? A l'évidence, oui. C'est à dire, on a, en somme, un certain nombre d'administrations qui ont, ou d'entreprises, qui ont rendu possible la déportation.

16 "… je crois que, il faut toujours mettre le focus sur ce qui rend toutes ces histoires insupportables, qui est que, on déporte pour assassiner."

17 Also see "*Das 'Octogon'- Komplott*" by Georg Hodel, in *Konkret 3* (2000), for something of a summary of preceding journalism and scholarship about the Octogon affair.

18 It is worth comparing, however, the role that American historian Robert Paxton (1972) played in setting off a round of intensive national debates in France about Vichy and the extent of French complicity with Nazi policies. In this case, an outsider was able to bring attention to a historical period that had largely (and likely willingly) gone ignored by intra-national historians. The impact Paxton's *Vichy France* suggests perhaps that it may not be outsiders per se that cannot comment upon certain kinds of sensitive national histories, but *particular* outsiders who may themselves be implicated in these histories and historiographies. (Thanks to Susan Rogers for this observation and insight.)

19 I use "scripts" and "scripting" here in contradistinction to Arjun Appadurai's (1990) use of these terms in his "Disjuncture and Difference in the Global Culture Economy" when he defines "mediascapes" (9); I refer to actual scripts and the ways these are taken up in discrete social contexts (in this case, ARTE's documentary department) to describe how they are given meaning and socially produced, rather than as a global metaphor that points, vaguely, to "cultural scripts" that are assumed to move, globally, as a result of unspecified transnational mediational processes.

5. culture, "culture," Culture

1 I use quotation marks when I mean to remind the reader of the fluidity of the word's meaning – that it is a particularly ambiguous term, especially as it circulates at ARTE – and should not be understood to have some sort of already commonly shared or intuited meaning.

2 I found that meanings of culture at ARTE differed from those bureaucratically produced and disseminated in Brussels (as described in Cris Shore's Building Europe [2000]), likely because ARTE staff were not charged with defining the term in any public, official, or institutionally uniform way.

3 Note that I am *not* arguing that there are objective differences between French culture and German culture, but in the ways culture is understood, by ARTE staff, to vary in France and Germany, and in French and German.

4 Douglas Holmes (2000) advances the argument that this particularly French logic – that society is a problem to be worked on – lay close to the core of the ideology of European integration, especially as conceived by French founding father Jean Monnet. Holmes traces the historical emergence of this doctrine through Catholic social doctrine to French technocrats. Of course, Emile Durkheim ([1893] 1912) can be considered to be one of the first French thinkers to frame the social and cultural community as a "problem" to be solved (through, for example, religion). Thanks to Susan Rogers for not letting me forget about Durkheim.

5 See Ruth Mandel's (2008) excellent discussion of Berlin's relatively new "cosmopolitan" spin and claims to *Weltoffenheit* in *Cosmopolitan Anxieties* (27–50, 87–108).

6 Jérôme Clément, "La création est au cœur de la mission d'ARTE," euractiv. com, 21 March 2007, accessed 21 July 2009. Translation mine.

7 Biographer of Malraux, Olivier Todd, quotes Jacques Chirac who explains why he approved the transfer of Malraux's ashes to a special honorary tomb at the Pantheon: "He was the General [de Gaulle]'s companion, he invented the Ministry of Culture … He had panache" (Todd 2002, x).

8 From Malraux's 1959 decree outlining the ministry's mission statement, here excerpted from David L. Looseley's *The Politics of Fun* (1997, 37). Translation mine.

9 Part of this "politics" has to do with the subsequent and ongoing debate about the extent to which administration of, and support for, the arts, should be centralized in Paris. Minister of Culture Jack Lang (1981–6, 1988–93) introduced a series of policies that allowed for the state to support more local and regional artists, for example, and which substantially widened the state's ideas of official culture; see chapter 1 of Mark Ingram's *Rites of the Republic* (2011) for a much more complete overview of French cultural policy.

10 "En ignorant la création de son temps ainsi que les nouveaux modes d'expression et de diffusion de la pensée … la politique des beaux-arts stérilise, sclérose, au lieu de vivifier, la culture dont elle se prétend la gardienne …"

11 "Jérôme Clément, Ecrivain et journaliste français," *Le Figaro Scope*, http://www.evene.fr/celebre/biographie/jerome-clement-17658.php, accessed 17 February 2017.

12 "Qu'est-ce que la culture, sinon un regard différent sur les autres, sur le monde? [C'est] une ouverture, une curiosité, une autre façon d'aborder le réel, qu'il soit exprimé par le talent des artistes (théâtre, cinéma, musique), ou saisi directement par ceux qui savent eux-mêmes regarder … [L]a télévision est au coeur d'un système de pensée et de relations sociales qui ne peut défendre des intérêts exclusifs de rentabilisation d'investissements. L'Etat doit assumer cette responsabilité sauf à accepter la domination de la sphère marchande sur les hommes et les esprits." It is worth noting that, in more recent years, the state's support of the arts has been challenged, both on the grounds that it continues to be heavily top-down (and elitist) and that protectionism of the arts spurns innovation. See Dubois et al. (2012) as well as the comparative edited volume by Poirrier (2011).

13 This etymology of *Kultur* and *culture* also happens to lie close to the centre of the fundaments of anthropological inquiry: "It is in the German intellectual tradition," writes George Stocking Jr. (1982), "that the roots of the culture idea, in both its humanist and anthropological forms, are most inextricably entangled" (201). The line between an ostensibly objective anthropological approach to culture, and "native" German ideologies out of which this analytical approach partly grew, here draws especially thin.

14 A point many critical anthropologists have asserted, including, and to list only a very few: Asad (1973), Fabian ([1983] 2002), Clifford and Marcus (1986), Rosaldo (1989), Abu-Lughod (1991), Fox (1991) (recapturing anthropology), Gupta and Ferguson (1992), Escobar (1995), and King (2002) (anthropology beyond culture).

15 "On trouve ici les limites de la télévision culturelle. Non seulement cell-ci ne résout pas le probleme actuel – redresser la qualité des programmes grand public concernant la culture – mais elle contribue à créer un ghetto culturel élitiste … Le risque de discrimination est particulièrement net avec la culture qui renforce les inégalités…et alimente snobisme et élitisme."

16 Indeed, in 2007, when Nicolas Sarkozy announced a plan to completely reorganize the public funding of television in France, and wanted ARTE to be included in the umbrella group of public channels *France Télévisions*, ARTE abdicated its French-ness altogether, declaring that it was a European channel that could not be subjected to French or any other national funding structures.

17 The French title drops the "four" (*vier*) of the German title.

6. trans/national audiences

1 On the other hand, there were some producers and programmers at ARTE who distanced themselves from ARTE audiences and viewers because they saw them either as lacking good taste or irrelevant to their work altogether. This parallels Sherry Ortner's (2013) findings among independent filmmakers in Hollywood who "make films to please only themselves and a small handful of people who share their tastes ... Independent filmmakers hope their films will find an audience ... but ultimately they are ready to say to hell with the audience if necessary" (51).

2 As Ang (1991) has written, "The television audience is taken-for-grantedly defined as an unknown but knowable set of people, not more, not less. In this way of thinking, the television audience becomes an object of discourse whose status is analogous to that of 'population,' 'nation,' or 'the masses.'" However, as Raymond Williams ([1961] 2001) has noted, masses are illusory totalities: there are no masses, "only ways of seeing people as masses" (289). In a similar vein, "'television audience' only exists as an imaginary entity, an abstraction constructed from the vantage point of the institutions, in the interest of the institutions" (Ang 1991, 2).

3 In French, these are referred to as *actions culturelles* (cultural initiatives) and in German usually, more broadly, as *Feste* (festivals).

4 The event at Sciences Po, entitled *Arrêtez le monde, je veux descendre!* (Stop the world, I want to get off!), began with a screening of the ARTE film *Générations 68* (ARTE France, 2008), directed by Simon Brooks, which was commissioned for the channel's 1968-themed programming. The event was filmed and is featured on ARTE's website, http://download.pro.arte .tv/archives/presse/2549882.pdf, accessed 12 April 2017.

5 I use both "public" and "audience" in this chapter, but not interchangeably. When I refer to "audiences" I mean aggregate viewers (television viewers and website visitors) that are measured and "imagined" by producers, programmers, and others, following Ang (1991); when I refer to publics, I refer to people who come in contact with ARTE's programming more broadly, who may or may not be counted, and who may or may not "count" in terms of ARTE's audiences, but who nevertheless are constituted (following Warner 2002) and self-constituted as having a collective interest.

6 See, for example, Muriel Frat, "Quand l'opéra descend sur les quais," *Le Figaro Magazine*, 30 September 2008; and, more recently, Antoine Pecqueur, "Filmer l'opéra autrement," *Le Monde*, 2 May 2010.

7 See "Le Téléprésident: Sarkozy Tightens His Grip over French State," *The Guardian*, 27 June 2008, https://www.theguardian.com/world/2008/jun/27/france.television, accessed 2 October 2011.

8 "Italy's RAI Hit by Double Whammy," *Variety*, 28 September 2009, http://variety.com/2009/biz/markets-festivals/italy-s-rai-hit-by-double-whammy-1118009259/, accessed 2 October 2011.

9 On this point, see the still very relevant enumeration of the various relationships between technology and ideology in Raymond Williams's first chapter of *Television: Technology and Cultural Form* ([1974] 2003).

10 See Serge Regourd's (1999) discussion of Channel 4 in the UK for what he proposes as an interesting compromise between public and private models of broadcast.

11 Read more about *Nya* at http://www.aboulagraa.fr/les-spectacles/nya, where you can also watch a video excerpt of the performance.

12 A Conseil Supérieur de l'Audiovisuel (CSA) study of mainstream French television revealed, for example, that 90 per cent of fiction, news, and documentary magazine program presenters are white. *Baromètre de la diversité à la television*, September 2009, http://www.csa.fr/Television/Le-suivi-des-programmes/La-representation-de-la-diversite/La-diversite-a-la-television/Le-barometre-de-la-diversite, accessed 15 March 2017.

conclusions and provocations

1 Indeed, during follow-up research in the summer of 2014, one of ARTE's program directors told me that he believed ARTE was, as a result of digitalization, in fact becoming *more* European as internet streaming (and platforms like YouTube) has, in effect, reduced obstacles that terrestrial and even digital television incurs as a result of disparate national distribution technologies, distribution rights, and so on.

2 I would add that, though present-day conditions of apparent "dispersion" or "fragmention" of mass media seem new, our contemporary circumstances may not be so dissimilar from the media pluralism of eighteenth- and nineteenth-century worlds of mediation. It may be worth reconsidering if "the mass media" have ever been able to produce the highly coherent imaginaries – national or otherwise – that the Andersonian theory posits.

3 I might quibble that we have never fully been able to ascertain the sense of "unity and belonging" that broadcast media, or any media for that matter, "retain the capacity to construct," except in the vaguest terms.

references

Abélès, M. 1992. *La vie quotidienne au Parlement européen*. Paris: Hachette.
– 1996. "La Communauté européenne: une perspective anthropologique." *Social Anthropology* 4 (1): 33–45.
– 2000. "Virtual Europe." In *An Anthropology of the European Union: Building, Imagining, and Experiencing the New Europe*, edited by I. Bellier and T.M. Wilson, 31–50. New York: Berg.
– 2004. "Identity and Borders: An Anthropological Approach to EU Institutions." Twenty-First Century Papers: On-Line Working Papers form the Center for 21st Century Studies. Milwaukee: University of Wisconsin. https://www4 .uwm.edu/c21/pdfs/workingpapers/abeles.pdf
Abu-Lughod, L. 1986. *Veiled Sentiments*. Berkeley: University of California Press.
– 1991. "Writing Against Culture." In *Recapturing Anthropology: Working in the Present*, edited by R. Fox, 137–62. Santa Fe, NM: School of American Research Press.
– 1997. "The Interpretation of Culture(s) After Television." *Representations* 59: 109–34.
– 2001. "Orientalism and Middle East Feminist Studies." *Feminist Studies* 27 (1): 101–13.
– 2002. "Egyptian Melodrama – Technology of the Modern Subject?" In *Media Worlds: Anthropology on New Terrain*, edited by F. D. Ginsburg, L. Abu-Lughod, and B. Larkin, 115–33. Berkeley: University of California Press.

– 2004. *Dramas of Nationhood: The Politics of Television in Egypt*. Chicago: University of Chicago Press.

Aksoy, A., and K. Robins. 2005. "New Complexities of Transnational Media Cultures." In *Media and Global Change: Rethinking Communication for Development*, edited by H. Oscar and T. Thomas, 41–58. Buenos Aires: CLASCO.

Althusser, L. 1971. *Ideology and Ideological State Apparatuses (Notes Towards an Investigation)*. New York: Monthly Review Press.

Amselle, J. 2003. *Affirmative Exclusion: Cultural Pluralism and the Rule of Custom in France*. Ithaca, NY: Cornell University Press.

Anderson, B. 1991. *Imagined Communities: Reflections on the Origin and Spread of Nationalism*. Revised and extended edition. New York: Verso.

Ang, I. 1991. *Desperately Seeking the Audience*. New York: Routledge. http://dx.doi.org/10.4324/9780203321454.

– 1996. *Living Room Wars: Rethinking Media Audiences for a Postmodern World*. New York: Routledge.

Angrand, B., and A. Marx. 2009. *Idées Reçues: L'Allemagne*. Paris: Le Cavalier Bleu.

Appadurai, A. 1990. "Disjuncture and Difference in the Global Cultural Economy." *Public Culture* 2 (2): 1–24. http://dx.doi.org/10.1215/08992363 -2-2-1.

– 1993. "Patriotism and Its Futures." *Public Culture* 5 (3): 411–29.

– 1996. "Patriotism and Its Futures." In *Modernity at Large: Cultural Dimensions of Globalization*, 158–77. Minneapolis: University of Minnesota Press.

– 2006. *Fear of Small Numbers: An Essay on the Geography of Anger*. Durham, NC: Duke University Press.

Asad, T. 1973. *Anthropology and the Colonial Encounter*. New York: Humanities Press.

– 1997. "Europe Against Islam: Islam in Europe." *The Muslim World* 87 (2): 183–95.

– 2000. "Agency and Pain: An Exploration." *Culture and Religion* 1 (1): 29–60.

– 2003. "Boundaries and Rights in Islamic Law: An Introduction." *Social Research* 70 (3): 683–6.

– 2007. *On Suicide Bombing*. New York: Columbia University Press.

Auslander, L. 2000. "Bavarian Crucifixes and French Headscarves: Religious Signs and the Postmodern European State." *Cultural Dynamics* 12 (3): 283–309. http://dx.doi.org/10.1177/092137400001200302.

Askew, K., and R.R. Wilk, eds. 2002. *The Anthropology of Media: A Reader*. Malden MA: Blackwell Publishers.

Balibar, E. 2004. *We, the People of Europe? Reflections on Transnational Citizenship*. Translated by J. Swenson. Princeton, NJ: Princeton University Press.

Balibar, E., and I. Wallerstein. 1991. *Race, Nation, Class: Ambiguous Identities*. New York: Verso.

Ballinger, P. 2003. *History in Exile: Memory and Identity at the Borders of the Balkans*. Princeton, NJ: Princeton University Press.

Barth, F. 1969. *Ethnic Groups and Boundaries: The Social Organization of Cultural Difference*. Long Grove, IL: Waveband Press.

Basch, L., N.G. Schiller, and C.S. Blanc. 1993. *Nations Unbound: Transnational Projects, Postcolonial Predicaments, and Deterritorialized Nation-States*. New York: Taylor and Francis.

Baudrillard, J. 1995. *Simulacra and Simulation*. Translated by Sheila Glaser. Ann Arbor: University of Michigan Press.

Beck, U. 2006. "Unpacking Cosmopolitanism for the Social Sciences: A Research Agenda." *British Journal of Sociology* 57: 1–23.

– 2007. "The Cosmopolitan Condition: Why Methodological Nationalism Fails." *Theory, Culture & Society* 24 (7–8): 286–90. http://dx.doi.org/10.1177/02632764070240072505.

Bellier, I. 2000. "The European Union, Identity Politics, and the Logic of Interests' Representation." In *An Anthropology of the European Union: Building, Imagining, and Experiencing the New Europe*, edited by I. Bellier and T.M. Wilson, 53–74. New York: Berg.

Berdahl, D., M. Bunzl, and M. Lampland, eds. 2000. *Altering States: Ethnographies of Transition in Eastern Europe and the Former Soviet Union*. Ann Arbor: University of Michigan Press. http://dx.doi.org/10.3998/mpub.15976.

Berger, S. 2007. *Writing the Nation: A Global Perspective*. New York: Palgrave MacMillan.

Berger, S., and C. Lorenz, eds. 2008. *The Contested Nation: Ethnicity, Class, Religion and Gender in National Histories*. New York: Palgrave MacMillan.

Beriss, D. 2004. *Black Skins, French Voices: Caribbean Ethnicity and Activism in Urban France*. Boulder, CO: Westview.

Bhabha, H.K., ed. 1990. *Nation and Narration*. New York: Routledge.

Billig, M. 1995. *Banal Nationalism*. London: Sage.

Bishara, A. 2012. "Circulating the Stances of Liberation Politics: The Photojournalism of the Anti-Wall Protests." In *Sensible Politics: The Visual Culture of Nongovernmental Activism*, edited by M. McLagan and Y. McKee, 139–48. Cambridge, MA: MIT Press.

Bitsch, Marie-Thérèse. 2004. *Histoire de la construction européenne de 1945 à nos jours*. Brussels: Editions Complex.

Boellstorff, T. 2008. *Coming of Age in Second Life: An Anthropologist Explores the Virtually Human*. Princeton, NJ: Princeton University Press.

Bonilla-Silva, E. 2006. *Racism Without Racists: Color-Blind Racism and the Persistence of Race Inequality in the United States*. 2nd ed. Lanham, MD: Rowman and Littlefield Publishers.

Born, G. 2004. *Uncertain Vision: Birt, Dyke and the Reinvention of the BBC*. London: Secker and Warburg.

Borneman, J. 1992a. *Belonging in the Two Berlins: Kin, State, Nation.* New York: Cambridge University Press.

– 1992b. "State, Territory, and Identity Formation in the Postwar Berlins, 1945–1989." *Cultural Anthropology* 7 (1): 45–62.

Borneman, J., and N. Fowler. 1997. "Europeanization." *Annual Review of Anthropology* 26: 487–514.

Bourdieu, P. 1984. *Distinction: A Social Critique of the Judgement of Taste.* Cambridge, MA: Harvard University Press.

Bowen, J.R. 2007. *Why the French Don't Like Headscarves: Islam, the State, and Public Space.* Princeton, NJ: Princeton University Press. http://dx.doi.org/ 10.1515/9781400837564.

– 2009. *Can Islam Be French? Pluralism and Pragmatism in a Secularist State.* Princeton, NJ: Princeton University Press. http://dx.doi.org/10.1515/ 9781400831111.

Boyer, D. 2000. "On the Sedimentation and Accreditation of Social Knowledges of Difference: Mass Media, Journalism, and the Reproduction of East West Alterities in Unified Germany." *Cultural Anthropology* 15 (4): 459–91. http://dx.doi.org/10.1525/can.2000.15.4.459.

– 2001. "Foucault in the Bush: The Social Life of Post-Structuralist Theory in East Berlin's Prenzlauer Berg." *Ethnos* 66 (2): 207–36. http://dx.doi.org/ 10.1080/00141840120070949.

– 2005. *Spirit and System: Media, Intellectuals, and the Dialectic in Modern German Culture.* Chicago: University of Chicago Press.

Briggs, A. 1995. *The History of Broadcasting in the United Kingdom.* Oxford: Oxford University Press.

Brubaker, R., and F. Cooper. 2000. "Beyond Identity." *Theory and Society* 29 (1): 1–47. http://dx.doi.org/10.1023/A:1007068714468.

Buonanno, M. 2008. *The Age of Television: Experiences and Theories.* Translated by J. Radice. Chicago: University of Chicago Press.

Bunzl, M. 2004. *Symptoms of Modernity: Jews and Queers in Late-Twentieth-Century Vienna.* Berkeley: University of California Press.

– 2005. "Between Anti-Semitism and Islamophobia: Some Thoughts on the New Europe." *American Ethnologist* 32 (4): 499–508. http://dx.doi. org/10.1525/ae.2005.32.4.499.

Butler, J. 1997. *Excitable Speech: A Politics of the Performative.* New York: Routledge.

Burns, T. 1977. *The BBC: Public Institution and Private World.* London: Macmillan.

Calhoun, C. 1997. *Nationalism.* Minneapolis: University of Minnesota Press.

– 2003. "The Class Consciousness of Frequent Travellers: Towards a Critique of Actually Existing Cosmopolitanism." In *Debating Cosmopolitics,* edited by D. Archibugi, 86-116. London: Verso.

– 2007. *Nations Matter: Culture, History, and the Cosmopolitan Dream*. New York: Routledge.

Cappelletto, F., ed. 2005. *Memory and World War II: An Ethnographic Approach*. New York: Berg.

Castells, M. 2000. *The Rise of the Network Society*. 2nd ed. Oxford: Blackwell Publishers.

Chalaby, J.K. 2005. *Transnational Television Worldwide: Towards a New Media Order*. London: I.B. Taurus.

– 2009. *Transnational Television in Europe: Reconfiguring Global Communications Networks*. London: I.B. Taurus.

Clément, J. 1992. "ARTE, enfin, l'Europe!" *Le Monde*, 26 September.

– 2002. "La culture n'est pas une marchandise comme les autres. C'est un bien précieux, notre âme." *La Tribune*, 30 May.

Clifford, J., and G.E. Marcus, eds. 1986. *Writing Culture*. Berkeley: University of California Press.

Coleman, J.S. 1958. *Nigeria: Background to Nationalism*. Berkeley: University of California Press.

Comaroff, J.L., and J. Comaroff. 2009. *Ethnicity, Inc*. Chicago: University of Chicago Press. http://dx.doi.org/10.7208/chicago/9780226114736.001.0001.

Connolly, W.E. 2005. *Pluralism*. Durham, NC: Duke University Press.

Critcher, C. 2006. *Critical Readings: Moral Panics and the Media*. London: Open University Press.

Cunningham, S. 2004. "Popular Media as Public 'Sphericules' for Diasporic Communities." In *The Television Studies Reader*, edited by R. C. Allen and A. Hill, 151-61. New York: Routledge.

Curtin, M. 2009. "Matrix Media." In *Television Studies after TV: Understanding Television in the Post-Broadcast Era*, edited by G. Turner and J. Tay, 9–19. New York: Routledge.

Daniel, E.V. 1996. *Charred Lullabies: Chapters in an Anthropography of Violence*. Princeton, NJ: Princeton University Press. http://dx.doi.org/10.1515/9781400822034.

Darian-Smith, E. 1999. *Bridging Divides: The Channel Tunnel and English Legal Identity in the New Europe*. Berkeley: University of California Press.

Dávila, A. 2001. *Latinos, Inc.: The Marketing and Making of a People*. Berkeley: University of California Press.

Debord, G. [1967] 1994. *The Society of the Spectacle*. Translated by Donald Nicholson-Smith. Brooklyn, NY: Zone Books.

de Swaan, A. 1994. *Social Policy Beyond Borders: The Social Question in Transnational Perspective*. Amsterdam: Amsterdam University Press. http://dx.doi.org/10.5117/9789053560693.

Debray, R., and Bernard-Henri Lévy. 1989. "Le prix de la culture." *Le Monde*, 19 September.

Delanty, G. 1995. *Inventing Europe: Idea, Identity, Reality*. New York: St. Martin's Press. http://dx.doi.org/10.1057/9780230379657.

Delassein, S. 1998. *Barbara, une vie*. Paris: Éditions L'Archipel.

Deleuze, G., and F. Guattari. 1972. *Anti-Oedipus: Capitalism and Schizophrenia*. Paris: Les Éditions de Minuit.

– 1980. *Capitalisme et schizophrénie*. Vol. 2: *Mille plateau*. Paris: Les Éditions de Minuit.

Den Boer, P., P. Bugge, O. Waever, K. Wilson, and W.J.V.D. Dussen, eds. 1995. *The History of the Idea of Europe*. New York: Routledge.

Depétris, F. 2008. *L'État et le cinéma en France: Le moment de l'exception culturelle*. Paris: L'Harmattan.

Derrida, J. 1967. *Of Grammatology*. Paris: Les Éditions de Minuit.

Dornfeld, B. 1998. *Producing Public Television, Producing Public Culture*. Princeton, NJ: Princeton University Press.

Dreyfus, H.L., and P. Rabinow. 1982. *Michel Foucault: Beyond Structuralism and Hermeneutics*. Chicago: University of Chicago Pres.

Dubois, V., C. Bastien, A. Frecermuth, and K. Matz. 2012. *Le politique, l'artiste et le gestionnaire: (Re)configurations locales et (dé)politisation de la culture*. Bellecombe-en-Bauges: Éditions du Croquant.

Durkheim, E. [1893] 1912. *The Division of Labor in Society*. New York: Simon and Schuster.

Ecker, A. 2004. *Initial Training for History Teachers: Structures and Standards in 13 Member States of the Council of Europe*. Strasbourg, France: Council of Europe Press.

Edmonds, A. 2010. *Pretty Modern: Beauty, Sex, and Plastic Surgery in Brazil*. Durham, NC: Duke University Press.

Elias, N.E. 2000. *The Civilizing Process: Sociogenetic and Psychogenetic Investigations*, edited and translated by E. Dunning, J. Goudsblom, and S. Mennell. 2nd ed. Malden, MA: Blackwell Publishers.

Escobar, A. 1993. "The Limits of Reflexivity: Politics in Anthropology's Post-'Writing Culture' Era." *Journal of Anthropological Research* 49(4): 377–91.

– 1995. *Encountering Development: The Making and Unmaking of the Third World*. Princeton: Princeton University Press.

Evans-Pritchard, E.E. 1940. *The Nuer: A Description of the Modes of Livelihood and Political Institutions of a Nilotic People*. Oxford: Clarendon.

Fabian, J. [1983] 2002. *Time and the Other: How Anthropology Makes its Object*. New York: Columbia University Press.

Fallers, L.A. 1974. "The Social Anthropology of the Nation-State." *The Lewis Henry Morgan Lectures, 1971*. Chicago: Aldine Publishing.

Fox, R.G., ed. 1991. *Recapturing Anthropology: Working in the Present*. Santa Fe, NM: School of American Research Press.

Friedman, S.S. 2002. *"Border Talk," Hybridity, and Performativity: Cultural Theory and Identity in the Spaces between Difference*. Vienna: Eurozine.

Fumaroli, M. 1991. *L'État culturel: une religion moderne*. Paris: Fallois.

Ganti, T. 2012. *Producing Bollywood: Inside the Contemporary Hindi Film Industry*. Durham, NC: Duke University Press.

Geiss, P. D. Henri, and G. Le Quintrec, eds. 2006. *Histoire/Geschichte: L'Europe et le monde depuis 1945*. Paris: Fernand Nathan.

Gellner, E. 1983. *Nations and Nationalism: New Perspectives on the Past*. Ithaca, NY: Cornell University Press.

– 2006. *Nations and Nationalism*. Malden, MA: Blackwell.

Geschiere, P. 2009. *The Perils of Belonging*. Chicago: University of Chicago Press.

Ginsburg, F. 1994. "Culture/Media: A (mild) Polemic." *Anthropology Today* 10 (2): 5–15. http://dx.doi.org/10.2307/2783305.

– 2003. "Atanarjuat Off-Screen: From 'Media Reservations' to the World Stage." *American Anthropologist* 105 (4): 827–31.

– 2005. "Black Screens and Cultural Citizenship." *Visual Anthropology Review* 21 (1–2): 80–97.

– 2008. "Rethinking the Digital Age." In *The Media and Social Theory*, edited by D. Hesmondhalgh and J. Toynbee, 287–306. New York: Routledge.

Ginsburg, F., L. Abu-Lughod, and B. Larkin. 2002. *Media Worlds: Anthropology on New Terrain*. Berkeley: University of California Press.

Gitlin, T. 2000. *Inside Prime Time*. Berkeley: University of California Press.

Goffman, E. 1959. *The Presentation of Self in Everyday Life*. Cambridge, MA: Harvard University Press.

– 1974. *Frame Analysis: An Essay on the Organization of Experience*. Cambridge, MA: Harvard University Press.

Griffiths, A. 2002. *Digital Television Strategies: Business Challenges and Opportunities*. London: Palgrave Macmillan.

Gupta, A., and J. Ferguson. 1992. "Beyond 'Culture': Space, Identity, and the Politics of Difference." *Cultural Anthropology* 7 (1): 6–23.

Habermas, J. 2009. *Europe: The Faltering Project*. Cambridge: Polity.

Hall, S. 1980. "Encoding/ Decoding." In *Culture, Media, Language*, edited by S. Hall, D. Hobson, A. Love, and P. Willis, 128–38. London: Hutchinson.

Handler, R. 1988. *Nationalism and the Politics of Culture in Quebec: New Directions in Anthropological Writing*. Madison: University of Wisconsin Press.

Hartigan, J. 2005. *Odd Tribes: Toward a Cultural Analysis of White People*. Durham, NC: Duke University Press.

Hedetoft, U.R. 1998. "Germany's National Identity: Normalisation by other Means." In *Break Out, Break Down or Break In? Germany and the European Union after Amsterdam*, edited by C. Lankowski, 1–11. Washington, DC: American Institute for Contemporary German Studies, Research Report No. 8.

Heidegger, M. [1954] 1977. "The Age of the World Picture." In *The Question Concerning Technology and Other Essays*. Translated by W. Lovitt. New York: Harper and Row.

Hellström, A. 2016. *Trust Us: Reproducing the Nation and the Scandinavian Nationalist Populist Parties*. New York: Berghahn Books.

Herrman, R. K., T. Risse, and M. B. Brewer, eds. 2004. *Transnational Identities: Becoming European in the EU*. New York: Rowman and Littlefield.

Herzfeld, M. 1985. "Of Horns and History: The Mediterraneanist Dilemma Again." *American Ethnologist* 12 (4): 778–80.

– 1987. *Anthropology through the Looking-Glass: Critical Ethnography in the Margins of Europe*. New York: Cambridge University Press.

– 2001. *Anthropology: Theoretical Practice in Culture and Society*. Malden, MA: Blackwell.

– 2004. *The Body Impolitic: Artisans and Artifice in the Global Hierarchy of Value*. Chicago: University of Chicago Press.

– 2005. *Cultural Intimacy: Social Poetics in the Nation-State*. New York: Routledge.

– 2015. "The Village in the World and the World in the Village: Reflections on Ethnographic Epistemology." *Critique of Anthropology* 35 (3): 338–43.

Hill, J.H. 1993. "Hasta La Vista, Baby: Anglo Spanish in the American Southwest." *Critique of Anthropology* 13: 145–76.

– 2007. "Crises of Meaning: Personalist Language Ideology in US Media Discourse." In *Language in the Media: Representations, Identities, Ideologies*, edited by S. Johnson and A. Ensslin, 70–88. London: Continuum.

Hobsbawm, E.J. 1992. *Nations and Nationalism since 1780: Programme, Myth, Reality*. New York: Cambridge University Press.

Holmes, D.R. 2000. *Integral Europe: Fast-Capitalism, Multiculturalism, Neofascism*. Princeton, NJ: Princeton University Press.

Holmes, D.R., and G.E. Marcus. 2005. "Cultures of Expertise and the Management of Globalization: Toward the Refunctioning of Ethnography." In *Global Assemblages: Technology, Politics, and Ethics as Anthropological Problems*, edited by A. Ong and S. J. Collier, 235–52. Oxford: Blackwell.

Hull, M. 2012. *Government of Paper: The Materiality of Bureaucracy in Urban Pakistan*. Berkeley: University of California Press.

Ingram, Mark. 2011. *Rites of the Republic: Citizens' Theatre and the Politics of Culture in Southern France*. Toronto: University of Toronto Press.

Irvine, J., and S. Gal. 2000. "Language Ideology and Linguistic Differentiation." In *Regimes of Language: Ideologies, Politics, and Identities*, edited by P. Kroskrity, 35–83. Santa Fe, NM: School of American Research Press.

Jarausch, K.H., and T. Lindenberger, eds. 2007. *Conflicted Memories: Europeanizing Contemporary Histories.* New York: Berghahn.

Jenkins, H. 2006. *Convergence Culture: Where Old and New Media Collide.* New York: New York University Press.

Judt, T. 2006. *Postwar: A History of Europe since 1946.* New York: Penguin Books.

Kahin, G.M. 1952. *Nationalism and Revolution in India.* Ithaca, NY: Cornell University Press.

Kastoryano, R. 2002. *Negotiating Identities: States and Immigrants in France and Germany. Princeton Studies in Cultural Sociology.* Princeton, NJ: Princeton University Press.

Kearney, M. 1995. "The Local and the Global: The Anthropology of Globalization and Transnationalism." *Annual Review of Anthropology* 24: 547–65.

Kelleher, W.F. 2003. *The Troubles in Ballybogoin: Memory and Identity in Northern Ireland.* Ann Arbor: University of Michigan Press. http://dx.doi.org/10.3998/mpub.16469.

Kim, E. J. 2010. *Adopted Territory.* Durham, NC: Duke University Press.

King, B. J. 2002. "On Patterned Interactions and Culture in Great Apes." In *Anthropology Beyond Culture*, edited by R.G. Fox and B.J. King, 83–104. Oxford: Berg.

Klumbyte, N. 2011. "Political Intimacy: Power, Laughter, and Coexistence in Late Soviet Lithuania." *East European Politics and Societies* 25 (4): 658–77.

Kondo, D. 1990. *Crafting Selves: Power, Gender, and Discourses of Identity in a Japanese Workplace.* Chicago: University of Chicago Press.

Kosnick, K. 2007. *Migrant Media: Turkish Broadcasting and Multicultural Politics in Berlin.* Bloomington: Indiana University Press.

La Croix. 1992. "ARTE: Enjeu Sans Frontières." 27 September.

Landau, A., and R.G. Whitman, eds. 1997. *Rethinking the European Union: Institutions, Interests, and Identities.* New York: Palgrave Macmillan.

Larkin, B. 2004. "Degraded Images, Distorted Sounds: Nigerian Video and the Infrastructure of Piracy." *Public Culture* 16 (2): 289–314. http://dx.doi.org/10.1215/08992363-16-2-289.

– 2008. *Signal and Noise: Media, Infrastructure, and Urban Culture in Nigeria.* Durham, NC: Duke University Press.

Lawrence, T., and N. Phillips. 2000. "Understanding Cultural Industries." *Journal of Management Inquiry* 11 (4): 430–41.

Lebow, R.N., W. Kansteiner, and C. Fogu, eds. 2006. *The Politics of Memory in Postwar Europe*. Durham, NC: Duke University Press.

Leggewie, C. 2010. *Seven Circles of European Memory*. Vienna: Eurozine.

Leibfried, S., and P. Pierson. 1992. *The Prospects for a Social Europe. Program for the Study of Germany and Europe Working Paper Series*. Cambridge, MA: Minda de Gunzburg Center for European Studies, Harvard University. http://dx.doi.org/10.1177/003232929202000305.

Lévi-Strauss, C. 1955. *Tristes Tropiques*. Paris: Librarie Plon.

Levy, D., and N. Sznaider. 2010. *Human Rights and Memory*. University Park, PA: Pennsylvania State University Press.

Lomnitz, C. 2001. *Deep Mexico, Silent Mexico: An Anthropology of Nationalism*. Minneapolis: University of Minnesota Press.

Looseley, D.L. 1997. *The Politics of Fun: Cultural Policy and Debate in Contemporary France*. New York: Berg.

MacDonald, S., ed. [1993] 1997. *Inside European Identities: Ethnography in Western Europe*. Providence, RI: Berg.

Mahon, M. 2000. "The Visible Evidence of Cultural Producers." *Annual Review of Anthropology* 29 (1): 467–92.

Mandel, R. 2008. *Cosmopolitan Anxieties: Turkish Challenges to Citizenship and Belonging in Germany*. Durham, NC: Duke University Press. http://dx.doi.org/10.1215/9780822389026.

Mankekar, P. 1999. *Screening Culture, Viewing Politics: An Ethnography of Television, Womanhood, and Nation in Postcolonial India*. Durham. NC: Duke University Press.

Martel, F. 2006. *De la culture en Amérique*. Paris: Gallimard.

Marshall, H. 2009. "Educating the European Citizen in the Global Age: Engaging with the Post-National and Identifying a Research Agenda." *Journal of Curriculum Studies* 41 (2): 247–67.

Mauchamp, N. 2006. *Idées Resçues: Les Français*. Paris: Le Cavalier Bleu.

Mayer, V., M.J. Banks, and J.T. Caldwell. 2009. *Production Studies: Cultural Studies of Media Industries*. New York: Routledge.

Mazzarella, W. 2013. *Censorium: Cinema and the Open Edge of Mass Publicity*. Durham, NC: Duke University Press.

McCarthy, A. 2010. *The Citizen Machine: Governing by Television in 1950s America*. New York: New Press.

Merry, S.E. 2006. "Transnational Human Rights and Local Activism: Mapping the Middle." *American Anthropologist* 108 (1): 38–51. http://dx.doi.org/10.1525/aa.2006.108.1.38.

Michaels, E. 1984. "The Social Organisation of an Aboriginal Video Workplace." *Australian Aboriginal Studies* 1: 26–34.

– 1994. *Bad Aboriginal Art*. Minneapolis: Minnesota University Press.

Miller, T. 2007. *Cultural Citizenship: Cosmopolitanism, Consumerism, and Television in a Neoliberal Age*. Philadelphia: Temple University Press.

Miller-Idriss, C. 2009. *Blood and Culture: Youth, Right-Wing Extremism, and National Belonging in Contemporary Germany*. Durham, NC: Duke University Press. http://dx.doi.org/10.1215/9780822391142.

Mitchell, T. 1991. "The Limits of the State: Beyond Statist Approaches and Their Critics." *The American Political Science Review* 85 (1): 77–96.

Myers, F.R. 2001. *The Empire of Things: Regimes of Value and Material Culture*. New York: School for Advanced Research Press.

Nairn, T. [1977] 2003. *The Break-up of Britain: Crisis and Neo-Nationalism*. 3rd ed. Champaign, IL: Common Ground Publishing.

Nardi, B. 2010. *My Life as a Night Elf Priest: An Anthropological Account of World of Warcraft*. Ann Arbor: University of Michigan Press.

Navaro-Yashin, Y. 2009. "Affective Spaces, Melancholic Objects: Ruination and the Production of Anthropological Knowledge." *The Journal of the Royal Anthropological Institute* 15 (1): 1–18.

Nelson, B., D. Roberts, and W. Veit. 1992. *The Idea of Europe: Problems of National and Transnational Identity*. New York: Berg.

Neveu, C. 2000. "European Citizenship, Citizens of Europe and European Citizens." In *Anthropology of the European Union: Building, Imagining and Experiencing the New Europe*, edited by I. Bellier and T. Wilson, 119–35. New York: Berg.

– 2002. "The Local Press and Farmers' Protests in Brittany: Proximity and Distance in the Local Newspaper Coverage of a Social Movement." *Journalism Studies* 3 (1): 53–67.

Niehaus, I. 2013. "Anthropology and Whites in South Africa: Response to Unreasonable Critique." *Africa Spectrum* 48 (1): 117–27.

Nolan, M.E. 2005. *The Inverted Mirror: Mythologizing the Enemy in France and Germany 1898–1914*. New York: Berghahn Books.

Nóvoa, A., and M. Lawn, eds. 2002. *Fabricating Europe: The Formation of an Education Space*. Dordrecht: Kluwer Academic Publishers. http://dx.doi.org/10.1007/0-306-47561-8.

Ong, A., and S.J. Collier. 2005. *Global Assemblages: Technology, Politics, and Ethics as Anthropological Problems*. Malden, MA: Blackwell Publishing.

Ortner, S. 2013. *Not Hollywood: Independent Film at the Twilight of the American Dream*. Durham, NC: Duke University Press.

Ouellette, L. 2002. *Viewers Like You? How Public TV Failed the People*. New York: Columbia University Press. http://dx.doi.org/10.7312/oull11942

Pagden, A. 2002. *The Idea of Europe: From Antiquity to the European Union*. New York: Cambridge University Press.

Partridge, D.J. 2008. "We Were Dancing in the Club, Not on the Berlin Wall: 'Black' Bodies, Street Bureaucrats, and Exclusionary Incorporation in New Europe." *Cultural Anthropology* 23 (4): 660–87.

Paxton, R. 1972. *Vichy France: Old Guard and New Order, 1940–1944*. London: Barrie and Jenkins, 1972.

Peterson, B. 2003. "The Politics of Leisure during the Early Days of South African Cinema." In *To Change Reels: Film and Film Culture in South Africa*, edited by I. Balseiro and N. Masilela, 81–121. Detroit, MI: Wayne State University Press.

Pingel, F. 2000. *The European Home: Representations of 20th Century Europe in History Textbooks*. Strasbourg, France: Council of Europe Press.

Poirrier, P. 2011. *Pour une histoire des politiques culturelles dans le monde (1945–2011)*. Paris: La Documentation Française.

Postill, J. 2006. *Media and Nation Building: How the Iban Became Malaysian. Asia Pacific Studies*. Vol. 1. New York: Berghahn Books.

Proust, M. [1913–1927] 1982. *Remembrance of Things Past*. New York: Vintage.

Rabinow, P. 1989. *French Modern: Norms and Forms of the Social Environment*. Cambridge, MA: MIT Press.

Regourd, S. 1999. "Audiovisual Liberalisation." In *Television and Broadcasting in Contemporary France and Britain*, edited by M. Scriven and M. Lecomte, 29–45. London: Berghahn Books.

– 2002. *L'exception Culturelle. Que Sais-Je?* Paris: Presses universitaires de France.

– 2004. "La culture comme enjeu politique." *Hermès* 40: 28–32.

Rey, H. 1996. *La peur des banlieues*. Paris: La Bibliothèque du Citoyen.

Richardson, T. 2008. *Kaleidoscopic Odessa: History and Place in Contemporary Ukraine*. Toronto: University of Toronto Press.

Ries, N. 1997. *Russian Talk: Culture and Conversation During Perestroika*. Ithaca, NY: Cornell University Press.

Rifkin, J. 2004. *The European Dream: How Europe's Vision of the Future Is Quietly Eclipsing the American Dream*. New York: Tarcher/Penguin.

Rodríguez-García, M. 2010. *Liberal Workers of the World, Unite? The ICFTU and the Defense of Labour Liberalism in Europe and Latin America (1949–1969)*. New York: Peter Lang.

Rogers, S.C. 1991. *Shaping Modern Times in Rural France: The Transformation and Reproduction of an Aveyronnais Community*. Princeton, NJ: Princeton University Press.

Rosaldo, R. 1989. *Culture & Truth: The Remaking of Social Analysis*. Boston: Beacon Press.

– 1994. "Cultural Citizenship and Educational Democracy." *Cultural Anthropology* 9 (3): 402–11.

– 2003. *Cultural Citizenship in Island Southeast Asia: Nation and Belonging in the Hinterlands*. Berkeley: University of California Press.

Rumford, C., ed. 2007. *Cosmopolitanism and Europe: Studies in European Regional Cultures*. Liverpool: Liverpool University Press.

Rupp, Stephanie. 2011. *Forests of Belonging: Identities, Ethnicities, and Stereotypes in the Congo River*. Seattle: University of Washington Press.

Sahlins, M.D. 1985. *Islands of History*. Chicago: University of Chicago Press.

Sandstrom, A.R. 1991. *Corn Is Our Blood: Culture and Ethnic Identity in a Contemporary Aztec Indian Village*. Tulsa: University of Oklahoma Press.

Sassen, S. 1996. *Losing Control? Sovereignty in an Age of Globalization. University Seminars/Leonard Hastings Schoff Memorial Lectures*. New York: Columbia University Press.

– 2002. "Towards Post-National and Denationalized Citizenship." In *Handbook of Citizenship Studies*, edited by E.F. Isin and B.S. Turner, 277–92. London: Sage.

– 2006. *Territory, Authority, Rights: From Medieval to Global Assemblages*. Princeton: Princeton University Press.

Schiller, N.G. 2005. "Racialized Nations, Evangelizing Christianity, Police States, and Imperial Power: Missing in Action in Bunzl's New Europe." *American Ethnologist* 32 (4): 526–32. http://dx.doi.org/10.1525/ae.2005.32.4.526.

Schiller, N.G., and A. Wimmer. 2002. "Methodological Nationalism and Beyond: Nation-State Building, Migration and the Social Sciences." *Global Networks: A Journal of Transnational Affairs* 2 (4): 301–34. http://dx.doi.org/10.1111/1471-0374.00043.

Schissler, H., and Y. Soysal, eds. 2005. *The Nation, Europe, and the World: Textbooks and Curricula in Transition*. New York: Berghahn Books.

Shohat, E., and R. Stam. 2014. *Unthinking Eurocentrism*. New York: Routledge.

Shore, C. 2000. *Building Europe: The Cultural Politics of European Integration*. London: Routledge.

Shotwell, A. 2016. *Against Purity: Living Ethically in Compromised Times*. Minneapolis: University of Minnesota Press.

Silverstone, R. 1985. *Framing Science: The Making of a BBC Documentary*. London: BFI Publishing.

Smith, A.D. 1971. *Theories of Nationalism*. London: Duckworth.

Sneath, D., M. Holbraad, and M.A. Pederson. 2009. "Technologies of the Imagination: An Introduction." *Ethnos* 74 (1): 5–30.

Sontag, S. 1977. *On Photography*. New York: Farrar, Straus and Giroux.

Soula, C. 1992. "ARTE: La Guerre des Cultures." *Le Nouvel Observateur*, August, 19–21.

Spitulnik Vidali, D. 1993. "Anthropology and Mass Media." *Annual Review of Anthropology* 22: 293–315.

Spivak, G.C. 2010. *Nationalism and the Imagination*. Chicago: University of Chicago Press.

Stankiewicz, D. 2011. "Discursive Disjunctions of Globalizing Media: Ideological Claims and Tensions at the French-German European Television Channel ARTE." In *Global Media, Cultures, and Identities*, edited by R. Chopra and R. Gajjala, 156–71. New York: Routledge.

– 2016. "Against Imagination: On the Ambiguities of a Composite Concept." *American Anthropologist* 118(4): 796–810.

Stocking Jr, G. 1982. *Race, Culture, and Evolution: Essays in the History of Anthropology*. Chicago: University of Chicago Press.

Stoller, P. 1997. *Contemporary Ethnography: Sensuous Scholarship*. Philadelphia: University of Pennsylvania Press.

Streeter, T. 1996. *Selling the Air: A Critique of the Policy of Commercial Broadcasting in the United States*. Chicago: University of Chicago Press. http://dx.doi.org/10.7208/chicago/9780226777290.001.0001.

Suny, R.G., and G. Eley, eds. 1996. *Becoming National: A Reader*. New York: Oxford University Press.

Thompson, E.P. 1967. "Time, Work-Discipline, and Industrial Capitalism." *Past and Present* 38: 56–97.

Todd, O. 2002. *André Malraux: Une vie*. Paris: Gallimard.

Tsing, A. 2000. "The Global Situation." *Cultural Anthropology* 15 (3): 327–60. http://dx.doi.org/10.1525/can.2000.15.3.327.

– 2005. *Friction: An Ethnography of Global Connection*. Princeton, NJ: Princeton University Press.

Turkle, S. 1997. *Life on Screen: Identity in the Age of the Internet*. New York: Simon and Schuster.

Turner, G. 2009. "Television and the Nation: Does This Matter Anymore?" In *Television Studies after TV: Understanding Television in the Post-Broadcast Era*, 54–64. New York: Routledge.

Turner, G., and J. Tay, eds. 2009. *Television Studies after TV: Understanding Television in the Post-Broadcast Era*. New York: Routledge.

Turner, T. 2002. "Representation, Politics, and Cultural Imagination in Indigenous Video: General Points and Kayapo Examples." In *Media Worlds: Anthropology on New Terrain*, edited by F. D. Ginsburg, L. Abu-Lughod, and B. Larkin, 75–89. Berkeley: University of California Press.

Verdery, K. 1991. *National Ideology under Socialism: Identity and Cultural Politics in Ceaucsescu's Romania*. Berkeley: University of California Press.

– 1993. "Nationalism and National Sentiment in Post-Socialist Romania." *Slavic Review* 52: 179–203.

– 2000. "Ghosts on the Landscape: Restoring Private Landownership in Eastern Europe." *Focaal: European Journal of Anthropology* 36: 145–63.

– 2003. *The Vanishing Hectare: Property and Value in Postsocialist Transylvania.* Ithaca, NY: Cornell University Press.

Verstraete, G. 2010. *Tracking Europe: Mobility, Diaspora, and the Politics of Location.* Durham, NC: Duke University Press. http://dx.doi.org/10.1215/9780822391364.

Vervotec, S. 2010. "Towards Post-multiculturalism? Changing Communities, Conditions and Contexts of Diversity." *International Social Science Journal* 61: 83–95.

Vianna, N. 2000. "Culture et télévision en Europe: le cas d'Arte." DEA thesis, University of Bordeaux. http://communicationorganisation.revues.org/2376

Warner, M. 2002. "Publics and Counterpublics." *Public Culture* 14 (1): 49–90.

White, H. 1973. *Metahistory: The Historical Imagination in Nineteenth-Century Europe.* Baltimore: Johns Hopkins University Press.

Williams, R. [1961] 2001. *The Long Revolution.* Orchard Park, NY: Broadview Press.

– 1983. *Keywords: A Vocabulary of Culture and Society.* New York: Oxford University Press.

– [1974] 2003. *Television: Technology and Cultural Form.* New York: Routledge.

Wilson, P., and M. Stewart, eds. 2008. *Global Indigenous Media: Cultures, Poetics, and Politics.* Durham, NC: Duke University Press.

Wilson, T.M. 2000. "Agendas in Conflict: Nation, State and Europe in the Northern Ireland Borderlands." In *An Anthropology of the European Union: Building, Imagining and Experiencing the New Europe,* edited by I. Bellier and T. M. Wilson, x, 205. New York: Berg.

Wilson, T.M., and H. Donnan, eds. 1998. *Border Identities: Nation and State at International Frontiers.* Cambridge, New York: Cambridge University Press. http://dx.doi.org/10.1017/CBO9780511607813.

Wimmer, A., and N.G. Schiller. 2002. "Methodological Nationalism, the Social Sciences, and the Study of Migration: An Essay in Historical Epistemology." *International Migration Review* 37 (3): 576–610.

Wogan, P. 2001. "Imagined Communities Reconsidered: Is Print-Capitalism What We Think It Is?" *Anthropological Theory* 1 (4): 403–18.

Wolton, D. 1992. "DÉBATS: ARTE, la culture et la television." *Le Monde,* 23 September.

Woolf, S.J. 1991. *Napoleon's Integration of Europe.* New York: Routledge.

Zabusky, S.E. 1995. *Launching Europe: An Ethnography of European Cooperation in Space Science.* Princeton, NJ: Princeton University Press.

index

ANTHROPOLOGICAL HORIZONS

Editor: Michael Lambek, University of Toronto

Published to date:
The Varieties of Sensory Experience: A Sourcebook in the Anthropology of the Senses / Edited by David Howes (1991)

Arctic Homeland: Kinship, Community, and Development in Northwest Greenland / Mark Nuttall (1992)

Knowledge and Practice in Mayotte: Local Discourses of Islam, Sorcery, and Spirit Possession / Michael Lambek (1993)

Deathly Waters and Hungry Mountains: Agrarian Ritual and Class Formation in an Andean Town / Peter Gose (1994)

Paradise: Class, Commuters, and Ethnicity in Rural Ontario / Stanley R. Barrett (1994)

The Cultural World in Beowulf / John M. Hill (1995)

Making It Their Own: Severn Ojibwe Communicative Practices / Lisa Philips Valentine (1995)

Merchants and Shopkeepers: A Historical Anthropology of an Irish Market Town, 1200–1991 / Philip Gulliver and Marilyn Silverman (1995)

Tournaments of Value: Sociability and Hierarchy in a Yemeni Town / Ann Meneley (1996)

Mal'uocchiu: Ambiguity, Evil Eye, and the Language of Distress / Sam Migliore (1997)

Between History and Histories: The Production of Silences and Commemorations / Edited by Gerald Sider and Gavin Smith (1997)

Eh, Paesan! Being Italian in Toronto / Nicholas DeMaria Harney (1998)

Theorizing the Americanist Tradition / Edited by Lisa Philips Valentine and Regna Darnell (1999)

Colonial 'Reformation' in the Highlands of Central Sulawesi, Indonesia, 1892–1995 / Albert Schrauwers (2000)

The Rock Where We Stand: An Ethnography of Women's Activism in Newfoundland / Glynis George (2000)

Being Alive Well: Health and the Politics of Cree Well-Being / Naomi Adelson (2000)

Irish Travellers: Racism and the Politics of Culture / Jane Helleiner (2001)

Of Property and Propriety: The Role of Gender and Class in Imperialism and Nationalism / Edited by Himani Bannerji, Shahrzad Mojab, and Judith Whitehead (2001)

An Irish Working Class: Explorations in Political Economy and Hegemony, 1800–1950 / Marilyn Silverman (2001)

The Double Twist: From Ethnography to Morphodynamics / Edited by Pierre Maranda (2001)

The House of Difference: Cultural Politics and National Identity in Canada / Eva Mackey (2002)

Writing and Colonialism in Northern Ghana: The Encounter between the LoDagaa and the 'World on Paper,' 1892–1991 / Sean Hawkins (2002)

Guardians of the Transcendent: An Ethnography of a Jain Ascetic Community / Anne Vallely (2002)

The Hot and the Cold: Ills of Humans and Maize in Native Mexico / Jacques M. Chevalier and Andrés Sánchez Bain (2003)

Figured Worlds: Ontological Obstacles in Intercultural Relations / Edited by John Clammer, Sylvie Poirier, and Eric Schwimmer (2004)

Revenge of the Windigo: The Construction of the Mind and Mental Health of North American Aboriginal Peoples / James B. Waldram (2004)

The Cultural Politics of Markets: Economic Liberalization and Social Change in Nepal / Katherine Neilson Rankin (2004)

A World of Relationships: Itineraries, Dreams, and Events in the Australian Western Desert / Sylvie Poirier (2005)

The Politics of the Past in an Argentine Working-Class Neighbourhood / Lindsay DuBois (2005)

Youth and Identity Politics in South Africa, 1990–1994 / Sibusisiwe Nombuso Dlamini (2005)

Maps of Experience: The Anchoring of Land to Story in Secwepemc Discourse / Andie Diane Palmer (2005)

Beyond Bodies: Rain-Making and Sense-Making in Tanzania / Todd Sanders (2008)

We Are Now a Nation: Croats between 'Home' and 'Homeland' / Daphne N. Winland (2008)

Kaleidoscopic Odessa: History and Place in Post-Soviet Ukraine / Tanya Richardson (2008)

Invaders as Ancestors: On the Intercultural Making and Unmaking of Spanish Colonialism in the Andes / Peter Gose (2008)

From Equality to Inequality: Social Change among Newly Sedentary Lanoh Hunter-Gatherer Traders of Peninsular Malaysia / Csilla Dallos (2011)

Rural Nostalgias and Transnational Dreams: Identity and Modernity among Jat Sikhs / Nicola Mooney (2011)

Dimensions of Development: History, Community, and Change in Allpachico, Peru / Susan Vincent (2012)

People of Substance: An Ethnography of Morality in the Colombian Amazon / Carlos David Londoño Sulkin (2012)

'We Are Still Didene': Stories of Hunting and History from Northern British Columbia / Thomas McIlwraith (2012)

Being Māori in the City: Indigenous Everyday Life in Auckland / Natacha Gagné (2013)

The Hakkas of Sarawak: Sacrificial Gifts in Cold War Era Malaysia / Kee Howe Yong (2013)

Remembering Nayeche and the Gray Bull Engiro: African Storytellers of the Karamoja Plateau and the Plains of Turkana / Mustafa Kemal Mirzeler (2014)

In Light of Africa: Globalizing Blackness in Northeast Brazil / Allan Charles Dawson (2014)

The Land of Weddings and Rain: Nation and Modernity in Post-Socialist Lithuania / Gediminas Lankauskas (2015)

Milanese Encounters: Public Space and Vision in Contemporary Urban Italy / Cristina Moretti (2015)

Legacies of Violence: History, Society, and the State in Sardinia / Antonio Sorge (2015)

Looking Back, Moving Forward: Transformation and Ethical Practice in the Ghanaian Church of Pentecost / Girish Daswani (2015)

Why the Porcupine is Not a Bird: Explorations in the Folk Zoology of an Eastern Indonesian People / Gregory Forth (2016)

The Heart of Helambu: Ethnography and Entanglement in Nepal / Tom O'Neill (2016)

Tournaments of Value: Sociability and Hierarchy in a Yemeni Town, 20th Anniversary Edition / Ann Meneley (2016)

Europe Un-Imagined: Nation and Culture at a French-German Television Channel / Damien Stankiewicz (2017)